Books by SAMUEL ELIOT MORISON

The Life and Letters of Harrison Gray Otis, 2 vols., 1913

The Maritime History of Massachusetts, 1921, 1941

The Oxford History of the United States, 2 vols., 1927

Builders of the Bay Colony, 1930, 1964

The Tercentennial History of Harvard University, 4 vols., 1929–36

Three Centuries of Harvard, 1936, 1963

Portuguese Voyages to America, 1940

Admiral of the Ocean Sea: A Life of Christopher Columbus, 1942

History of U. S. Naval Operations in World War II, 15 vols., 1947–62

By Land and By Sea, 1953

The Intellectual Life of Colonial New England, 1956

Freedom in Contemporary Society, 1956

The Story of the "Old Colony" of New Plymouth, 1956

John Paul Jones: A Sailor's Biography, 1959

The Story of Mount Desert Island, 1960

One Boy's Boston, 1962

The Two-Ocean War, 1963

Vistas of History, 1964

Spring Tides, 1965

The Oxford History of the American People, 1965

Old Bruin: Commodore Matthew C. Perry, 1794–1858, 1967

Harrison Gray Otis, The Urbane Federalist, 1969

The European Discovery of America: The Northern Voyages A.D. 500–1600, 1971

Samuel de Champlain: Father of New France, 1972

WITH HENRY STEELE COMMAGER AND WILLIAM E. LEUCHTENBURG

The Growth of the American Republic, 2 vols., 1930, 1969

WITH MAURICIO OBREGÓN

The Caribbean as Columbus Saw It, 1964

SAMUEL
de CHAMPLAIN

SAMUEL DE CHAMPLAIN
The only authentic portrait, by himself. Enlarged from his drawing of the 1609 fight on Lake Champlain, in Les Voyages *(1613). Courtesy Harvard College Library.*

Samuel de Champlain
FATHER OF NEW FRANCE

SAMUEL ELIOT MORISON
With illustrations

An Atlantic Monthly Press Book

LITTLE, BROWN AND COMPANY · BOSTON · TORONTO

LIBRARY OF CONGRESS CATALOG CARD NO. 71–186963

FIRST EDITION

T06/72

ATLANTIC–LITTLE, BROWN BOOKS
ARE PUBLISHED BY
LITTLE, BROWN AND COMPANY
IN ASSOCIATION WITH
THE ATLANTIC MONTHLY PRESS

Published simultaneously in Canada
by Little, Brown & Company (Canada) Limited

PRINTED IN THE UNITED STATES OF AMERICA

To PRISCILLA BARTON MORISON

Amiable and beloved companion in following
Champlain's courses from Pemaquid
to Port-Royal, this book is
affectionately dedicated

The names of those who in their lives fought for life,
Who wore at their hearts the fire's center.
Born of the sun they traveled a short while towards the sun,
And left the vivid air signed with their honor.

—STEPHEN SPENDER

Preface

SAMUEL de Champlain was the most versatile of colonial founders in North America; at once sailor and soldier, writer and
man of action, artist and explorer, ruler and administrator. Sailors
admire him, not only for exploring the rugged coast of New England without serious mishap, but for his *Treatise on Seamanship*,
in which his description of "The Good Captain" well applies to
himself: "An upright, God-fearing man, not dainty about food
or drink, robust and alert, with good sea legs." Canoeists admire
him for his explorations up rugged Canadian rivers, and his un-
complaining acceptance of hardship and danger in the long, long
carries and the *sault*. Historians admire him for his detailed records
of voyages and of events in Canada, the best source we have for
the first third of the seventeenth century.

Champlain's accounts of his coastal cruises and explorations of
the interior were embellished with drawings of flora, fauna, and
fights with the natives, which, though not of great artistic merit,
are marvelously informing; and they are accompanied by maps
which for fifty years were not surpassed in accuracy. Loyal to
his king, his church and his wife, he endeavored with success to
lead the New Testament life in an age of loose morals. The life

of this great man encompassed those efforts which led to the Founding of New France.

My interest in Champlain goes back to boyhood, when in 1904 I saw the tercentennial monument to him erected on Mount Desert Island — at the wrong place. His *Voyages*, in the Slafter translation, were my companions in sundry cruises along the coasts of New England and L'Acadie — Nova Scotia and New Brunswick. Later I became the proud possessor of the Champlain Society edition of his *Works*, and as early as 1950, when my wife and I resumed cruising along the Maine coast, I planned to write a new biography of my hero. Other and more pressing matters interrupted the work; but herein it is brought to fruition.

Strange how someone's offhand remark sticks. More than forty years ago I conducted a seminar at Harvard on early American history, and one of my Canadian students was Arthur R. M. Lower, who has since become a distinguished professor of history at Queen's University, Kingston. When I opened up the Harvard copy of Champlain's 1612 map, Lower pointed out the surprising accuracy of its delineation of the Ottawa River valley. Then and there I determined some day to explore this region, by air if not by canoe; and finally the chance came this very year. My friend James F. Nields, with Robert D. Huntington Jr. as co-pilot, flew me up the Ottawa and Mattawa River valleys to Lake Nipissing, then over the 30,000 islands of Georgian Bay, and then across Old Huronia to Lake Simcoe. We next followed Champlain's route, surprisingly close to the Trent Canal system, to Lakes Ontario and Oneida, where we checked the little pond where Champlain met his first defeat. Thence we crossed the Adirondacks to Schroon Lake, New York, and spent a night pleasantly and profitably at hospitable Ticonderoga as guests of John Pell and Colonel Edward P. Hamilton. Before returning to my Boston base, we paid a visit to Plymouth and Cape Cod — Champlain's

Port Saint-Louis, Mallebarre, and Port Fortuné. But I hope that Canadian sportsmen will follow Champlain's entire inland course by canoe, and give us a photographic report of it.

Now for a few practical matters.

The spelling of French personal names at this period is a problem. Champlain's name seldom varies; but Pont-Gravé, for instance, is given five or six different names in the sources. I have therefore followed the usage of Marcel Trudel, the eminent Canadian historian.

The scales on Champlain's harbor charts are in *toises*, each of which was equivalent to 1.96 meters or 6.4 feet, a little more than a fathom, which the French generally called *brasse*. The soundings are in *brasses*. On the big maps the scale is in *lieues*, leagues. W. F. Ganong, who studied this subject very thoroughly, states in the Champlain Society edition of the *Works* I 200 that Champlain's league represents "about two and a half of our geographical (i.e., nautical) miles." It is evident that Champlain used *la petite lieue marine*, which various plottings on charts indicate to be somewhere between 2.2 and 2.7 nautical miles long. For discussion, see my *European Discovery of America: Northern Voyages* A.D. *500–1600* (1971), pp. 288, 382, 387. In my opinion, 2.5 nautical miles, or 4633 meters, is a fair average for Champlain's league.

To conclude, here is my best effort to honor one of the greatest pioneers, explorers and colonists of all time.

S. E. Morison

"*Good Hope*"
Northeast Harbor, Maine
1 August 1971

Contents

[xv]

Illustrations

SAMUEL
de CHAMPLAIN

I

Canada Before Champlain

CANADA, before Samuel de Champlain made his first visit in 1603, was a "desert," as both French and English then called a wilderness. Not that it was uninhabited. Beothuk, Souriquois, Etchimin, Montagnais, Huron and Algonkin, all forest people, occupied the woodlands east of the Great Lakes and north of the New England coast, and Eskimo were lords of the Labrador. They led good lives according to their own ideas, with excellent hunting and fishing, and plenty of fighting with neighboring tribes. But they were subject to starvation from changes in the ecology, and often were forced to migrate in search of food. With Europeans who came by water they began exchanging peltries for axes, knives, and various knickknacks early in the sixteenth century, but before that they did considerable trading among themselves, as archaeologists have proved by finding in their midden heaps copper discs and stone pipe bowls from around Lake Superior, the Hiawathan "Land of Gitche Gumee."

Baffin Island, the Labrador and Newfoundland, all now parts of Canada, were discovered by Leif Ericson from Greenland A.D. 1001; but his efforts and those of his family to found a colony on the northern peninsula of Newfoundland were frustrated by the hostility of the natives. John Cabot discovered and named Newfoundland, and took possession for England, on 24 June 1497; but England did nothing about it for more than half a century. The Corte Real brothers of Terceira came shortly after Cabot, and they and the fishermen who quickly followed in their wake left Portuguese names along the outer coast of Newfoundland. French fishermen began to frequent the shores of that great rugged island in 1504, having learned that the coastal waters and the Grand Banks teemed with codfish which, when salted and cured, became a popular foodstuff in Europe.

The first French voyage of discovery and exploration along these coasts that is known to history came in 1524. *La Dauphine*, commanded by Giovanni da Verrazzano for King François-premier of France, made the North American shores at Cape Fear, North Carolina, and sailed thence to latitude 50° N in Newfoundland. Verrazzano is the first European known to have put in at the sites of New York and Newport, Rhode Island. And he was responsible for the name Arcadia, happily recalling the ideal Arcadian landscape of ancient Greece, which has become L'Acadie or Acadia. Ninety-odd years later Champlain, who had read Hakluyt's translation of Verrazzano's unique narrative, in the dedication of one of his *Voyages* to Marie de Medici reminded the Queen Regent that the Florentine navigator was her compatriot, hoping thus to give her a personal interest in supporting his efforts to colonize Canada. But Marie did not "bite." Champlain, however, profited by one of Verrazzano's mistaken methods — sailing so very far off shore that he missed all the big bays. Champlain always sailed close to shore in a small vessel, and he missed nothing between Newfoundland and Cape Cod, or in the Laurentian basin.

For ten years after Verrazzano's remarkable voyage, nothing was done by France to follow it up. The first real efforts to nail down French rights to this northern country were the voyages of

Jacques Cartier in 1534–41. This master mariner of Saint-Malo, the leading seaport of Brittany, made three voyages of exploration in the Gulf and River of St. Lawrence, and twice attempted to found a French colony at or near the site of Quebec. His prime objects were to find that northwest passage to the Orient which Verrazzano had sought in vain, and to turn up new sources of precious metals. On his first voyage he made landfall at Cape Bonavista, Newfoundland, sailed through the ice-cluttered Strait of Belle Isle and along the northern shore of the Gulf, which he reported to be "a land of Cain," all rock and scarcely any verdure. His account of this shore was so discouraging that Champlain never went near it, but Basque whale fishers found it to be a convenient base for their operations. Cartier discovered the Magdalen group, remarking that he would rather have one *arpent* of Brion Island than the whole of Newfoundland; Prince Edward Island; and the New Brunswick shore of the Gulf, exploring the Baie de Chaleur in the hope that it was the sought-for passage to the Indies. There he met a group of friendly Micmac Indians who offered peltry for trade, indicating that Europeans had already been there. At Gaspé harbor in Gaspé Bay he encountered a summer fishing party of Indians from around Quebec, and they too were friendly. Cartier persuaded their chief, Donnaconna, to allow his two sons to be given a trip to France and trained as interpreters. Off Anticosti on 1 August 1534, Cartier decided to turn back, as wind and tide were strong against him, and he had insufficient provisions to last through a deep-freeze.

François-premier, favorably impressed, ordered a second voyage to be organized. Cartier now commanded a big ship, *La Grande Hermine*, a small one named *La Petite Hermine*, and a little *galion* or pinnace named *L'Emerillon*. His objects, according to his commission, were "to explore beyond *les Terres*

Neufves" (Newfoundland and what he had already discovered), and "to discover certain far-off countries." Departing Saint-Malo in May of 1535, he sailed through the Strait of Belle Isle and about mid-August entered what he aptly named La Baie de Sept Isles. It is still the Bay of Seven Islands, a prosperous railhead for iron ore from northern Labrador.

Donnaconna's two boys, whom Cartier had brought along as guides and interpreters, now told him he was about to enter the Great River of Hochelaga (Montreal), which was *le chemin de Canada*. This, recorded in Cartier's *Brief Récit* of the voyage, is the first appearance in any European literature of the name Canada, which then and there entered the stream of history.

The name St. Lawrence entered it a few days earlier. On 10 August, feast of that saint, Cartier anchored in a small harbor on the north coast of the Gulf and named it "La Baye Sainct Laurins." Through a misunderstanding by later writers, this name in the following century became applied to the entire Gulf and River of St. Lawrence. Never, since the Roman Empire, have two local names received such a vast extension as Canada and St. Lawrence.

During the voyage, if not earlier, the two Indian boys began filling up Cartier with wonderful stories about a fabulous, miraculous, mysterious Kingdom of Saguenay, lying somewhere up north. It was rich in gold, silver and precious stones, and the people were almost white; it contained extraordinary creatures such as pygmies and unipeds. Cartier swallowed it whole. If what the boys (and subsequently their father) said were true, here was a northern Mexico or Peru from which France could extract vast wealth to rival Spain. And it appeared to be ripe for the plucking. Cartier first sailed a few miles up the beautiful Moisie River in his longboat to see if that was the way to Saguenay, or to

China; decided it was not, and so continued up the St. Lawrence, which he always called La Grande Rivière.

On 30 August he reached the site of Tadoussac, at the mouth of a deep river flowing from the north which the natives called Saguenay, suggesting that here was the principal route to the mythical kingdom. Cartier sailed a short distance up it; but at the urgency of the two native boys, who "wanted home" and alleged that there was another and better route (the Ottawa River), he postponed investigating the Saguenay and continued up the St. Lawrence. He believed that he had already hit upon the passage to China. Native stories about the Great Lakes he took to indicate bays of the Pacific Ocean.

On 7 September he reached a big island in the river which he named Orléans after the king's son. There he was welcomed with enthusiasm by Donnaconna, who had expected never to see his sons again. This, wrote Cartier, "marks the beginning of the land and province of Canada."

Donnaconna, after hearing from his sons about the good time they had enjoyed in France, embraced Cartier and led him with a fleet of canoes to his capital, a village of bark lodges called Stadaconé, on Cape Diamond, nestling under the Rock of Quebec. That name Cartier apparently did not pick up, but he did hear "Canada" and applied it to the immediate vicinity. The whole of Eastern Canada he called La Nouvelle France.

Desceliers, an eminent Dieppe cartographer who obtained his information from Cartier, extended the name Canada over the whole Laurentian region in his maps of 1542 and 1550, so that by the next century it was commonly understood as covering the Gulf and Valley of St. Lawrence, and all New France westward — but not L'Acadie (Nova Scotia) or Newfoundland, which the English had pre-empted by virtue of Cabot's voyage.

Cartier was not content with locating Canada. He must get on, toward Cathay. On 19 September 1535, in pinnace *L'Emerillon*, towing two shallops or longboats, he started up-river in search of the passage to the Indies. Leaving the pinnace in Lac Saint-Pierre (future scene of the classic "wreck of the *Julie Plante*"), he pushed on in his longboats, and on 2 October landed at the site of Montreal close by the modern bridge named after him. There he encountered another friendly tribe who spoke the same language as Donnaconna's people. They lived in a fortified village called Hochelaga, built on much the same plan as the Iroquoian fortress later attacked by Champlain. Cartier made friends with these natives, climbed to the top of Mont Royal, which later gave the great city her name, but was deeply disappointed at seeing a series of roaring rapids on the St. Lawrence, barring his way westward. These Champlain called Le Sault Saint-Louis. Robert Cavelier de La Salle, who acquired an estate nearby a century later, ironically changed this name to La Chine because the rapids marked the nearest approach of the French to China by this route.

On 11 October, Cartier was back at what he called "the port of Sainte-Croix," the mouth of the St. Charles River adjoining Quebec. Here the sailors of the two ships had already built a fort ashore — Champlain found the ruined chimney in 1603. The French now prepared for winter, mooring their ships near the fort for mutual protection, salting fish and game, and piling up stores of firewood. This winter of 1535–36 proved to be unusually cold, and a scurvy epidemic made it even worse for the French. After many had been struck down and only three or four men were healthy enough for sentry duty, an Indian showed Cartier how to cure the disease by concocting and drinking a broth made from the leaves of an evergreen tree. *Annedda*, as the natives called it, has been identified by Jacques Rousseau, the eminent

Canadian botanist, as *Thuja occidentalis*, the common arborvitae. Strangely enough, Champlain and other French pioneers of the next century, who had read Cartier's narrative, never could find a tree that cured their scurvy.

Donnaconna amused himself and the Frenchmen during the long winter by filling their ears with tall tales of the wonders of Saguenay (he claimed to have been there), where immense quantities of gold, rubies, and even spices could be had for the asking, and all manner of marvels were to be seen. Indians always enjoyed pulling the legs of palefaces, but Donnaconna paid heavily for his fun. Cartier kidnapped him and several more to take home, in order to help him "sell" Saguenay to the king. He sailed for France 6 May 1536, using Cabot Strait, the passage between Cape Breton and Newfoundland, and reached Saint-Malo in mid-July.

This second voyage of Cartier's was the most profitable. It opened up the St. Lawrence–Great Lakes route to the interior, the greatest of all axes of penetration of North America from the sea — except possibly the Mississippi. On the other hand, the fabulous though mythical splendors of Saguenay, of whose existence Cartier and Donnaconna had no trouble convincing François-premier, raised false hopes and created mischievous expectations.

By the time this second voyage ended, the king was too busy preparing to fight Spain to pay any attention to Cartier or Canada, and it was only after he had been defeated and captured at Pavia, and concluded peace with Charles V and been released from captivity, that he took up Canada again. The object now was to establish a colony on the St. Lawrence as a base for discovering and conquering the Kingdom of Saguenay — recalling the relation of Old Panama to Pizarro's conquest of Peru. The king, regarding old-salt Cartier of insufficient rank to be a governor, appointed over him, as general and viceroy, a young and adventurous nobleman named Jean-François de la Roque, sieur de Roberval. Preparations for this third voyage were so elaborate and took so many ships and people that all Europe was agog. Spanish, Portuguese and English spies in the seaports reported immense fleets being gathered, but were unable to find out whether they were destined for the West Indies, Portuguese Africa, Canada or Newfoundland.

Cartier's half of the expedition, *La Grande Hermine, L'Emerillon* and three more vessels, their decks uncomfortably crowded with cattle, their 'tween decks with colonists (mostly convicts), and their holds crammed with goods and provisions for a proper colony, left Saint-Malo 23 May 1541; Roberval's fleet started almost a year later.

Anticipating a cool reception at Stadaconé, since Chief Donnaconna had died in France, Cartier built a palisaded and fortified settlement a few miles up-river on Cap Rouge, which he named Charlesbourg-Royal. He then took his fleet's longboats with sundry "gentlemen, masters and pilots," up-river to the site of Montreal. There he engaged native guides who promised to show him the Ottawa route to Saguenay; but as it was already late in the season, he returned empty-handed down-river to Charlesbourg-Royal and there passed the winter of 1541–42, his second in Canada, as miserably as the first. The natives attacked the habitation and killed some thirty-five Frenchmen.

In the spring of 1542, since Roberval's fleet had not turned up and no report of it had reached him, Cartier assumed that the viceroy had been lost at sea, and sailed for home. Putting in at St. John's, Newfoundland, about 10 June, he encountered Roberval's fleet of three new merchant vessels carrying some two hundred men and women. These included gentlemen passengers who, hoping to be granted a gold mine in Saguenay, expected to stay; peasants engaged for work only; thirty or more convicts for the labor force, and a quantity of materials for building a colony. Roberval ordered Cartier to turn back with him to Canada; but the master mariner, estimating correctly that their combined strength would not be sufficient to defend themselves against the natives, refused. He returned forthwith to France with samples of "gold ore" which proved to be marcasite, and of quartz crystals supposed to be diamonds. Cartier then retired from the sea and lived peaceably at Saint-Malo until 1557.

In the meantime, Roberval pushed ahead by the Strait of Belle Isle to Cap Rouge, which he renamed France-Roy, and built a new fortified camp to replace Cartier's Charlesbourg-Royal. There he and his people spent a miserable winter, losing some fifty persons to scurvy and other diseases; possibly also to Indian attack. In June 1543 Roberval led a longboat expedition up-river to the site of Montreal. After one boat had capsized and all hands drowned, he turned back to France-Roy and, as no relief expedition showed up, sailed for home that summer with his entire company and arrived at Saint-Malo in September.

Neither he nor Cartier had anything to show for all this trouble, expense and loss of life but a mess of "gold ore" that was not gold and of quartz crystals that were not diamonds. The very word Canada became a joke in France; anything that sparkled like a diamond, but was not a real one, from now on was called "a diamond of Canada." The only useful results of these voyages were a series of maps, based on information from Cartier's explorations, by the Dieppe cartographers Desceliers and Vallard, showing fairly accurately the Gulf of St. Lawrence and the Great River up to the rapids. They proved very useful later to Champlain; but for over sixty years after Roberval's failure, no European went to Canada with the intention of staying.

Champlain was born too late to have talked with Cartier or

Roberval, but he studied attentively what records were available of their voyages, and from them learned a great deal. Especially, what not to do. First, to enter the Gulf by Cabot Strait rather than the ice-ridden Strait of Belle Isle, and not to bother with the barren north shore of the Gulf. Second, to treat the Kingdom of Saguenay as a myth, and spend no time or effort searching for nonexistent gold or diamonds. Third, to give the natives good usage, tolerate their manners and customs, and not kidnap or otherwise misuse them; but if possible, bring out missionaries to convert them. Finally, to accept the cold northern winter and come to terms with it by snug buildings, fresh game and fish, and even amusements. Champlain never gave up altogether the quest for a passage to China, but he devoted himself primarily to making the original Canada, the Great River between Quebec and Montreal, a viable French colony based on fish, fur, timber and agriculture.

It did not escape him that the basic cause of Cartier's failure to establish a colony was arrogance toward the natives. As yet the savages had no firearms, but their numbers, and their excellent archery, were more than a match for the feeble number of soldiers and colonists that French merchants or kings cared to send to Canada. There was no use building a strong fort for protection if every person who left its walls to fish, dig clams, cut firewood or shoot game was likely to be picked off by an arrow and dispatched by a tomahawk. Champlain decided very early that he must make and keep the friendship of all tribes in the Laurentian region if his colonies, too, were not to be snuffed out.

In the sixty years between Roberval's return and Champlain's first voyage to Canada, neither the French government nor the English did anything significant to secure Canada or Newfoundland. England, although she claimed all North America by virtue of Cabot's discoveries, never asserted jurisdiction over Newfoundland until Sir Humfry Gilbert put in at St. John's in 1583, and she never challenged French sovereignty over the Gulf and River of St. Lawrence until 1628, when the two countries were at war. English explorers such as Martin Frobisher and John Davis explored Baffin Island and part of the Labrador, looking for riches that did not exist, and for the Northwest Passage, which was first threaded by sail in 1905. Sir Humfry Gilbert and Sir Walter Raleigh bypassed the Laurentian region to try settlements in Norumbega (New England) and in Virginia (Roanoke Island, North Carolina) in the last twenty years of the century; but no Englishman even attempted a Newfoundland colony until 1610. Not long after the Cartier-Roberval voyages ended, France became torn apart by a civil war which only ended in 1594 when the jolly, bearded Béarnais, Henry of Navarre, was crowned King Henri IV at Chartres. During this period of civil war the only French colonizing enterprises were directed to Brazil and Florida, and all ended in disaster.

This does not mean that European individuals left Canada to herself. Fishing vessels by the score sailed annually to the Grand Banks and to Newfoundland for codfish, and the so-called dry-fishermen, who cured their catch on the Laurentian shores instead of sailing it directly home, found a profitable by-product. They traded for beaver, marten and other furs with the Montagnais and Souriquois (Micmac) Indians. Every summer the outer waters of Newfoundland and those of the Gulf of St. Lawrence were sprinkled with sail; you might have thought a great yachting regatta was under way. In the deliciously cool northern summer, living high on venison, fresh fish, native berries and all manner of wildfowl, the French, English, Portuguese, Spanish and (at the end of the century) Dutch seamen enjoyed themselves as yachtsmen now do in those waters. And in the sixteenth century, sailors made money there instead of just spending it. In the Paris fur market the peltry they brought home in 1583 was said to be worth 20,000 écus, say $12,000 in gold. The fishing-fur traders put forth in late winter or early spring, and by late September most of them were home — at Dieppe, Saint-Malo and La Rochelle; at Viana, Lisbon and Cadiz; at Exeter, Dartmouth, Brixton, Barnstaple and Bristol. Until the following spring the fishing banks, the harbors, Gulf, islands and rivers, indeed the entire further territory of Eastern Canada, were left to the fish, the deer, the birds, and the natives.

Great changes took place in the natives' distribution through the Laurentian region during the fifty years between Cartier and Champlain. Eskimo, migrating from the Labrador, occupied the north shore of the Gulf of St. Lawrence. Donnaconna's subjects disappeared from Quebec and the Great River, even beyond the site of Montreal. When Champlain arrived in these waters, he found only scattered groups of Algonkin on the upper river, and of Montagnais around Tadoussac and Quebec, and nobody at the site of Montreal. The elaborate fortified town of Hochelaga had completely disappeared, as had the village of Stadaconé and those between the two sites. It was formerly assumed that, defeated by attacks of the Five Nations, they had returned to a region around Lake Huron, but it seems to be now agreed that the Hurons of Lake Huron had been there for over a century when Champlain called. Historians are still discussing what happened. Probably a series of raids by one or more of the Five Nations, possibly an epidemic, from germs planted unwittingly by Cartier or Roberval. We simply don't know.

The only attempted French colony before the turn of the century was, of all places, on tiny Sable Island, away off the Acadian shore. A Breton nobleman, Troïlus de Mesgouez, *dit* Marquis de La Roche, who had a patent from Henri IV for the whole of New

France, selected about the worst place he could find within it, and in 1598 settled Sable Island with two shiploads of convicts. They, needless to say, did not prosper, and finally eleven long-haired and rugged survivors were repatriated in 1603. In the meantime, the king confiscated La Roche's monopoly and granted it, or most of it — the transactions were very complicated — to Pierre Chauvin, a Protestant gentleman and merchant-shipowner of Honfleur. He in 1600 sent out the most formidable fleet that had gone to Canada from France since Roberval's. His second in command was François Pont-Gravé of Saint-Malo, the inseparable companion of Champlain for over a quarter-century. And with Chauvin sailed an important person who, this time, came simply for pleasure, but who became deeply involved in colonizing Canada. This was Pierre du Gua, Sieur de Monts.

Chauvin's fleet sailed straight to Tadoussac at the mouth of the Saguenay, already an important rendezvous of fishermen, fur traders and Indians. He built a wooden habitation (shown on Champlain's chart of Tadoussac, p. 28) and left sixteen men to winter there. A sad, sickly winter they all had; those who did not die were so desperate as to take refuge with the Indians in order to eat. Chauvin made another voyage in 1602, and was trying to get new blood into his company when he died, early in 1603.

Henri IV now granted the same monopoly to a company organized at Rouen by Aymar de Chaste, vice-admiral of France, governor of Dieppe, and French ambassador at the Court of St. James's. An imposing personage of advanced age, he appointed Pont-Gravé as his lieutenant to take a fleet to Tadoussac; and on Pont-Gravé's ship sailed, as a sort of observer-chronicler, a thirty-three-year-old seaman from Brouage, hitherto unknown to fame, named Samuel Champlain.

II

Early Life and West Indies Voyages

CONSIDERING that Samuel de Champlain has generally been accepted as the "Father of New France," it is surprising how little is still known about his early life. He was born *about* 1570 — natal day unknown and year doubtful — at Brouage, a little seaport in Saintonge, the French province next south of Brittany, and not far from La Rochelle. Nothing is known about his parents except their names; in Samuel's marriage contract they are called Antoine de Complain, captain in the merchant marine, and Marguerite Le Roy. We know the names of only two other relations, an uncle who followed the sea and a cousin, Marie Cameret, who married the chief whip in the royal kennels and became Samuel's residuary legatee.

Brouage at the time of Champlain's birth was an important seaport and center of the salt industry, where that indispensable preservative was evaporated from seawater. Fishermen destined for the Grand Bank of Newfoundland came to Brouage to fill their holds with dry salt crystals, which preserved their catch until they could reach shore and dry the cod in the sun. Little vessels from Brittany and Normandy came to Brouage to buy salt for preserving beef, pork and herring in casks. Before refrigeration, pickling in brine was the only known way to keep fresh meat and fish from spoiling.

Brouage still has salt pans, but no harbor; the Bay of Biscay receded at this point, leaving the town high and dry, so that the old stone walls which once defended its sea gate now border miles of salt marsh. But in Samuel's childhood and youth it was a very active place. We may assume that the boy went fishing or coasting, because in later life he wrote to Marie de Medici, Queen Regent of France, "The art of navigation from childhood has stimulated me to expose almost all my life to the impetuous waves of the ocean, and has made me navigate and coast along a part of the lands of America, especially of New France." We know from his later maps and illustrations that he somehow learned to draw passably well, but that is all we positively know about his education. He was probably born and certainly brought up a Catholic. Only after becoming an author of consequence did he call himself Le Sieur de Champlain; but from the two kings he served so faithfully he received neither title nor honors.

Our earliest positive records of Samuel are for service in the royal army in the last decade of the century, as *fourrier* (quartermaster) in the army of Brittany, with 75 livres ($15 in gold) monthly pay. He fought under Henri IV when the Béarnais was engaged in driving out the Spanish invaders of France. One of the important actions in that war was an Anglo-French assault on Fort Crozat near Brest, 7 November 1594. Young Champlain here fought side by side with the English contingent under Sir Martin Frobisher, who led the assault. Frobisher received a mortal wound in storming the fort, but Samuel Champlain came through unscathed. It is noteworthy that in the French army documents our young hero is called "sieur" and is given a "de" — to neither of which he was strictly entitled.

When the war ended four years later, all Spanish troops still in France were repatriated and the French army demobilized. Thus Samuel found himself unemployed at the age of twenty-eight — if 1570 is the correct year of his birth. By good luck the 500-tun ship *Saint-Julian*, commanded by his uncle Guillaume Hellaine or Allène, known as *le capitaine provençal* because his home port was Marseilles, was chartered to repatriate Spanish troops; and uncle invited nephew to be his guest. He gratefully accepted and put this voyage to good use by learning how to handle a large sailing vessel, to speak Spanish, and then to make a tour of the West Indies. *Saint-Julian*, after spending four months in Spanish ports, was chartered for the annual fleet which took Spanish goods to the West Indies and brought back treasure. That was just what Samuel wanted — to see Spanish America, which few Frenchmen had even approached. He made his first transatlantic voyage in 1599, in what capacity we know not.

Samuel kept a mental account of every island or port that he visited, and of the Indians, fruits and animals. He saw most of the Lesser Antilles, Puerto Rico and Cuba. At San Juan de Ulua, the principal seaport of Mexico, he left the ship and managed to visit Mexico City. "After having remained a month in Mexico," he wrote, "I returned to Saint-Jean-de-Luz, where I embarked in a *patache* [pinnace] for Portouella" — Porto Bello. Thence he crossed the Isthmus to Old Panama, and expressed the opinion that a transcontinental canal, built there, would shorten the passage to the Pacific by "more than 1500 leagues." After spending a month at Porto Bello, Champlain crossed to the same Basque port, "where we sojourned fifteen days waiting for our ships to be careened" in order to cleanse their bottoms of foul tropical growth. From Saint-Jean-de-Luz he took passage to the Havana, "rendezvous of armies and fleets." The fleet was blown apart by a northerly gale off Portugal, the pilot of the ship in which

The ramparts of Brouage in the twentieth century. In Champlain's day they rose directly from the sea. From Lucien Pledy, Brouage, ville forte (*La Rochelle, 1925*).

Champlain sailed lost his reckoning, and but for a providential encounter with a pinnace whose master knew his position, the ship would have piled up on the coast of Yucatán. After spending some time at the Havana he visited Cartagena de las Indias, returned to the Havana, and sailed back to Spain with the treasure *flota* of 1600 or 1601. Thus, he made six South Atlantic crossings in different ships and must have become an accomplished seaman even before his Canadian career began. We would like to know on what ships he sailed after he left his Provençal uncle, and in what capacity. But of that Champlain, reticent as usual about himself, tells us nothing.

He was impressed by the magnificence of the capital, admired the fertility of Mexico, and deplored the cruelty of the Spaniards to the Indians. He evidently resolved to prevent anything of that sort in New France, if ever he were in authority there, and in this he remained consistent. No early European explorer was anywhere near so successful as Champlain in making friends of the natives, or so humane in protecting them.

After this series of West Indian voyages he returned to France, and for a year or two we know nothing about him except that he was writing a *Brief Discours des Choses plus Remarquables que Sammuel Champlain de Brouage a reconneues aux Indes Occidentalles, au voiage qu'il en a faict en icelles en l'année 1599 et en 1601, comme ensuit.**

We would all like to have a physical description of Champlain in his young manhood, or at any other time. Unfortunately there is none. No contemporary has left a record of his appearance; only of his character. No court or other painter recorded his lineaments. The best portrait of him is the rough, crude sketch from

---

* "Brief Discourse of the most remarkable things which Samuel Champlain of Brouage has observed in the West Indies during the voyages he made thither in the year 1599 and the year 1601, as follows." Printed, with black-and-white reproductions of his drawings, in the Champlain Society *Works* I 1–80.

Two paintings from Champlain's Brief Discours of his West Indies voyage. ABOVE: *Extracting gum from the* canime *or* locust tree. BELOW: *The* palmiste (cabbage palm) *about to be cut down with a sword. The pith, he says, is sweeter than sugar, and the Indians make a fermented drink of it. Courtesy John Carter Brown Library.*

his own pen, shooting an arquebus at the Mohawk, and that we have used as frontispiece; other self-portraits in his sketches of battles give us even less. As one who has lived with Champlain for many years, I may be permitted to give my own idea of him. A well-built man of medium stature, blond and bearded, a natural leader who inspired loyalty and commanded obedience. A man of unusually rugged constitution, never complaining of discomforts in his voyages or on his canoe and other overland journeys, sleeping in the open with no covering and only evergreen boughs between his body and the snow, eating the natives' often loathsome food. A proud man among his fellows, demanding the respect due to his position, but humble before God.

III

First Voyage to Canada

A MARINER with a talent for drawing and map-making as well as navigation could not long remain unemployed, although Samuel would have to wait many years for a command. An opportunity now opened for him at the age of thirty-three to join an exploring and colonizing voyage to Canada as a privileged passenger. He snapped at it, little suspecting that the entire second half of his life would be devoted to bringing Canada into the French empire and converting *les sauvages*.* Champlain always accepted whatever came his way and made the best of it. It so turned out that whilst all the officers placed over him are forgotten, this passenger-observer has become the Father of New France.

Since Cartier and Roberval had abandoned their attempted colonies in and near Quebec in 1541, the Gulf and River of St. Lawrence and the coasts of Newfoundland had become the seats of summer colonies — not in the modern sense, but strictly for business. Their shores, completely deserted by Europeans for half the year, were thronged increasingly during the summer by

---

* Whilst Champlain referred to the natives of Spanish America as *les Indiens*, neither he nor any other early French writer called those of Northern America anything but *les sauvages*. By this they did not mean what we do by the word "savage," but rather "uncivilized."

[23]

ships of France and England, decreasingly by those of Spain and Portugal. Europeans came primarily to catch codfish and cure it on shore. Very early the fishermen discovered that the coastal natives, if treated decently, could be depended on to exchange furs and pelts which they had cured during the winter for knives, hatchets, fishhooks and other European products, and at a rate which for a few years brought astronomical profits. Furs were then the height of fashion; all gentlefolk wore fur hats, fur coats, fur muffs and so on, for which the trappers of Europe could not begin to satisfy the demand. Hence, as the turn of the sixteenth century to the seventeenth approached, fur began to be the main export of yet unsettled Canada, although it was still a bad second to fish, if you include the off-shore fisheries of the Grand Banks with those of the Gulf. The way independent traders operated was this. Anchoring in some suitable harbor of L'Acadie or the Gulf, or up the St. Lawrence, they established friendly relations with the local Indians, exchanged axes, knives, and other European goods for peltry, caught and dried codfish, and then sailed home in the fall, returning to the same place early next summer. If the men had behaved well they would be met by the same group of savages with an even greater supply of peltry. This went on year after year at so many tiny harbors and "gunk holes" that the monopolists could never cope with them. These independent operators erected no buildings for storage or other purposes, but took home at the end of every summer the peltry they had obtained by barter, and fish they had caught and cured. The only place one can call an entrepôt, which several traders frequented, competing with each other, was Tadoussac. Typical of the rough practices of that era was that of a Malouin captain who marooned three of his men at Tadoussac as punishment. Henri Couillard, master of Pierre Chauvin's 200-tun *Don de Dieu,* rescued them and was paid 18 livres ($3.60) each upon landing them at Honfleur in the fall of 1602.

Both the English and French governments realized that only year-round permanent colonies of their own subjects could hold down these northern lands for their respective countries. But colonies cost money, not much of which could be spared from "defense," so the only practical way for a government to promote them was through private enterprise. The king would give a group of seaport merchants a monopoly of the Canadian fur trade in return for their promise to bring out a certain number of their countrymen to set up a year-round fishing and trading post. This had been tried by several groups of Frenchmen before Champlain came into the picture, but always with the same result: independent traders who had been making a good thing out of the fur trade raised so loud a clamor against the monopoly that it was revoked and the trading post abandoned.

One of these monopolies, held in succession by the Marquis de La Roche, Pierre Chauvin and Aymar de Chaste, became the means of Champlain's entry into Canada. King Henri IV, eager to support de Chaste, beefed up his company with new blood and capital. In 1603, by order of the king, de Chaste sent out a fresh expedition under François Pont-Gravé, who had already made fishing voyages to the St. Lawrence. He was a big jolly chap pushing fifty years of age, with a voice so loud that he was always called upon to hail passing ships at sea. Pont-Gravé, possibly at the king's prompting, invited Samuel Champlain to come along and record the voyage. They liked each other from their first meeting and were partners for nigh thirty years. I imagine that Champlain was thinking of Pont-Gravé when he wrote in his *Treatise on Seamanship* that the good captain should have a strong voice in order to carry commands to the sailors when the

Vive Henri IV! From the engraving by Thomas de Leu and F. Quin, about 1601–1602. Courtesy Museum of Fine Arts, Boston.

waves were roaring and the wind whistling through the rigging.

This fleet sailed from Honfleur, a lively little port on the Seine estuary in Normandy, on 15 March 1603. Honfleur seems to have been a favorite port of embarkation for Canada; it was not only handy to Rouen and Paris, but an important recruiting area for mariners. On a cliff on the starboard hand entering the harbor you may still see their own proper church, Notre-Dame-de-Grâce, established as a votive chapel to the Virgin by Duke Robert I of Normandy after the Queen of the Sea had saved his expedition against King Canute from disaster in a terrible tempest. Sailors always made a barefoot pilgrimage to Notre-Dame-de-Grâce before sailing, and again after returning, if return they did.

De Chaste's fleet consisted of *La Bonne Renommée* of 120 tuns, owned and commanded by Pont-Gravé; and two smaller vessels, names unknown, outfitted by merchants of Rouen and Saint-Malo. At about mid-passage they were beaten back by a westerly gale which lasted seventeen days. After making up the lost distance, and avoiding a great mass of ice, they struck soundings on the Grand Bank of Newfoundland on 2 May. Steering west in order to thread what is now Cabot Strait, they experienced a danger common to those waters, which still takes its toll of mariners' lives. In a thick fog the lookout cried, "Breakers ahead!" Just in time they managed to luff up and claw off a high rocky cliff. Next morning the fog lifted, and Pont-Gravé recognized Cape St. Mary's on the Avalon Peninsula of Newfoundland. Another westerly gale blew them out to sea again, so it was not until 5 May that the three vessels made Saint-Pierre, the little island which, together with Miquelon, still fosters a cozy vestige of colonial France. After dodging more ice, they entered the Gulf of St. Lawrence, sighted the already famous landmark Cap Percé, picked up the mountains of the Gaspé Peninsula, and sailed up the Great River to Tadoussac. This was then the center,

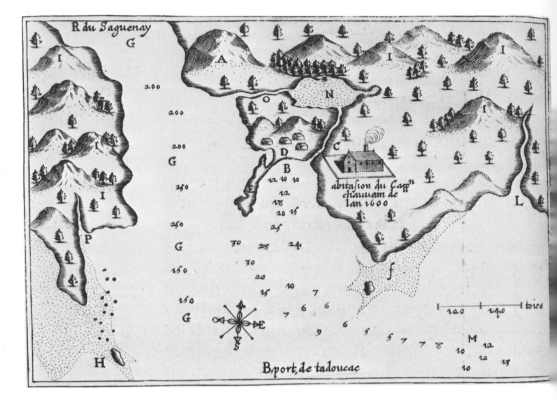

Champlain's chart of Tadoussac roadstead and mouth of the
Saguenay. From Les Voyages (1613). The house is the one
built by Captain Chauvin in 1600. KEY: A. "Round mountain on
edge of river." C. "Little stream." D. "Spot where the savages
camp when they come to trade." f. "Pointe de tous les Diables"
(Pointe des Vaches). H. "Pointe des Alouettes" (Lark Point).
I. Mountains covered with birch and pine. L. "Moulin Bode."
M. "Roadstead where ships anchor awaiting wind and tide."
N. "Petit lac." P. "Grassy Point." Courtesy Harvard College
Library.

almost the emporium, of the Laurentian fur trade. Montagnais Indians brought furs down the Saguenay River; Etchimin brought their packs by a series of rivers, lakes and portages from New Brunswick and Maine, and a detached Algonkin tribe brought theirs from the upper St. Lawrence.

In Champlain's first book to be published, *Des Sauvages, ou Voyage de Samuel Champlain, de Brouage*, he vividly describes the Montagnais Indians whom they interrupted at Tadoussac in the midst of a great feast. One member of that tribe, whom Pont-Gravé had taken to France on an earlier voyage and now brought back as interpreter, made an oration in which he told about his good usage at the hands of the French and assured the assembled multitude that they came as friends and would protect them against their implacable enemies the Five Nations. Anadabajin, the sagamore, after passing around a pipe of peace, replied that he was delighted to receive the French, that they were welcome to inhabit the country, and his hundred or more subjects present gave their assent in a chorus of "Ho! Ho! Ho!" A feast of moose venison, beaver meat and seal blubber, all boiled together in great kettles, followed. Champlain found this stew not too bad, but was disgusted by his hosts' table manners, cleaning their greasy hands, which had handled the meat, on the backs of dogs or in their own hair. He would have to eat hundreds of such meals, most of them even nastier, and would learn not to be so nice. You could, he found, if very hungry, be grateful for even Indian cooking and keep it down.

It may well be doubted whether Anadabajin or any of the other sagamores who so generously invited the French to live among them realized what they were in for. The French, unlike the English and Dutch pioneers, never attempted to buy land from the natives. Why should they, when the Indians invited them to settle down, free gratis for nothing? North American Indians never understood land cession, or at least not until the late eighteenth century. They regarded land as a gift from the Great Spirit to those who could use it, and defend it.

A few days after this *tabagie* (formal feast), a party of Algonkin allies arrived in two hundred birch bark canoes and held an even bigger feast with their Montagnais hosts, to celebrate a recent defeat of an Iroquois raid. Champlain was somewhat shocked by one of the numbers of the victory dance: the women and girls stripped themselves stark naked, except for their jewelry of beads and porcupine quills; then put on their furs and skins while the men performed a similar act. The Algonkin presented gifts to their hosts and organized running races. Champlain remarked that if these savages could be taught to till the ground, and worship the true God, they would make good French subjects.

Similar scenes occurred hundreds of times during the next two centuries whenever French, English or Dutch encountered a concourse of friendly Indians.

On 18 June 1603 Champlain, in a 12-tun pinnace carried over in parts by *La Bonne Renommée* and assembled at Tadoussac, together with a longboat or shallop for shoal-water exploration, started up-river with Montagnais guides. Although they discovered nothing that Cartier had not seen and reported, we first find the name "Kébec" in Champlain's narrative, applied to the narrow bend of the river now commanded by the city of Quebec. Aside from the ruined chimney he found at the site of the fort built by Cartier's sailors in 1535, all the works of man described by the French explorers over sixty years earlier — the native village of Stadaconé, the French habitation at Cap Rouge, and the native fortified town at Hochelaga (Montreal) — had disappeared. There was no trace of the teeming native life observed by Cartier and Roberval along the river valley. These Indians had vanished.

Such signs of abandonment by both races might have seemed ominous to a superstitious man, but not to Champlain. He fell in love with the Quebec site at once. It satisfied every need for a trading post and future colony — focal point of a network of waterways, highly defensible, abundant fisheries, rich soil. It amply fulfilled what he later wrote in his *Voyages* of 1632, "One must not neglect to lodge oneself strongly, both in peacetime and in wartime, in order to withstand anything that may happen; that is why I advise all pioneers to seek out a place where they may sleep in safety."

Passing Quebec, Cap Rouge, and the site of Sorel and Trois-Rivières, Champlain reached the site of Montreal and encountered the formidable La Chine rapids, which he named Sault Saint-Louis.* He there learned that it was no use trying to explore the interior with heavy ships' boats; one must have bark canoes with friendly *sauvages* as guides. From his own Montagnais he obtained a remarkably accurate description of the portages and lakes above La Chine as far as Lake Ontario, and of the Ottawa River. He even heard about Niagara Falls and Lake Erie, and somehow got the impression that that lake was salt. This raised once more the old frustrated hope of a "passage to Cathay," nourished by every explorer of North America for two centuries. Champlain believed that such a passage must begin somewhere in the Great Lakes. Apart from this blooper, he showed great skill in getting geographical information out of the natives. If they tried any of the old Kingdom of Saguenay nonsense on him, he laughed and never even reported it; comb

* See his chart of the St. Lawrence at Quebec (pp. 104–105).

[31]

through his writings and you will find absolutely no mention of Canadian gold or diamond mines.

At Tadoussac the officers and sailors of the three ships traded for furs with the natives and cured codfish by drying it in the sun. Before starting for home in mid-August 1603, Pont-Gravé and Champlain rescued from the Montagnais an Iroquois woman prisoner about to be killed and eaten by her captors, and a saga-more lent them his son to visit France and learn the language. We do not know what became of the woman, but the boy was made a page to the three-year-old dauphin, the future Louis XIII, at the Château de Saint-Germain. Apparently *le petit Canada,* as the dauphin called this poor boy, was killed by kindness; eating rich foods caused his death within a year.

Pont-Gravé's fleet made a fast passage of fifteen days from the Grand Bank to Le Havre, arriving 20 September 1603. The first news they heard was bad — Aymar de Chaste had died. But their voyage proved very profitable to the company; the peltry and dried fish that they brought home yielded between 30 and 40 per cent on the investment.

Champlain now made his contribution by writing an account of the voyage, published by royal license in Paris before the end of 1603. It is a little duodecimo of 36 pages entitled *Des Sauvages, ou, Voyage de Samuel Champlain, de Brouage, fait en la France nouvelle, l'an mil six cens trois* (Paris: chez Claude de Monstr'oeil, au nom de Jésus, avec Privilège du Roy). This, in comparison with Champlain's later works, is a dry, factual account of coasts, waters, natural products, and native manners and customs. One concession he made to public taste: he reported the Micmac legend of *"un monstre épouvantable* whom the savages call *Gougou,"* a female beast of enormous size and horrible aspect, which ate men. All the savages he met believed in her, and some claimed to have heard her roaring in the forest.

This probably helped to sell the book, since all travelers since Sir John Mandeville were supposed to report monsters and marvels. Marc Lescarbot, much to Champlain's annoyance, later accused him of having believed in the Gougou; and he did lend himself to the charge by writing that, having heard so much about her from so many people, he thought that some sort of devil must live in the Canadian wilderness.

IV

L'Acadie and Norumbega

D E Chaste having died, the king reorganized his company by giving it a fur-trading and colonizing monopoly between latitudes 40° and 46° N — those of Philadelphia and Cape Race, Newfoundland. The patent in 1604 was conferred upon Pierre du Gua, Sieur de Monts, a Protestant gentleman of Saintonge, Champlain's native province. He had fought under Henri IV, who made him governor of the château de Pons; a Huguenot and a solid merchant, he had invested in Aymar de Chaste's company, went out on his 1603 voyage, and now drew in other investors from Rouen, Saint-Malo, La Rochelle and Saint-Jean-de Luz. The capital subscribed amounted to 90,000 livres tournois (about $18,000 in gold). The company had a fur-trading (but not fishing) monopoly for ten years, and Henri IV published an edict forbidding all and sundry to trade with the natives between the granted latitudes. In return, the company promised to send out at least one hundred settlers, including convicts. It looked as if France at last had a really solid joint-stock corporation, like England's Virginia Company. But the individual French mariners and merchants, who had been fishing and trading in Canadian waters for nigh one hundred years, refused to abdicate what they considered to be their rights, and wrecked the entire scheme. In official documents, Pierre du Gua is described as *Le sieur de Montz, lieutenant général pour Sa Majesté ès terres de la Cadie, Canada et aultres endroits de la Nouvelle France.*

Despite their differences in religion, de Monts and Champlain became warm friends; and they shared the same ideal, to make a good part of North America a French dependency. Until 1628, when the then viceroy, the Duc de Vantadour, forbade Protestants to go to Canada, Huguenots were equally prominent with Catholics in pioneering.

De Monts, who had been to chilly Tadoussac, decided to pitch his trading post several degrees further south in the area called, on the latest maps, Arcadie, L'Acadie, La Cadie or La Cady. This name, originally applied by Verrazzano in 1524 to Kitty Hawk, North Carolina, because its beautiful trees and hills reminded him of the Virgilian Arcadia in ancient Greece, had been gradually moved eastward by the whims of successive cartographers. By the turn of the century, maps available to Champlain applied it to the area now covered by Nova Scotia, New Brunswick and easternmost Maine. During the 1603 voyage, one of the ships, commanded by Captain Prevert, peeled off from the fleet and explored the outer coast of Nova Scotia and the Bay of Fundy. Prevert reported a warmer climate than that of Tadoussac and — even more to the point — sure signs of copper in the red sandstone cliffs on what he named Le Bassin des Mines. Eventually this became the "Evangeline country" beloved of the Nova Scotia tourist bureau. Prevert persuaded Champlain, and he de Monts, to establish their colony in L'Acadie rather than on the St. Lawrence; and Champlain imagined that he could find a water route to "Cathay" easier thence than from Canada proper. How wrong they were, the next events will show. Except for possible survivors of Raleigh's Virginia colony, not one Englishman or European was then alive north of Florida. This French company had the entire New England–New York–New Jersey coast to choose from, and what they picked out was a not very intelligent choice.

De Monts's fleet of 1604 consisted of *La Bonne Renommée*, a second ship of 120 tuns commanded by Pont-Gravé, and a third which went ahead to Tadoussac to buy furs and (hopefully) to chase away the interlopers. Champlain sailed with de Monts in the flagship. Pont-Gravé agreed to rendezvous with them at Canso, after scouring the Acadian coast.

De Monts had embarked a considerable number of gentlemen, one hundred and twenty *artisans* — workmen to set up the colony and stay there — and two ministers of religion, a Catholic and a Protestant. Their arguments, sometimes concluded but never settled by fist fights, greatly amused the sailors. The most important gentleman was the valiant and accomplished Jean de Biencourt de Poutrincourt of Picardy, generally called Poutrincourt to distinguish him from his son Charles, who is referred to as Biencourt. Poutrincourt was well educated in the classics, a competent musician, and a brave soldier.

La Bonne Renommée, which de Monts himself commanded, sailed from Le Havre 7 April 1604, and Pont-Gravé's ship followed shortly. They sighted Sable Island 1 May, Champlain noting somewhat mischievously that the pilots thought they were over a hundred miles further west. A week later they sighted Cape La Have, Nova Scotia, and here Champlain made the first of his excellent harbor charts. He had mastered the difficult art of drawing correct outlines of an island-studded bay from an anchorage, and he carefully sounded the approaches. Any yachtsman today, lacking modern charts, would be happy to enter port with one of Champlain's in hand.

At the next harbor *La Bonne Renommée* encountered a fur

poacher named Rossignol. De Monts seized his ship but compensated him by naming the port after him. Unfortunately the English later changed it to prosaic Liverpool, but the poacher's name is preserved in Lake Rossignol. The French then made an extended stay at a harbor that they named Port à Mouton because a sheep fell overboard and was captured swimming. It is still so called, and a beautiful harbor it is. My visit to Port Mouton many years ago, with one of her native sons, my sailing master Enos Verge, is among my most pleasant memories of following Champlain's course in Nova Scotia.

While waiting for Pont-Gravé's vessel to catch up, de Monts gave Champlain his first independent command: that of an eight-tun pinnace with eleven men, to examine the Acadian coast to the west and north in the hope of finding a suitable place for settlement. This pinnace had undoubtedly been brought over knocked down, in the flagship's hold, and assembled ashore. Such was the practice of the time, also adopted by the English after losing several pinnaces that they tried to sail across the Atlantic.

For three weeks from 19 May 1604, Champlain ranged this coast, many harbored but dangerous by reason of the very heavy tides that surge in and out of the Bay of Fundy. He passed and named Cape Negro from an unusually black rock, threaded Barrington Passage behind Cape Sable Island (now closed by a permanent causeway), passed through the Tusket Islands, remarked the enormous number and variety of wildfowl, and described accurately the harbor which the English later named Yarmouth. He then sailed (which few modern yachtsmen would care to do without power) up to the Minas Basin and the head of the Bay of Fundy. Somewhere on the shores of the bay he found a wooden cross covered with moss. This had probably been erected by Richard Hakluyt's friend Étienne Bellinger, who

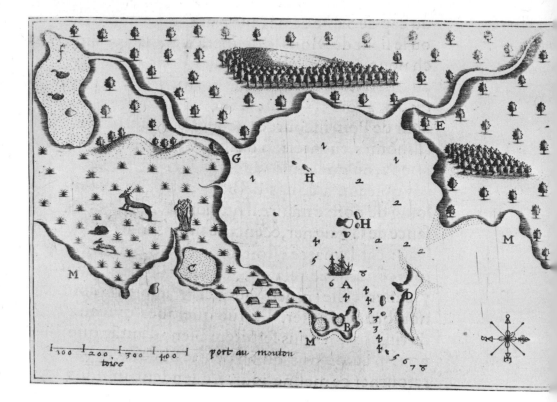

Champlain's chart of Port Mouton, Nova Scotia. From Les
Voyages *(1613).* KEY: *A. The anchorage, with de Monts's ship.
B. Bull Point, "where we camped." C. "A Pond" in Little Joli
Bay. D. Mouton Island, named after the sheep. E. Broad
River. f. "The Pond," still so named. G. Brook flowing from
The Pond. H. "Six small islands." M. "Line of the Sea Coast."
Courtesy Harvard College Library.*

in 1583 made a fur-trading voyage along the Acadian coast and up La Baie Françoise, as the Bay of Fundy is called on Champlain's maps.

Champlain returned to Port à Mouton and started off again in the flagship with de Monts to see whether one of the places he had reconnoitered would do for at least a temporary settlement. Passing Gulliver's Hole, they sailed through Digby Gut into Annapolis Basin and noted a good spot behind Goat Island; there the Port-Royal habitation was built a year later. Up the Bay again, they discovered samples of real copper in the rocks at Advocate Harbor, which they named Port aux Mines. They then crossed the Bay of Fundy to the New Brunswick shore, noted and named (as it was 24 June) the St. John River with its reversing falls; but evidently regarded this site as inadequate. It was far more suitable than the one they chose — Sainte-Croix Island in the like-named river.

The historian Francis Parkman, who sailed along this coast in the summer of 1871, has an unrivaled description of an overcast day, anywhere between St. John and Machias Bay: "The dull grey sky, the dull grey sea; the dark waste of ridgy forests; the mists that float around the brows of cold, stern cliffs; the reefs and rocks that lie in sullen slumber on the leaden waters. Now the fog rolls in and all is veiled from sight, till the seamed and scarred front of some grisly headland, crowned with bristling firs, looms grimly through the mists." Often have I seen the coast like this, both here and in Newfoundland; but memory cherishes the day when the wind changes to off-shore, bringing the smell of verdure, and both mist and fog vanish, the sun comes out, bringing out colors in the granite cliffs, lighting the ocean to a deep amethyst while the northwest wind flecks it with the brightest of whitecaps. Then each headland no longer "looms

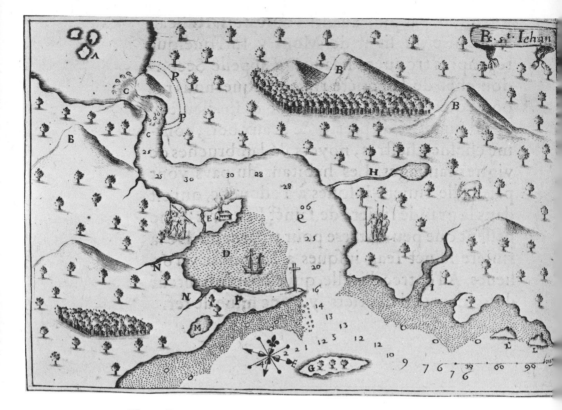

Champlain's chart of the St. John River, New Brunswick. From Les Voyages (1613). The city of St. John now covers all the eastern half, and most of the western too. KEY: A. *"Three Islands above the Falls."* B. *"Hills seen from seaward" (from west to east, sites of the Martello tower, Fort Howe, and the City Hospital).* C. *The reversing falls.* D. *"Shoals where ships can ground out at low water."* E. *"Hut where the Savages fortify themselves."* F. *"A gravelly point, where stands a cross" erected by Champlain.* G. *Partridge Island.* H. *"A little Brook which flows from a Little Pond" (now the railway yards).* I. *Courtenay Bay (much too small).* O. *"Dangerous Shoals, dry at Low Water."* P. *Portage around the falls.* Q. *Best anchorage. Courtesy Harvard College Library.*

grimly" but shines brilliantly, inviting the sailor to seek the snug little harbor which it marks.

Entering Passamaquoddy Bay and sailing north up that tidal river,* de Monts and Champlain encountered midstream a little island that they named after the Holy Cross.† Here they set up the second European year-round settlement in the eastern United States north of Spanish Florida. (The first, which Champlain knew about, was at Ingonish by the Portuguese Fagundes.)

It was now mid-June, and de Monts's men were tortured by black flies and mosquitoes as they labored to set up a prefabricated village. The sawn timbers, doors and windows had been brought from France in the ships' holds. Champlain, who sketched the settlement for his next book, shows a single house for the commander, a long covered gallery "where we passed the time during the rain," a communal kitchen overhanging the cliff, barracks for the workmen and *les Suisses* — apparently a company of Swiss mercenaries — a forge, two blocks of houses for the officers, and one for the curé adjoining a little chapel. They also built an out door oven for baking bread, and planted kitchen gardens. Every building was attractively located around a central plaza shaded by a great elm. Guns from the flagship, mounted on a rocky ledge facing south, commanded the river. In summertime, Sainte-Croix was very pretty and cozy, but winter there was dramatically different.

Many have speculated why English and French pioneers had such a predilection for pitching their first settlements on islands — Roanoke and Jamestown, Sable Island, the one in Rio de Janeiro Bay, and here. Probably the main reason was defense; the notion

---

* Champlain called it Rivière des Etchemins; later it took the name of the island, Sainte-Croix.

† Renamed Dochet Island in the colonial régime, in recent years it has been made part of the National Park system, with the original name restored. It is about four miles north of the western entrance to the harbor of St. Andrews, N.B., which is indicated on Champlain's map but not named.

Champlain's chart of Sainte-Croix Island. From Les Voyages (1613). KEY: *A. The habitation. B. "Garden." C. and D. Islets. E. "Cemetery." F. "Chapel." G. "Rocky reefs around said Island." I (on mainland). "Place where de Monts began a water mill." L. "Place where we made charcoal." M and N. Mainland gardens. P. "Rivière des Etchemins passing around Sainte-Croix Island." Lower left, de Monts's ship is firing a salute; upper right, a shallop. Courtesy Harvard College Library.*

that an island would be immune to a surprise attack by Indians in canoes, or European enemies approaching by sea. But Sainte-Croix Island could not support de Monts's colony of well over a hundred men, even in summer. Vegetables would not grow in the sandy soil; de Monts had to plant gardens and sow wheat on the mainland. The spring of fresh water went dry, and as the river at this point was still very salty, water as well as firewood had to be boated from the mainland. Power for the grist mill could be found only on a mainland rivulet, and the hand mill for turning wheat into flour was so difficult to grind that nobody wanted to do it.

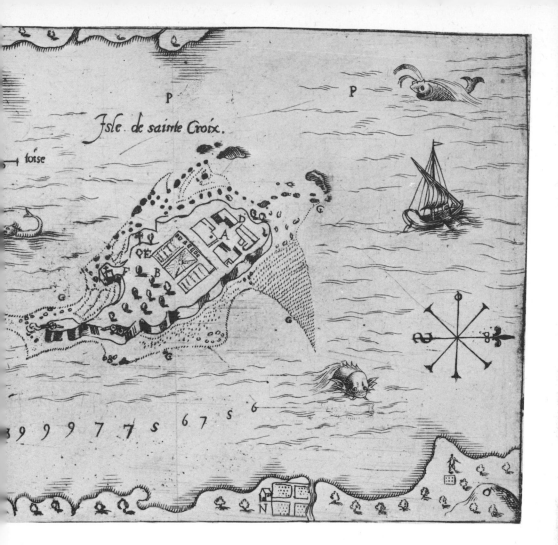

Isle de sainte Croix.

The paid workmen were sulky and miserable because there were no Indian girls.

Champlain now made two pinnace cruises from Sainte-Croix. The purpose of the first, up the Bay of Fundy, was to check the alleged copper deposit. He brought back a few samples of copper ore, not enough to cause excitement; but he did attend an assembly of Indians at the site of St. John, New Brunswick. These natives he called Etchemins (Englished as Etchimin); they were also known as the Souriquois and the Micmac; only the last name has survived. They were one of the tribes or subdivisions of what

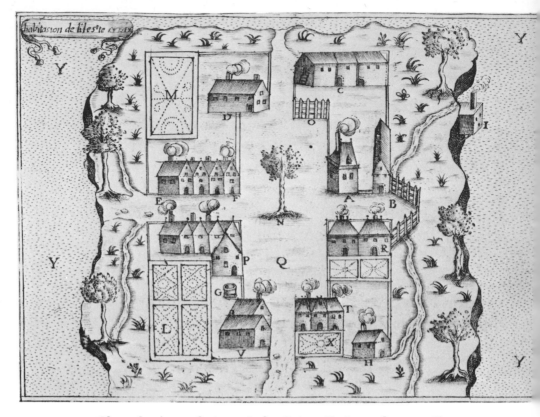

Champlain's rendering of the Sainte-Croix settlement. From Les Voyages (1613). KEY: *A. "The Sieur de Monts's Lodging." B. Covered gallery and shelter from rain. C. "Storehouse." D. "Barracks of the Swiss." E. "Forge." F. "Carpenter's Lodgings." G. "The Well." H. "The Oven where we baked bread." I (overhanging the river). "The Kitchen." L and M. "Gardens." N. "The Square, with a tree in the middle." O. "Palisade." P. "Lodging of the Sieurs d'Orville, Champlain and Champdoré." Q, R, T. Lodgings of several other sieurs and artisans. V. "Lodging of our curé." X. "Other Gardens." Y. "The River which surrounds the Island." Courtesy Harvard College Library.*

modern ethnologists call the Abnaki Confederacy, which occupied the coast between Cape Breton and Casco Bay, Maine. This Algonkin-language race were noted for their friendliness by all European explorers. Of the Etchimin encountered by Champlain in 1604 he wrote, "When we were seated they began to smoke, as was their custom before making any discourse. They made us presents of game and venison. All that day and the night following they continued to sing, dance and feast until day reappeared. They were clothed in beaver skins." Here, as elsewhere, Champlain appreciated the natives' good qualities, and they took a great liking to him. It is not too much to say that Champlain's Indian relations, in contrast to those of Cartier, were responsible for the Abnaki becoming faithful allies to France throughout the colonial period. Unfortunately they did not pick the winner; and their rather pitiful remnants in small reservations on Passamaquoddy Bay and at Old Town, Maine, are still struggling to survive against the pressure of surrounding "civilization."

The purpose of Champlain's second cruise was "to explore the coast of Norumbega" and find a suitable place for a permanent French settlement. This cruise, starting from Sainte-Croix 2 September 1604, was conducted in a *patache* or pinnace of 17 to 18 tuns with twelve sailors and two friendly Etchimin as pilots and interpreters. These two cruises were Champlain's first definite sea command (not counting his tour of the Bay of Fundy), and he was justly proud of them. Every old-time sailor or modern yachtsman who has sailed in those waters admires Champlain, not only for avoiding submerged rocks but for his remarkably accurate maps and harbor charts, the best ever made of northern America in that century.

The pinnace ran into a "thick o' fog" and did not really get started until 5 September; she sailed outside a big island which Champlain called Le Grand Manan, since *menan* or *manan* was the Abnaki name for island. Once clear of it, Champlain sighted a group of rocky islets so covered with puffin that he called them Iles des Perroquets, the French-Canadian name for those remarkable little parrot-billed birds. Several big islands such as Cross, the Libbys, Head Harbor, Steel Harbor and Great Wass he called Les Iles Rangées because their outer coasts are remarkably in line; you may steer twenty miles from one end of them to the other without altering course, unless the tides surging in and out of Machias Bay catch you. He then reached a tiny, rocky, spruce-covered islet at the end of a long bar which he called Le Petit Manan; and Petit (or, as the natives call it, 'Tit) Manan it is to this day, when a tall lighthouse has replaced the spruce trees. For the night he put in at one of the little harbors (Birch, Wonsqueak or Prospect) on the east side of Schoodic Peninsula.

Next day he rounded that peninsula and headed for a mountainous island which he had sighted the day before. Owing to its bare granite summits, Champlain named this L'Isle des Montsdéserts, and Mount Desert Island it still is, the most beautiful of all the islands discovered by him, or anyone else, on the New England–Nova Scotia coast.

This 6th of September 1604 was a halcyon day, with calm sea and a light easterly breeze. Champlain, seeing smoke arising from a cove on the south side of Mount Desert Island, steered for it, but his lookouts were so careless that the pinnace struck a submerged rock off Otter Cliff and punctured a hole in her garboard strake. That required repairs, which were quickly effected at the nearest mud flat, in Otter Creek. The Etchimin, who came there every summer to fish and dig clams, were friendly and furnished Champlain with a guide to the Penobscot River, where their head chief resided. The Frenchman's consistent courtesy to the natives paid off here as elsewhere. Nine years later, when a French colony arrived off Mount Desert Island, Asticou, sagamore of the summering Indians at the entrance to Somes Sound, invited them to settle over against his own village.

As the pinnace passed along the outer shore of Mount Desert and out to sea by the Western Way, more *monts déserts* opened up, until one could count ten different peaks, not including the two little Bubbles. None were given names by the French; the easternmost, the first that he saw, is now called after Champlain himself. And his name for Nova Scotia and eastern Maine has been adopted in the present century for the Acadia National Park, which covers parts of Mount Desert Island, Schoodic Peninsula and Isle au Haut.

Since 1529, when the fjord-like Somes Sound of Mount Desert first appeared on Diogo Ribero's map as Río de las Montañas, this island had been mapped as a part of the mainland. Champlain ascertained from his Indian acquaintances that it was an island indeed, separated from the main by a narrow channel bare at low water. And so it appears with surprising accuracy on his 1607 map.

Having repaired his pinnace and floated her, Champlain on 7 September 1604 left the great harbor of Mount Desert, passing the sites of the future villages of Seal Harbor, Northeast Harbor and Southwest Harbor, and headed out to sea by the Western Way. Once outside, he sighted another conspicuously high island, steered for it, and named it Isle Haulte; and Isle au Haut it still is. The Indian guide then piloted him west of the Fox Islands, up Penobscot Bay. He mapped the bigger islands such as Sears and Islesboro, dubbed in numerous small islets and rocks, depicted the Camden chain of hills, and clearly indicated the harbors named Camden, Castine and Rockland. When the wind is fair and the sun shining, this sail up Penobscot Bay, with island after island rising over the northern horizon and becoming more beautiful as you approach, is something to remember. Woe, woe to those who

"L'Isle des Monts-déserts" from over Mount Desert Rock.
Photo by Augustus Phillips of Northeast Harbor.

L'Isle des Monts Déserts. ABOVE: *Otter Cliff; the rock that Champlain struck is breaking.* BELOW: *Otter Creek, where Champlain beached his pinnace.*

Isle au Haut (above) and Georges Islands. From foreground: Davis, Benner and Allen islands; Monhegan in background. Photos by James F. Nields, 1971.

would ruin Penobscot Bay with an oil refinery or other abomination!

Champlain had reached the region known to both English and French as Norumbega. Passing the Bucksport Narrows, he searched in vain for the turreted stone city which earlier map-makers had placed a little north of that point, and for the highly sophisticated natives clad in sumptuous furs with gold trimmings which the famous foot traveler David Ingram reported. Champlain concluded that none of these tellers of tall tales or depicters of imaginary cities had ever been up the Penobscot; for his part, he would "tell the truth of what I have discovered and seen from the mouth of the bay, as far as I have been." That was a typical Champlain statement, and true. No magic, mythical kingdoms of Saguenay or El Dorado are in his writings and (even more surprising) not one hint or promise of gold or precious stones.

He used the Algonkins' names for Penobscot Bay (Pentagoët) and for the mainland (Bedabedec), and gave the correct latitude, 44° N, for the river mouth. Near the site of Bangor, then covered by a beautiful oak grove, two local sagamores named Bessabez and Cabahis parleyed with Champlain through his interpreter. They seemed to be pleased with his assurance that the French wished to settle among them, to make peace with their enemies, and to show them how to farm their land properly. Cabahis, whose seat lay near Belfast, told Champlain about the portage between the headwaters of the Penobscot and the Sainte-Croix, and via Chesuncook Lake to the Chaudière River, which empties into the St. Lawrence. It is strange that, after ascertaining these natives to be friendly, and the Penobscot to be key to a maze of inland waterways and to peltry, Champlain did not persuade de Monts to pitch his permanent colony there. The probable reason is that Poutrincourt, as we shall see, fell in love with the Annapolis Basin in Nova Scotia. In the long run, Quebec proved to be far better than the Penobscot as the center of New France; it drained a much greater territory for the fur trade, and the English and other enemies found it more difficult to get at. Pentagoët, like Mount Desert, was too near Virginia to be healthy for Frenchmen.

The conference with Bessabez and Cabahis took place on 16 September, and next day the pinnace dropped down the river with the ebb tide, passed the "Mountains of Bedabedec" (the Camden Hills), and anchored in Rockland Harbor. Here, when the captain intimated that he wished to visit "Quinebequy" (the Kennebec), his guides left him in their canoes; for the Armouchiquois Indians in that part of Maine were not, at that time, friendly, and the Etchimin feared trouble. Champlain's pinnace rounded Owls Head, threaded the Muscle Ridge channel, passed Mosquito Island, sailed outside Muscongus Bay, and put in at an island harbor ten leagues short of the Kennebec. This was the one which George Weymouth visited the following year and named after St. George. And Georges Island Harbor it still is.

It was now 23 September, the weather turned foul and provisions were running short; so Champlain, hoping to extend the Maine cruise next year, turned eastward and arrived at Sainte-Croix on 2 October. He found all the buildings erected and everything (as they thought) made snug for winter. Poutrincourt had sailed for home with the two ships, leaving the Sieur de Monts and seventy-eight other Frenchmen at Sainte-Croix. Also the two pinnaces, which were hauled out for the winter.

It often happened that North American explorers who spent the winter had the good luck to hit a comparatively mild one, which aroused false expectations. The contrary happened here. The winter of 1604–1605 set in early and severely, like that of 1970–71. On 6 October, even before the autumn foliage reached its brilliant height, snow fell; on 3 December ice floes began floating down-river, cutting the Frenchmen off from their gardens, woodlots, and springs of fresh water. Let us quote the maestro, Francis Parkman, for a vivid description of what that hard winter meant for this "one weak band of Frenchmen, clinging as it were for life, to the fringe of the vast and savage continent":

"The gray and sullen autumn sank upon the waste, and the bleak wind howled down from the St. Croix and swept the forest bare. Then the whirling snow powdered the vast sweep of desolate woodland, and shrouded in white the gloomy green of pine-clad mountains. Ice in sheets, or broken masses, swept by their island with the ebbing and flowing tide, often debarring all access to the main, and cutting off their supplies of wood and water. A belt of cedars, indeed, hedged the island; but de Monts had ordered them to be spared, that the north wind might spend something of its force with whistling through their shaggy boughs. Cider and wine froze in the casks, and were served out by the pound. As they crowded round their half-fed fires, shivering in the icy currents that pierced their rude tenements, many sank into a desperate apathy.

"Soon the scurvy broke out, and raged with a fearful malignity. Of the seventy-nine, thirty-five died before spring, and many more were brought to the verge of death. In vain they sought that marvellous tree which had relieved the followers of Cartier. Their little cemetery was peopled with nearly half their number, and the rest, bloated and disfigured with the relentless malady, thought more of escaping from their woes than of building up a transatlantic empire. Yet among them there was one, at least, who, amid languor and defection, held to his purpose with indomitable tenacity; and where Champlain was present, there was no room for despair."

Champlain himself wisely concluded, "It was impossible to know this country without having wintered there, for on arriving in summer everything is very pleasant owing to the woods, the fair landscape, and the good fishing for cod and other species which we found. *But winter in this country lasts six months.*" It surely did in 1604–1605!

The first break came in March. A band of friendly Indians called at Sainte-Croix and, for trading truck, sold game that they had recently killed; that stopped the scurvy. Poutrincourt was expected back any day, but he came not, and the "mocking spring's perpetual loss" (as a New England poet put it) proved less fatal, but even more discouraging than the winter. By 15 May the situation seemed so desperate that de Monts made preparations to abandon Sainte-Croix; he ordered the two pinnaces to be launched and rigged, planning to sail all survivors to Gaspé, where they would be sure to find fishermen to take them to France. But on 15 June, before they were ready for sea, there arrived a shallop from Captain Pont-Gravé's ship (she had been to France and back), anchored in Quoddy roads, and the ship came up shortly after. She was joyfully hailed with sound of trumpet and roar of cannon. Now assured of support from home, de Monts shifted his plans and took command of the big pinnace on a cruise westward to seek out a better place than Sainte-Croix to settle down. Champlain became his first officer, navigator and artist. For pilots they selected a local Etchimin named Panounias and his wife, because she came from the tribe that lived around the Kennebec and so could help the French communicate with the natives of those parts, whom Champlain called Almouchiquois or Armouchiquois.*

Sailing 18 June 1605 from Sainte-Croix, our explorers enjoyed

---

* This term was loosely applied to the Algonkin tribes of southern Maine and eastern Massachusetts, who spoke a different language from the Abnaki and were frequently at war with them.

the best season of the year to range the New England coast under sail. Seventeen hours of daylight, little fog, balmy breezes wafting out to sea the odor of growing things, birch and maple flinging out their tassels and light green leaves against the dark evergreen background; and as you threaded a narrow passage or entered a harbor, a tumult of birdsong. After passing through Grand Manan Channel, the pinnace anchored in a sheltered harbor of the Isles Rangées — probably the one now called Head Harbor, with an inner basin so completely landlocked as to be called the Cow Yard. There the men shot a large number of crows, and Champlain named the conspicuous Black Head of Head Harbor Island, Cap Corneille. Without stopping, he passed outside Mount Desert and Isle au Haut and anchored in a harbor near Bedabedec (Owls Head). Next day with a fine off-shore wind the pinnace zoomed along to the mouth of the Kennebec. The lofty island that we call by its Indian name, Seguin, they noted and named La Tortue; *seguin* means turtle. De Monts decided to sail up this Rivière de Quinebequy, as he called it, partly because a heavy fog lay on the waters outside. Entering, Champlain noted the two islands later called Pond and Stage and the bare pinnacle rocks now called the Sugar Loaves, and anchored in a cove of Stage Island where his pinnace is depicted. The chart of the Kennebec entrance reproduced here is one of Champlain's best — it is amazing that he could get so many details accurately with only two nights' stay.

Indians who had come to fowl and fish were encamped on Sabino Head on the west side of the entrance. A canoe full of them was accosted by Panounias and wife, who satisfied them that the Frenchmen were friendly and persuaded one or two to volunteer as river pilots. They led the pinnace not up the main channel but up their regular canoe route; the narrow, sinuous Back River, which only small power boats dare use today. This took the pin-

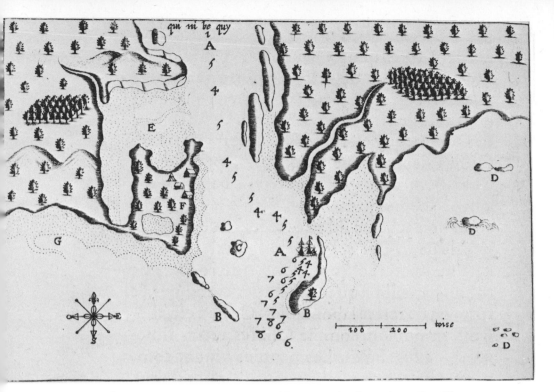

Mouth of the Kennebec River. ABOVE: *Champlain's chart, from* Les Voyages
(1613). KEY: A. *"Main stream of the river," with a ship at Champlain's
anchorage. B. "Two islands which make the river entrance" (Pond and
Stage). C. "Two very dangerous rocks" (the Sugar Loaves). D. "Islets and
rocks along the coast" (the one awash is Black Rock). E. "Mud flats where
6o-tun ships may be grounded" (Atkins Bay). F. "Place where the savages
camp when they come to fish" (Sabino Head). Courtesy Harvard College
Library.* BELOW: *View of the same site in 1971, from the west. Photo by
James F. Nields.*

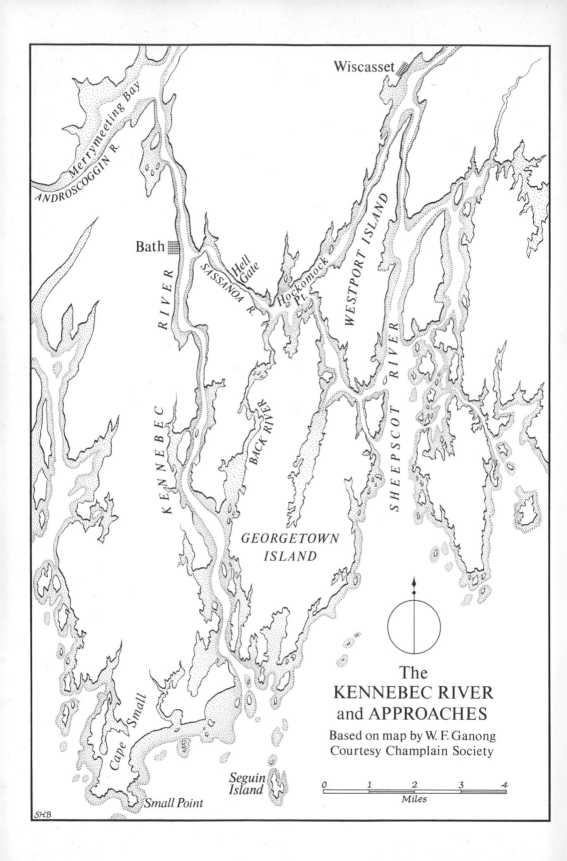

Wiscasset

Merrymeeting Bay

ANDROSCOGGIN R.

Androscoggin R.

Bath

KENNEBEC RIVER

SASSANOA R.

Hell Gate

Hockomock Pt.

WESTPORT ISLAND

SHEEPSCOT RIVER

BACK RIVER

GEORGETOWN ISLAND

Cape Small

Seguin Island

Small Point

SHB

The
KENNEBEC RIVER
and **APPROACHES**

Based on map by W. F. Ganong
Courtesy Champlain Society

0   1   2   3   4
Miles

nace to Hockomock Bay, a widening of the inland passage between Bath and Boothbay much frequented in days of sail. The pinnace turned east and then north, leaving Westport Island on the starboard hand, to the site of the town of Wiscasset. There de Monts and Champlain parleyed with a chief named Manthoumermer, who welcomed them warmly, inviting the French to become his allies in war and (somewhat inconsistently) to mediate peace with the Abnaki. The chief then provided pilots to take the pinnace by a short route to the main channel of the Kennebec. They passed Hockomock Point, upon which each Indian pilot cast an arrowhead for good luck in passing the next stage, the tidal rapids which the English named Upper Hell Gate. Although they had a fair wind and bellying sails, the French got through only by attaching hawsers to trees and all hands pulling with full strength against the current. Your author, more fortunate, calculated the hour of quiet water and triumphantly sailed through. That was sixty-five years ago, but he could not do it now, when this beautiful tidal passage is closed by bridges.

Reaching the Kennebec at the site of Bath, the pinnace sailed up Merrymeeting Bay, where the Androscoggin River joins. But there was then no meeting, merry or otherwise — they waited a day for two sagamores who were to meet them there, but who never showed up. Champlain, however, learned about the canoe portage route via Dead River and the Chaudière to *"le grand fleuve S. Laurens."* The pinnace sailed quickly downstream, passing shores which Champlain dismissed as of slight value and (on the starboard hand) Sabino Head, where the Northern Virginia Company would pitch its Sagadahoc settlement only two years later. De Monts anchored his pinnace off Stage Island as before, and next day continued along the coast westward.

All the way to Cape Cod the Indians were very friendly, dancing and shouting welcome on every headland that the Frenchmen approached; and they approached most of them, since Champlain had learned how to sail close to shore by keeping a sharp lookout and frequently heaving the lead. They called at Richmond Island (which Champlain named Ile de Bacchus for its wild grapes), sailed up the lower Saco (Chouacoit) River, where they encountered a handsome young chief named Honemechin, who wore his hair in a carefully cultivated roach topped by feathers and braided behind. Here, for the first time in L'Acadie or New England, Champlain found cultivation. The Indians manured their corn hills with the *signoc,* the curious horseshoe crab, which greatly interested Champlain and is depicted on two of his maps. In the same gardens they grew bush beans (which he called *febues du Bresil*), pumpkins, and tobacco, which he called *petun,* the name which the French had picked up in Brazil. "The fixed abodes, the cultivation, and the fine trees" — hickory, oak, beech, ash, elm — wrote Champlain, "caused us to believe that the climate is more temperate here than that where we wintered. . . . This is a very pleasant place, as attractive a spot as one can see anywhere."

Champlain's chart of Saco Bay is one of his best, although the distance between Fletcher Neck and the mouth of the Saco River is too great in proportion to the distance to Prout's Neck. The soundings, too, are on the conservative side; and he missed the narrow entrance to Biddeford Pool. In mid-nineteenth century the Pool and Old Orchard Beach, north of the river mouth, became famous summer resorts; and Prout's Neck, where Champlain shows his boat going ashore to greet Chief Marchin on his return trip, is where the artist Winslow Homer did some of his best work. Even earlier this bay became noted for shipwrecks, owing probably to schooners and brigs missing Portland harbor, so in 1808 a lighthouse was erected on Wood Island, which Champlain shows large as life, off Fletcher Neck. Everyone who sailed

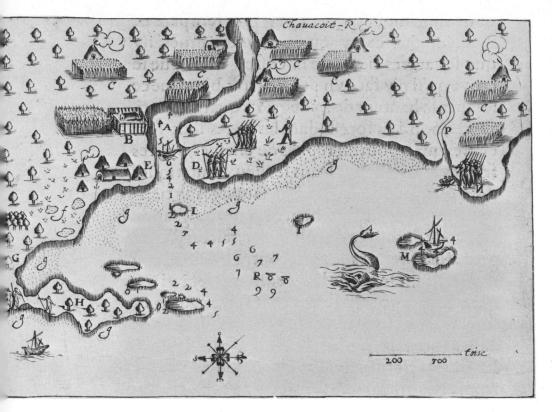

Champlain's chart of Chouacoit (Saco Bay). From Les Voyages
(1613). KEY: *A. The Saco River, with the pinnace at anchor. B. The
savages' "fortress." C. "Cabins which are in the fields, near which
they . . . grow Indian corn." D. "Extensive plain, covered with
grass." E. "Place where they camp together . . . after planting their
corn." F. "Marsh, where there's good pasturage." G. "Spring of fresh
water." g. Old Orchard and other beaches. H. Fletcher Neck, "all
cleared except for some fruit trees and wild grapes." I. Ram and
Eagle islands. M. "Two islands where vessels may find a sheltered
anchorage with good holding ground." These are Stratten and Bluff
islands, and the pinnace is depicted in the 4-fathom anchorage between them. N. Prout's Neck, with boat going ashore to greet Chief
Marchin, on the French return journey. O (letter not on map). "Four
islands" off Fletcher Neck, now Wood, Tappan, Stage, and Basket.
R. "Roadstead where vessels may anchor awaiting the flood tide."
Courtesy Harvard College Library.*

along that coast around the middle of this century will remember the lighthouse keeper's dog, who would respond to a signal by grasping the fog bell's lanyard in his teeth and tolling the bell.

One infers from Champlain's enthusiastic account that he would have chosen Saco Bay for a settlement, but the Sieur de Monts would have none of it.

On 12 July the pinnace made sail and continued westward. She anchored off Wells Neck, owing to adverse wind, and Champlain admired a flock of redwing blackbirds. This anchorage being unprotected, the pinnace backtracked a few miles and took refuge in the completely landlocked harbor of Cape Porpoise. He did not complain of the swarms of mosquitoes from nearby salt marshes, but for which Le Cap aux Iles, as Champlain called this place, would be a yachtsman's paradise. He took the latitude of the harbor only four miles short of correct, and the sailors shot a quantity of wild pigeon which were feeding on wild currants, the *groseille rouge* depicted on his map of 1612.

Departing Cape Porpoise 15 July 1605, de Monts and Champlain passed Boon Island without noting it, and stretched across Ipswich Bay, inside the Isles of Shoals, which they called Iles Gettées, to Cape Ann. Champlain named this majestic cape Le Cap aux Isles, one of the islands being the Dry Salvages about which T. S. Eliot built a great poem. Indians dancing a welcome on the beach were approached in a boat by Champlain, who gave to each a knife and a ship-biscuit, and they helped him with a stick of charcoal to draw a crude chart of Massachusetts Bay. After anchoring behind Salt Island and passing the sites of Marblehead and Nahant, the pinnace entered Boston Bay. Champlain well named it Baye des Isles and anchored close to an island, probably the future East Boston, where Logan Airport is now located. Here Champlain saw dugout canoes for the first time since his West Indies voyages; south of Cape Ann the paper birch did not grow big enough to make bark canoes. He did not like them, as they were much more tiddly than the bark kind. Nor did he care for the future Boston harbor; he probably estimated that the Charles River was too small to be an artery for fur trade. He named it, however, Rivière du Gua, after the family of the Sieur de Monts.

One may speculate endlessly as to the course of history if the French had settled at the site of Boston and had received enough support from home to defend it against the English Puritans. The Pilgrim Fathers, in that event, would have been forced to settle at the mouth of the Hudson, as they originally intended to do, and a town on the Rivière du Gua would have become the capital of a New France extending from Cape Cod or Long Island to the North Pole. This is all fantasy, for de Monts and Champlain did not like this location nearly as well as the Penobscot, or Annapolis Basin, Nova Scotia.

On 17 July the pinnace sortied from Boston harbor and steered for the cliffs of Scituate, then for Brant Rock, a peninsula situated about five miles short of the Gurnet. After turning back briefly because the Indians there were sending up smoke signals (which the French had learned to be an invitation), the pinnace hit Bartletts Rock on a falling tide, and it took quick work to get her off. "God preserved us," wrote Champlain. Natives who came out in big dugout canoes were ready to trade and gave the French small green squashes or pumpkins the size of one's fist, which Champlain said made "good salad." The pinnace then rounded the Gurnet and anchored in a fair harbor which the Captain named Port Saint-Louis after the royal saint of France.

This was the famous Plymouth, where the Pilgrim Fathers settled fifteen years later. The Aptucxet Indians, whom de Monts and Champlain found there in large numbers, were exterminated by a pestilence several years before the Pilgrims occupied their

territory. Governor Bradford, while thankful for this dispensa-
tion of Providence, would have been saved a lot of trouble finding a good anchorage for the *Mayflower* had he owned a copy
of Champlain's chart.

In entering Plymouth harbor, Champlain grounded his pinnace
on Brown Bank, and while awaiting the flood tide to float her off,
landed on Long Beach, where he climbed a convenient dune from
which to sketch his chart.

Two English voyagers, Bartholomew Gosnold and Martin
Pring, had already coasted this area, and the merry greetings that
the French pinnace received from all natives, prior to Nauset, indicate that these Englishmen had given them good usage.

On 19 July the pinnace departed the site of Plymouth. De
Monts, not knowing the bearing or distance of Cape Cod (so
named by Gosnold in 1602), followed the shores of Cape Cod Bay,
doubling Cap Blanc as Champlain called it. He described it as "a
sandy point which turns south some six leagues." The pinnace
stood south and put into Port Mallebarre, as he named Nauset
Harbor. It was low tide when she entered, with but four feet of
water in the channel, but she scraped through safely. Here the
French encountered the Nauset tribe who, although they came
dancing down to the beach in welcome, later misbehaved.

On 21 July some gentlemen went ashore with an armed guard
and found the natives pleasant enough, but were unable to communicate except by signs. A northeast gale blew up, detaining the
pinnace in the harbor for four days. On the 23rd, four French
sailors went ashore, each carrying a big kettle to fill with spring
water. The Indians snatched one of the kettles, and a fight ensued
in which a sailor was struck down by arrows and dispatched
with knives. The French fired a fusillade from the pinnace, but
hit nobody. Champlain said it was no use trying to catch them,

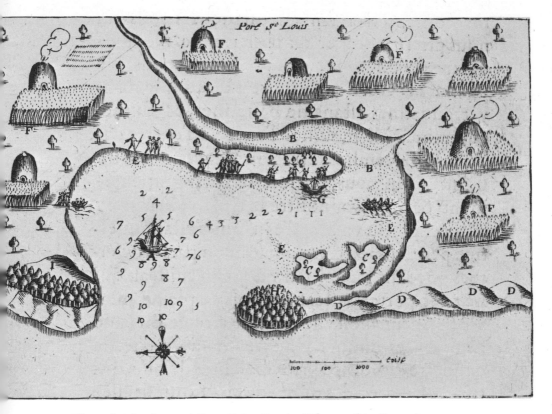

Champlain's chart of Port Saint-Louis (Plymouth). From Les
Voyages *(1613).* KEY: *A. "Anchorage," with his pinnace.*
B. "The Channel" (to the inner harbor). C. "Two Islands"
(Clarks, where the Pilgrim Fathers spent their first night
ashore in 1620, and Saquish Head). D. "Sand Dunes" (along
Duxbury Beach to the Gurnet). E. "Mud Flats" and a much
foreshortened Duxbury Bay. F. "Cabins where the savages till
the soil." G. "Spot where our pinnace ran aground" (Brown
Bank; the point adjacent is Long Beach). H. The Gurnet. Cour-
tesy Harvard College Library.

W. F. Ganong in the Champlain Society edition of Cham-
plain's Works *(I 346) has most interesting notes on this chart.*
He observes that Champlain's soundings are about double
those of today, owing doubtless to silting.

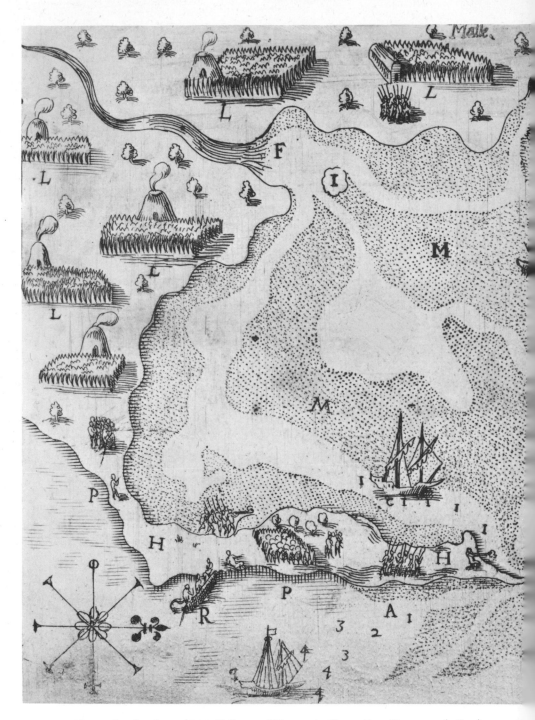

Champlain's chart of Mallebarre (Nauset). From Les Voyages *(1613).* KEY:
*A. "Two entrances to the harbor." These have since closed up, and one en-
ters about where Champlain places a P. B. "Sand dunes where the savages
killed a sailor." C. "Anchorage of the Sieur de Monts's pinnace." D. "Spring
on the edge of the harbor." E. Nauset Meadow beach. F. "A brook" — outlet
of Roberts Cove. G. "Brook where one takes a lot of fish" — eel trap included.*

H. "Sand dunes where there's a little wood and a lot of grapevines" (since washed away by the sea). L. "Houses and habitations of the savages who till the soil." M. "Shoals and sand-banks without and within said harbor." O. "Sand Dunes." q. "The Sieur de Poutrincourt's pinnace when he came here two years later." R. "Landing of the Sieur de Poutrincourt's people." Courtesy Harvard College Library.

Nauset Harbor, 1971

"for they ran fast as horses," and de Monts was too humane to kill an Indian hostage on board, or to fire into a fresh group of natives who came down to the beach protesting that they had had no part in the kettle-snatching episode.

Champlain concluded that the natives of the New England coast were great thieves who, when they could not lay hands on a desirable object, filched it with their toes; but he remarks charitably that if they had had anything to sell they might not have stolen. The Nauset had no spare furs at this season, and so bartered their implements of archery for pins and lace-points, and gave the French a quantity of tobacco which they had grown, dried, and reduced to powder. They brayed corn in wooden mortars and made the resulting meal into cakes and biscuits, or boiled it in earthen pots. The Indians talked about a bird which he guessed to be the wild turkey, but he never saw one.

Returning from "the discoveries on the Armouchiquois coast," as Champlain called this cruise, and without finding any place that he or de Monts considered suitable for a permanent settlement, the pinnace set sail from Nauset harbor 25 July 1605. She was nearly cast away on the harbor bar, the Mallebarre, through the carelessness of two pilots, Cramolet and Champdoré, who had supposedly buoyed the channel, but they got clear with very little damage. Cramolet, whom we never hear of again, seems to have been sacked; but Champdoré piloted many more expeditions. The pinnace rounded Cape Cod, then sailed fifteen leagues on the same tack to Cape Ann, and east-northeast sixteen leagues to Chouacoit, the Saco. There, on Prout's Neck, Champlain and de Monts held a parley with Chief Marchin, whom they had missed at Merry-meeting Bay. Champlain recorded that "savage though he was," Marchin impressed him as a man of impressive port and grave gestures, so he named the bay after him on his 1607 map. De Monts gave Marchin many gifts, and in return he entrusted the French with an Etchimin boy, a war prisoner, to return to his people.

Thence the pinnace sailed fifteen leagues northeast by east to the mouth of the Kennebec, where a local chief informed them that there was an English ship about, whose people had killed five Indians under cover of friendship. This was Captain George Weymouth's *Archangel,* which had kidnapped, not killed, five Indians at Monhegan. That is the high island well off the coast which Champlain saw from a distance and named La Nef, the ship, because it looked like one. His pinnace next sailed east-northeast twenty leagues to Isle au Haut, where she anchored; and on 1 August made twenty leagues by the outside route to Cap Corneille on Head Harbor Island. Another day's sail of seven leagues took them to Quoddy roads, where de Monts pushed off in a canoe, paddling up-river to Sainte-Croix.

V

Port-Royal and Cruise to Cape Cod

D E MONTS now rejected the idea of removing to one of the good harbors which he and Champlain had discovered in the pinnace, in favor of Port-Royal on the upper part of Annapolis Basin, Nova Scotia, which they had discovered in 1604. With them on that trip had been the attractive young nobleman Poutrincourt, who fell in love with Port-Royal. He promised to bring his family out and spend the rest of his life there if de Monts would cede it to him, and de Monts did just that. It was doubtless he who persuaded the leader to pitch his permanent settlement there rather than on the Penobscot, the Kennebec, the Saco or the St. John.

So, all buildings (except the storehouse) erected at Sainte-Croix were taken down, their planks and timbers stowed in the two pinnaces and freighted across the Bay of Fundy to Port-Royal. There, behind Goat Island (Lescarbot's *belle île forêtière*), at a place now called Upper Granville, the same materials were used to erect a single habitation in the form of a hollow square. Fortunately, Champlain sketched it, which has made possible the erection of a replica in the present century. Most units of the Sainte-Croix community were re-erected, in blocks; but a fine new kitchen, at one angle of the habitation, replaced the cliff-hanging one on the island. There were lodgings for sailors and for the workmen, of whom only a minority had survived the previous winter; separate lodgings for the four leaders, a *salle d'armes* for the soldiers, and two platforms facing the water for mounting ships' cannon. This habitation was very well sited, with its front on the well-protected Annapolis Basin and its back to a range of hills of 500 to 700 feet elevation, which afforded protection from winter northers. A further asset was the friendship of Membertou, the local sagamore, a great warrior of tall stature, bearded like a Frenchman and, by exception, monogamous. He allowed himself to be baptized, became a faithful friend to the French, and saw to it that they never starved. Later, in the long, dreary spring of 1609 at Quebec, when provisions gave out, Champlain must often have felt, "Oh if only we had Membertou and his Souriquois here, instead of these lazy Montagnais who can't even feed themselves!"

When every building had been set up, de Monts sailed for France, carrying souvenirs for the king such as a live caribou, a live moose calf, and bright bird feathers. He left Pont-Gravé in charge, with Champlain as second in command.

As an example of how Frenchmen made themselves at home in the New World, Champlain created a little garden near the habitation, with a *cabinet*, a sort of gazebo where he might take his ease. Close by he dammed up spring-fed brooks to make a pond for live trout, and on the harbor's edge he constructed a "little reservoir" of salt water for keeping sea perch and rock cod alive. "We often went there," he wrote of this place, "to pass the time; and it seemed to please the little birds of the neighborhood; for they assembled there in great numbers and made such a pleasant warbling and twittering, of which I have never heard the like."

The winter of 1605–1606 that followed at Port-Royal was not so severe as the preceding one at Sainte-Croix, but bad enough. Snow first fell on 20 December. Scurvy again took its toll; one wonders why Cartier's cure, of arborvitae broth, which Champlain had heard about, was not successful in these early seventeenth-century colonies. Twelve of the forty-five men who moved thither from Sainte-Croix died, and among the victims were the squabbling priest and minister; the sailors insisted on burying them in a common grave, "to see if dead they would live in peace, which they never had alive." Membertou's men brought in supplies of game and peltry, and the French had enough wheat for baking bread; only the wine gave out.

At the first signs of spring, the search for a better place was resumed, and Champlain made his third New England cruise. He called it "a voyage of discovery along the coast of Florida" — but never got within a thousand miles of Florida. His plan was to sail directly to Cape Cod and then start exploring west and south, but Pont-Gravé, who now commanded, was curious to see the coast already explored and insisted on covering Maine and Massachusetts Bay first.

The cruise started much too early to enjoy fine weather, and the first two attempts ended in disaster. First night out, 16 March 1606, the pinnace had to anchor in an exposed roadstead off Whitehead, close to Grand Manan. A furious gale and high waves beat on her in the night; she dragged, the anchor cable parted, and before they could make sail, she fetched up on a small rock. Fortunately an unusually big wave floated her clear and she grounded on a gravelly beach. There she was partly unloaded and repaired, Champlain giving the credit to Champdoré, the master. Finally on 21 March, with the return of fair weather, "We left this wretched place," says Champlain, and ran before a gentle southerly to Port aux Coquilles (Shellfish harbor), which his 1607 map indicates to have been Head Harbor, Campobello. Snow still lay on the ground, fog came in frequently, and the pinnace remained in this beautiful sheltered place for a week. Pont-

Champlain's chart of Port-Royal (Annapolis Basin and River, Nova Scotia).
From Les Voyages (1613). KEY: *A. Site of the habitation. B. Champlain's*
garden. C. "Wood road that the Sieur de Poutrincourt caused to be built."
D. Goat Island. E. Digby Gut. F. Shoals which "dry out at low water."
G. "Rivière St. Antoine" (Bear River). H. "Fields where we sow wheat" (site

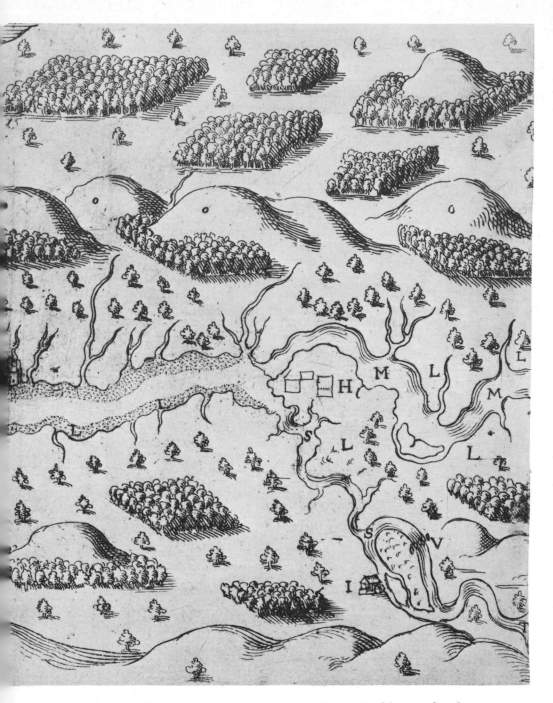

of Annapolis Royal). I. Poutrincourt's water mill. L. "Fields inundated at spring tides." M. "Rivière de l'Equille" (sand eel, now Annapolis River). N. "Seacoast." O. "Mountain slopes." P. Bear Island. R. Moose River. S. "Mill River" (Allens). X. "The trout brook." Y. "Wood road which the Sieur de Champlain caused to be built." Courtesy Harvard College Library.

Gravé then insisted on crossing the Bay of Fundy to Port-Royal to see how the people were doing, and at Port-Royal he suffered a slight heart attack and could not leave until 9 April.

On that day the pinnace made a second false start. First day out she anchored well within the Gut, about a mile north of the site of Digby. Early on the morning of the 10th Champdoré, in thick fog and a heavy rain, weighed anchor, hoisted the *bourcet* (the triangular mizzen), and tried to sail out of narrow Digby Gut with a north wind. He had not given the pinnace enough sail to breast the strong tidal current, which threw her on Man of War Rock, a ledge about a mile inside the Gut. Pont-Gravé, still sick, could not leave his bunk, but Champlain rushed on deck and ordered the square mainsail set to drive her still further on the rocks, for fear that the ebb tide — and there is twenty-five feet of tide at Digby — would cause her to slip off into deep water and sink. The rudder and part of the keel having been broken and three or four planks stove in, the pinnace filled and had to be abandoned. Secoudon, the local Micmac chief, and several of his subjects helped the Frenchmen with a fleet of canoes to unload and get ashore. "We were glad enough to have saved our lives," wrote Champlain, "and returned to our habitation with our poor savages, who stayed there a good part of the winter, and praised God for having preserved us from shipwreck, from which we never expected to escape so cheap." "For us this was a great misfortune," he concluded, "and due to the lack of foresight on the part of the master, who was stubborn, little versed in seamanship, and would listen to nobody. He was a good ship-carpenter, skilled in building vessels and careful in fitting them out, but in no way qualified to sail them." Champdoré, he means you! Old seafarers will recognize the type — a shipmate who is very clever at carpentry (or, nowadays, diesel engines and electronics) but ignorant and pigheaded as a navigator; the type who would risk a collision or a grounding rather than admit that he had shaped a wrong course. Champlain was ready to forgive Champdoré, but Pont-Gravé insisted on having him tried for barratry — intentional wrecking in order to escape another New England cruise. Found guilty, Champdoré was handcuffed; but since a new pinnace whose keel had already been laid needed his attention, he was set free to do what he did well.

De Monts, when he left Port-Royal, had ordered his men to clear out and seek some means of getting home if he himself had not returned by 15 July 1606. So, nothing having been heard of de Monts by that time, Pont-Gravé left the habitation in charge of two Frenchmen and friendly Membertou. All the rest piled into two pinnaces (the newly built one of 18 tuns and the old 8-tun one) and set forth along the Acadian coast for Cape Breton in the hope of speaking a fisherman who would return them to France. A series of accidents marked this short cruise. The anchor cable of one pinnace parted in the Grand Passage into St. Mary's Bay, and she barely managed to clear the rocks; in a heavy squall off Cap Fourchu, the rudder irons of the bigger pinnace broke. This time Champdoré recovered the good opinion of all hands by securing the rudder with rope. On Champlain's plea, the "bracelets" were not clapped on again, and Pont-Gravé quashed the indictment for barratry. Before rounding Cape Sable, they met a shallop manned by Jean Ralleau, de Monts's secretary, who told them that ship *Jonas* was on the way with Poutrincourt as governor of Port-Royal. So they turned back to Port-Royal, and there found *Jonas* already at anchor.

Although Poutrincourt had been the founder, as it were, of Port-Royal, both he and de Monts were now disenchanted with the place and wished to make a further search for a substitute. To that end they equipped the pinnace just completed, leaving *Jonas* at Port-Royal; for, as Champlain well said, a pinnace is far superior to a big vessel for coastal exploring since it draws less water and so can *ferreter* (ferret out) the inner bays, where the likeliest dwelling sites would be found. Champlain has not been recognized as a master of French prose, but his flair for *le mot juste* when describing anything maritime is notable.

On 28 August the newly built pinnace set forth from Port-Royal. An unseasonable line storm and unexpected leaks forced her back twice, and this third and last cruise of Champlain in New England waters did not really get going until 9 September 1606, too late in the season for exploring. The pinnace should have sailed straight to Cape Cod as Champlain wished; but Poutrincourt, who apparently owned her, insisted first on seeing the Maine coast for himself. And they also stopped at Sainte-Croix just to see how the winter wheat planted the year before was doing. Not badly, they found.

Passing through Quoddy roads and the Grand Manan channel, the pinnace sailed well outside Mount Desert and, after passing Isle au Haut, looked in at the Penobscot. Thence she sailed to the Saco River where, on 21 September, Poutrincourt and Champlain held parley with the Indian chiefs Marchin and Onemessin. One of their native passengers, Messamouet, sachem of the Souriquois around La Have, overwhelmed the Saco sagamore with all kinds of presents, native and foreign, hoping to make him an ally; the recipient made what Messamouet considered to be an insulting return of maize, beans and pumpkin. This unfortunate example of "Indian giving" became the first link in a chain which led to a minor war. Messamouet nursed his grudge, and next year led a war party in canoes against Saco. The Indians there killed Panounias, Champlain's former guide; and Membertou retaliated by leading a war party in two hundred canoes from Port-Royal along the Maine coast; he routed the enemy, killing both Saco sagamores.

The pinnace's next port of call was Beau Port (Gloucester harbor), which Champlain had missed on his 1605 voyage. She spent two or three nights and days there, anchoring between Ten Pound Island and Rocky Neck. This gave him time to make one of his best harbor charts. But he barely escaped a fight. When he landed with some sailors who were seeking a place to wash clothes, a band of Indians approached, apparently planning an ambush; but unknown to them Poutrincourt and a squad of arquebusiers were covering their shipmates. In Champlain's chart he is shown throwing his limbs about to signal to Poutrincourt. When the Indians observed this, they dropped their weapons, pretended peaceful intentions, and traded tobacco for French goods. Gloucester harbor seemed to Champlain the best locality he had yet seen on this coast for a permanent settlement; but he and Poutrincourt decided against it because the attitude of the large native population was ambiguous.

On 30 September 1606 the pinnace departed Beau Port, and after picking up Cap Saint-Louis (Brant Rock), sailed all night and made the waters off Wellfleet on Cape Cod before daylight 1 October. She anchored on Billingsgate Shoal in five feet at low water, enough for her in calm weather. After a shallop had explored Wellfleet harbor, which they named Port aux Huistres — and Wellfleet for three centuries has been famous for its oysters — the pinnace rounded Cap Blanc (Cape Cod), looked in briefly at Mallebarre (Nauset) and then became involved in Pollock Rip, the shoals that were to baffle the *Mayflower* fourteen years later. Unlike her, Poutrincourt's pinnace could not turn back, as the wind was blowing strong from the east. She had to take her chance, wrote Champlain, among the breakers and shoals, wherever they hoped to find the best water; at one time the pinnace, which drew four feet, had only six inches under her keel, and several times she struck; but "finally, by God's grace, we got

Champlain's chart of Le Beau Port (Gloucester, Massachusetts). From Les Voyages *(1613).* KEY: *A. "Spot where our pinnace lay" — but the ship shown there is much bigger than a pinnace. B. "Prairies." C. "Small isle" (Ten Pound). D. "Rocky Cape" (Eastern Point). E. "Place where we caulked our shallop" (Oaks Cove, Rocky Neck). f. Salt Island. G. "Savages' cabins, and where they till the soil." Frenchmen are landing from a shallop. H. "Little river where there are meadows" (Fresh Water Cove). I. "A brook." L. "Tongue of land" (Eastern Point) "covered with woods where there are lots of sassafras, hickory and grapevines." M (in northeast corner). "A cul-*

de-sac of the sea, in rounding Cap aux Isles" (Cape Ann). The cul-de-sac is Annisquam Harbor and canal. N. "A small river." O. "Small brook issuing from marshes" (now part of the canal). P. "Another small brook where we washed the linen." Q. "Troop of savages coming to surprise us." R. "Sandy Beach." S. "Seacoast." T. "Sieur de Poutrincourt in ambush, with 7 or 8 arquebusiers." V. "The Sieur de Champlain" (throwing his limbs about) "perceives the Savages," and thwarts their intended mischief. Courtesy Harvard College Library.

through." They doubled the long, sandy Monomoy Point, which he named Cap Batturier, and anchored in two and one-half fathom off the modern Chatham. The Nauset Indians who lived thereabouts seemed friendly enough, and piloted the pinnace to a protected anchorage in Stage harbor, where she dried out at low water and her rudder, broken on the Rip, could be repaired.

Here, for the first and only time in his New England cruises, Champlain remarked on the scenery; the coves, cornfields and meadows, he wrote, and the fine hardwood trees "gave beauty to the landscape." Rugged shores of Maine did not appeal to him, but the soft contours of Stage harbor, with its creeks, ponds and salt meadows, may well have reminded him of his native Brouage. The Nauset tribe who lived here were the best corn planters he had yet encountered, and he described how they made caches of maize in baskets which they buried four feet deep for protection from vermin and frost. He counted five to six hundred Indians at this place, described their garments, lodges and customs in detail, and dwelt on the abundance of game and fish.

Here the French tarried for two weeks. Poutrincourt, noting on 14 October that the natives were folding their tents and sending women and children away, guessed that something sinister was cooking and ordered his crew to come on board for the night. Four or five men disobeyed and stayed ashore, for the trivial reason that they wished to bake themselves some bread in the oven built by their shipmates in a tent on the beach. During the night these men were surrounded by a band of some four hundred Indians and killed with arrows. One body was found later with a little dog on his back, both transfixed by the same arrow. It was impossible for the French to take revenge because every time they landed to bury the dead, the Indians scampered into the woods. As Marc Lescarbot relates:

"The last duty towards the dead was not neglected, which were buried at the foot of the Cross that had been there planted. . . . But the insolency of this barbarous people was great, after the murders by them committed." During the funeral service, "These rascals did dance and howl a-far off," and when the French had re-embarked, "it being low water and having no means to come a-land," these wretches threw down the cross, exhumed one corpse and paraded around in his shirt, after which they conferred their supreme insult: "Turning their backs toward the barque, they did cast sand with their two hands betwixt their buttocks in derision, howling like wolves." The French opened fire, but the range was too great, and the Nauset threw themselves flat when they saw the match put to a gun. As soon as the flood tide allowed the French to land, the Indians "ran away as swift as greyhounds." Before they left, the Frenchmen "set up the Cross again with reverence, and reinterred the bodies which had been thrown here and there among the bushes. . . . On the 16th we departed from Port Fortuné, which we had named this place for the misfortune which happened to us there." This logic is hard to understand.

During a few days' sailing about in Nantucket Sound, Champlain named an island La Soupçonneuse or La Douteuse because vaguely seen in the offing; both names appear on his maps. This probably represents a distant glimpse of Martha's Vineyard, possibly of Nantucket. He then returned to Stage harbor, hoping to take revenge on the savages by kidnapping a few and using them as slaves to turn the unpopular hand mill at Port-Royal. He planned to attract a group of Indians under pretense of trade, when he and a group of arquebusiers, making a sort of lariat out of their *paternosters* — long rosary chains — would rope them like steers, bind them with the match-cords, and drag them on

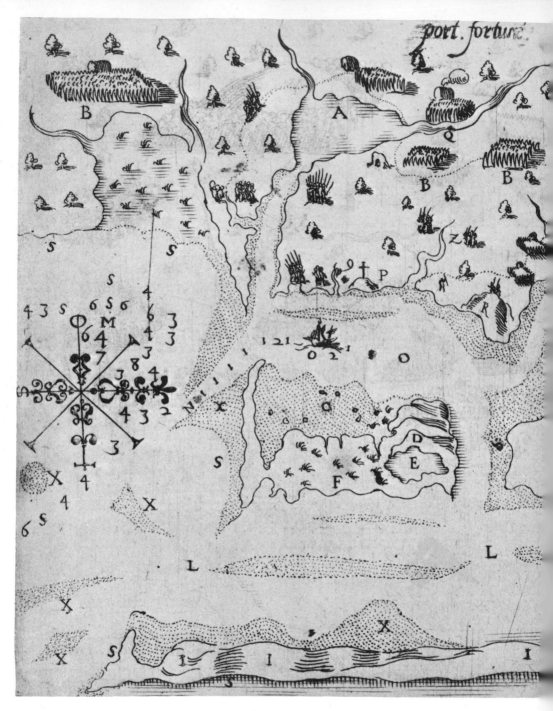

Champlain's chart of Port Fortuné (Stage Harbor, Cape Cod). From Les Voyages *(1613).* KEY: *A. "Salt Pond" (Oyster Pond). B. "Savages' cabins and land that they till." C. "Island marshes covered every tide" (Morris Island). D. "Hillocks on the island, covered with wood, vines and wild plum." E. "Fresh water pond" on the island, "where there's lots of game." F. "Meadow on the Island." G. "Island full of woods, with a great cul-de-sac (Ram Island, destroyed by a gale in 1851). H. "Sort of salt pond, where there's a heap of shellfish, including oysters" (Mill Pond). I. "Sand dunes on a little tongue of land" (this has been washed away). L. "Cul-de-sac."*

M (*on wind rose*). *"Roadstead where we anchored outside the harbor."*
N. *"Entrance of the Harbor"* (*this has shifted eastward*). O. *"Harbor and place where our pinnace lay"* (*Stage Harbor, and the pinnace is sketched*).
P. *"The cross that we planted."* Q. *"Little brook"* (*inlet to Oyster Pond*). The dotted line, also indicated by V, is the route of Poutrincourt and Champlain on a cross-country walk. R. *"Mountain which is seen from afar"* (*Sand Bluff*).
T. *"Small River."* X. *"Banks and mud."* Y. *"Small mountain"* (*Great Chatham Hill*). 9 (*next to cross*). *"Place where our people were killed by the savages."*
Courtesy Harvard College Library.

The fight at Stage Harbor. From Champlain's own picture in Les Voyages *(1613).* KEY: *A. "Place where the French were baking bread." B. "Savages surprising the Frenchmen." C. "French burned by the savages." O. "The Harbor." P. "Little brook" (Cedar Swamp Brook). Courtesy Harvard College Library.*

Air view of Stage Harbor, 1971

board the shallop. The Nauset were much too nimble to be caught that way; and in the scuffle that ensued, more Frenchmen were killed.

As provisions were now running low, and the wounded were dying for want of medicaments, Poutrincourt decided to head for Port-Royal. They had explored but a few miles further toward Florida than de Monts had done on the 1605 cruise. Their passage to Port-Royal took a month. Shortly after they made Isle au Haut on 31 October, the rudder again broke. That was most embarrassing and dangerous, but they coped with it as we in ketch *Mary Otis* once had to do off the Azores, steering by the sails with tack and sheet in hand. By this means they made a harbor — probably the Cow Yard, where Champlain had been before — beached, and installed a jury rudder. That in turn broke on the passage between Maine and Port-Royal, because the towed shallop gave it and the whole stern a terrific crack in a seaway. Champdoré, the Mr. Fixit of this crew, frapped the poor thrice-broken rudder with ropes, and they reached Port-Royal 14 November 1606, so late in the season as to have been given up for lost. The French garrison showed joy by greeting them with verses, laurel wreaths and a feast.

This was the last exploration of the New England coast by Champlain. He was bitterly disappointed that Poutrincourt had not allowed him to sail directly to Cape Cod and follow the coast westerly. Had they done so, they might have seen Newport harbor and New York Bay before either the English or the Dutch got there, and a French colony might have been established on Narragansett Bay or Manhattan Island before they became respectively Rhode Island and New Amsterdam.

VI

The Order of Good Cheer

Two interesting characters who had come out in the *Jonas* were ready to welcome the pinnace at Port-Royal. These were Poutrincourt's cousin, a thirty-year-old Parisian apothecary named Louis Hébert, and lawyer Marc Lescarbot. Maître Lescarbot, sick of Paris intrigues, hoped to serve God and the king in L'Acadie "by agreeable labor," and to help "establish the Christian faith and the French name among barbarous people." Classically educated, Marc had already acquired a literary reputation as translator of a Latin history of Russia; and he intended to turn this voyage to good literary account   as indeed he did.

During the pinnace cruise to Cape Cod, Lescarbot remained in charge at Port-Royal and, to welcome Poutrincourt and Champlain, he had the enterprise and good taste to prepare a masque, as symbolical plays were then called. Fortunately for us, he had the words printed as *Les Muses de la Nouvelle France* after his return to Paris.

The cast consisted of Neptune, six tritons and four savages; and among the audience were the venerable Membertou, "Sagamos de Souriquois," his family and people. On 14 November 1606, after the returned voyagers, dressed in their best, had taken their seats in a shallop in the bay fronting the habitation, Neptune approached in another shallop, and the tritons in bark canoes. Neptune, dressed in a blue robe, crowned, bearded, and holding a trident, came alongside Poutrincourt's boat and addressed him thus:

> Arrête, Sagamos, arrête-toi ici
> Et écoutes un Dieu qui a de toi souci!
>   *   *   *   *
>
> Si l'homme veut avoir une heureuse fortune
> Il lui faut implorer le secours de Neptune.
> Car celui qui chez soi demeure casanier
> Mérite seulement le nom de cuisinier!
>
> Stop, Sagamore, stop here a spell
> And listen to a god who wishes thee well!
>   *   *   *   *
>
> If man would wish to make his fortune,
> He must implore the help of Neptune.
> A lubber who won't quit his own house
> Deserves no better name than louse!

Neptune then observes that without his aid one cannot reach the China Sea, the North or the South Pole; that he was responsible for transporting the Sultan's gift of an elephant to Charlemagne, and for the Portuguese who sailed to the Orient, and for bringing French ships to New France. He applauds the courage of their officers and crews; he predicts their destiny:

> Préparer à la France un florissant Empire
> En ce monde nouveau, qui bien loin fera bruire
> Le renom immortel de de Monts et de toi,
> Sous le règne puissant de HENRY vôtre Roi.

Prepare for France a flourishing Empire
In this New World, where ages will inspire
Th' immortal fame of de Monts and of thee,
Under the puissant reign of great HENRY.

A trumpet sounds, and the six tritons in succession address Poutrincourt in complimentary and prophetic verses. It is a pity we do not know who took the part of Neptune, because the fifth triton adds a note of comedy by warning the company in his Gascon dialect that Neptune is an accomplished old lecher who has been caught kissing the Indian girls, and their parents had best keep watchful eyes on him, and them.

The four *sauvages* (played by Frenchmen) now appear in their canoes. The first offers a quarter of venison as homage "to the sacred Fleur-de-lis" and declares to Poutrincourt:

Nos moyens sont un peu de chasse
Que d'un coeur entier nous t'offrons,
Et vivre toujours en ta grace
C'est tout ce que nous désirons.

Our little talent in the chase
We beg you use, from hearts entire.
To live forever in thy grace
Is all our wish, our whole desire.

Second Indian presents beaver pelts; third Indian, a porcupine quill headdress made by his own mistress; and a fourth quaintly excuses himself for coming empty-handed, owing to bad luck in the chase, but if Poutrincourt can spare some bread, will he give him a little?

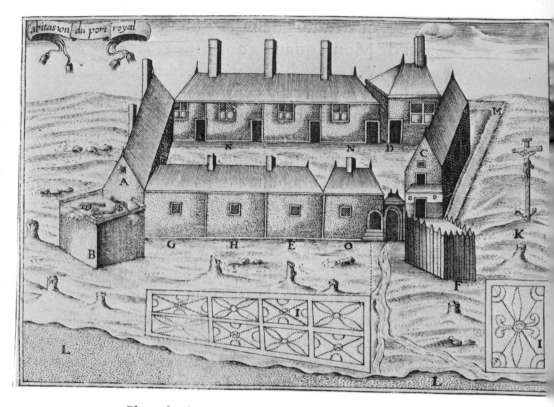

Champlain's picture of the Port-Royal habitation. From Les Voyages (1613). KEY: A. "Lodgings of the artisans." B. "Platform for cannon." C. Storehouse. D. "Lodging of the Sieurs de Pont-Gravé and Champlain." E. "The forge." F. Palisade of stakes. G. "The bakery." H. "The kitchen." I. Gardens. K. "The cemetery." L. The harbor. M. Drainage ditch. N. Officers' dwellings. O. "Little house where we stored the equipment for our pinnace." Courtesy Harvard College Library.

After Poutrincourt has thanked Neptune and tritons for their good will to him and to France, the entire troupe sings, in four parts, a concluding Hymn to Neptune:

> Vrai Neptune, donne nous
> Contre tes flots assurance,
> Et fais que nous puissions tous
> Un jour nous revoir en France,
> *Et fais que nous puissions tous*
> *Un jour nous revoir en France.*

> Pledge to us, great god Neptune,
> Against thy ocean arrogance;
> Grant us all, as highest boon
> That we may meet again in France,
> *Grant us all, as highest boon*
> *That we may meet again in France.*

This undoubtedly expressed the unanimous wish of a homesick company.

The masque being concluded, trumpets sounded, cannon roared, and at the entrance to the habitation "a comrade in a merry mood" welcomed Poutrincourt with "unbelievable grace." He called on cooks, scullions and volunteer waiters to break out their entire *batterie de cuisine,* to roast goose, duck and other poultry on spits, and to draw an overflowing tankard of wine for each man. He concluded:

> Entrez dedans, Messieurs, pour vôtre bien-venuë;
> Qu'avant boire, chacun hautement eternuë,
> A fin de décharger toutes froides humeurs
> Et remplir vos cerveaux de plus douces vapeurs.

Enter, Messieurs, your welcome gladly seize;
And each man, ere he drink, give vent to one big sneeze,
To throw out chilly humors brought in from sea,
And for winy vapors leave his brain quite free.

So we may imagine everyone taking snuff to stimulate a bout
of sneezing, after which Lescarbot says grace and all hands sit
down to a big feast of fish, meat and corn, washed down by
flagons of wine. Friendly merchants of La Rochelle had sent over
forty-five butts of Bordeaux to Port-Royal in the *Jonas*, so that
no shortage developed. And this feast was a mere sample of many
to come.

"We spent this winter very pleasantly," wrote Champlain, "and
had good fare, owing to L'Ordre de Bon Temps [Order of Good
Cheer] that I founded." He and Lescarbot, who had a pretty
talent of versification, and Poutrincourt, who could play and
compose music, put their heads together and decided that the only
way to get through an Acadian winter was to have fun. So every
gentleman in turn became chief steward and caterer, wearing a
chain of office; he had to provide food and make out menus for
the next day. Each steward vied with the others to produce game
and fish in abundance, in addition to the usual bread and salt codfish. Each dinner began with ceremony. The steward marched in,
"napkin on shoulder, wand of office in hand, and around his
neck the collar of the Order; . . . after him the other members
of the Order, each bearing a dish." After grace, the steward re-
signed his insignia to his successor, and drank with him a cup of
wine. They sang old favorite songs as well as new ones composed
on the spot, everyone had plenty to drink, and, "In short," wrote
Lescarbot, that merry man of law, "we made as good cheer as
in the rue aux Ours," where the best Paris cook-shops were then
located.

On the menus were an abundance of wildfowl such as mallard, goose and ruffed grouse; venison of moose, deer and caribou; beaver tail (a delicious morsel), meat of otter, bear, rabbit, and even wildcat; sturgeon and other fresh fish. Most of this was brought in by the Micmac. Membertou, their ancient chief, and visiting sagamores sat at high table with the gentlemen, whilst native women, offspring and favored subjects to the number of twenty or thirty squatted on the floor all around the hall. They particularly liked the French bread, baked in an outdoor oven and made of wheat imported from France.

Although this winter of 1606–1607 was unusually mild, there was some sickness; four Frenchmen died, as did the black interpreter. This man, of whom we would like to learn more, was the first black known to have come to New France. His name was Mathieu da Costa or d'Acosta, a well-educated and baptized Negro who had been to L'Acadie before in a Portuguese ship and learned the Micmac language. A Rouen merchant associated with the Dutch had kidnapped him in Portugal or the East Indies, and sold or lent him to the Sieur de Monts. The merchant sued de Monts for his presumed value as a slave, and the suit dragged on for years.

On 14 January 1607 all hands had a picnic in the open air with music accompaniment. Pretty soon, trout, alewives and smelt began running up the brooks. Kitchen gardens were prepared in March for May planting, and Poutrincourt caused a water-powered grist mill to be constructed on the little river which flows into Annapolis Basin, which saved them the hard labor of the hand mill. Two pinnaces were built, and Poutrincourt found out how to make pitch from spruce trees, for caulking. All winter the *artisans* were allowed to observe a three-hour day; and since they were not under union rules, they consented to perform jobs for which they had not been hired. One sawyer, for instance,

Champlain's 1607 chart of L'Acadie and Norumbega.
Courtesy Library of Congress.

turned charcoal-burner; a stonemason baked "as good bread as that of Paris," and a cordwainer provided all hands with *galoches*, wooden-soled overshoes with deerskin uppers which enabled them to pad about in the snow dryshod.

On Ascension Day, 24 May 1607, a sail appeared before Port-Royal: a pinnace sent from Canso by ship *Jonas*, bringing bad news. The Sieur de Monts's monopoly had been revoked, owing to pressure of rival fur traders on the king; and his imperial domain between the latitudes of Philadelphia and Newfoundland was now free-for-all.

While the pinnace made a trip to Sainte-Croix in search of furs, Champlain and Poutrincourt made their last Acadian exploration up the Bay of Fundy to look for Prevert's elusive copper. Then the pinnace and three longboats took most of the Port-Royal colony to Canso for repatriation. Champlain sent word to wait for him another month, so that he could reap their planted wheat and take some home as proof of Acadian fertility. Only Poutrincourt and eight men remained at Port-Royal to hold down the ambitious habitation.

In a shallop with nine men Champlain now explored the Acadian coast between La Have and Canso, observing and mapping Mahone and St. Margaret's bays, Sambro, Chebucto Bay (seat of the future Halifax), Jeddore, Country Harbor, and St. Mary's River. At Tor Bay he found an old Basque skipper named Savalette who had been coming there annually to fish for forty-two years, from St. Jean-de-Luz. His 80-tun vessel could carry a hundred thousand dry codfish, and he was making a good living. Arriving Canso near the end of August, Champlain found Lescarbot and Champdoré on board *Jonas*, not quite ready to sail. So he had time to investigate and map the Gut of Canso and the beautiful Bras d'Or which honeycombs the interior of Cape Breton Island. He noted Port aux Anglais, which later became Louisbourg, and

Ingonish, where the Portuguese Fagundes had tried to settle almost a century earlier. He reported this Acadian coast to be full of excellent harbors but with poor soil and the climate no warmer than that of Annapolis Basin.

Poutrincourt, in another shallop, joined them shortly, and *Jonas*, with all three leaders on board and a heavy lading of dried codfish, sailed from Canso 3 September 1607. After a fair passage of 23 days they sighted the Scillies, and on 28 September entered the little port of Roscoff in Brittany. Thence they proceeded to Saint-Malo.

Never again did Champlain see L'Acadie. His project of making it the center of New France had failed. Supposing he had persuaded de Monts to locate on the Penobscot, or at one of the good harbors of New England such as Saco, Gloucester or Newport? Would it then have succeeded? He thought so in 1632, when he wrote with unwonted bitterness against those who had frustrated de Monts's plans; but he was probably wrong. Adrian Gilbert's Northern Virginia colony, which crossed Champlain at sea as he was going home, lasted but one winter; and the people were as miserable as the Frenchmen at Sainte-Croix. The promising Jesuit colony at Mount Desert Island was assaulted in the summer of 1613, a few weeks after its establishment, by the Anglo-Virginian Samuel Argall, who then proceeded to rub out the almost deserted Port-Royal. Champlain, discussing the causes of the failure of Port-Royal, attributed it to the selfish lawlessness of French shipowners, and the king's failure to abide by his promises; but he admitted that it was impossible for de Monts to police his overseas empire, where more than eighty ships annually poached on his domain.

After three and three-quarters centuries, it is clear that a French colony in North America could have survived only if it enjoyed more military and naval support than any French king was willing to give and, also, if it kept out of the way of the now ambitious and energetic English.

Something was salvaged from the Acadia experiment. Poutrincourt hung on, and his son Biencourt set up trading posts on Cap Nègre, Cape Sable Island, and elsewhere. Champlain was able to plot six little French flags on his last map of the Acadian coast, representing as many posts. But he had nothing more to do with that part of New France after leaving Canso in the autumn of 1607.

One very important thing salvaged from these frustrating years in Acadia was Champlain's map *Les Côtes et Grandes Isles de la Nouvelle France,* dated 1607, most of which we have reproduced (p. 96). This remained a manuscript, which after many vicissitudes, has come to rest in the Library of Congress. The coastline on this chart, first to be drafted with regard to compass variation, is remarkably accurate. It replaced the Riberan concept as the standard map of the future Nova Scotia and New England.

It is a tribute to Champlain's charts that many of his names have endured even on coasts never settled by French people. From east to west today's map shows: Grand and Petit Manan, Sainte-Croix, Roque Island (Iles des Perroquets abbreviated and moved inshore), Mount Desert, Isle au Haut, Saco (Chouacouit abbreviated), and Mallebarre (Nauset) which, transferred to the "elbow" of Cape Cod, remained on maps and in books as late as 1898, when it was superseded by Monomoy. The outer coast of Nova Scotia, which remained tenuously under French sovereignty until 1713, still shows plenty of Champlain's names: Canso, Sambro (corrupted from Cézembre), La Have, St. Margaret's Bay, Port Mouton, Cape Negro, Cape Sable, Cape Fourchu, St. Mary's Bay, and the Grand and Petit Passages through Isle Longue. St. John, New Brunswick, also owes its name to Champlain, and one wonders why he and de Monts did not choose the

St. John River, with its fertile meadows and good protection, for
their Acadian colony.

Partly to escape unlawful competition from both French and
English, partly to tap a vast watershed for valuable peltry, de
Monts and Champlain now attempted to found a permanent trading post at Quebec. And, owing to Champlain's persistence and
wisdom, this one did last, and developed into a great city.

So let us sing with Lescarbot in his *Muses de la Nouvelle
France*, "Adieu à L'Acadie, du 30 juillet 1607":

> Adieu donc, beaux coteaux et montagnes aussi,
> Qui d'un double rempart ceignez ce port ici.
> Adieu, vallons herbus que le flot de Neptune
> Va baignant largement deux fois à chacque lune,
> Pour donner nourriture aux arborés élans
> Et autres animaux que ne sont pas si grands.
>
>   *   *   *   *
>
> Adieu, mon doux plaisir, fontaines et ruisseaux,
> Qui les vaux et les monts arrossé de vos eaux,
> Pourrai-je t'oublier, belle île forêtière,
> Riche honneur de ce lieu et de cette rivière?

> Adieu, then, pretty hills and mighty mountains drear,
> Which like a double wall surround this port so near.
> Adieu those grassy fields which the tide of Neptune
> Flows completely o'er twice in every moon,
> To nourish noble herds of antlered moose
> And lesser beasts designed for human use.
>
>   *   *   *   *
>
> Adieu, O my delight, thy springs and tiny rills
> Which flow down from mountains, watering the hills.
> And could I forget thee, O lovely wooded isle,
> Which honoreth this place, and gives this basin style?

And so on, for some hundred lines, in which Lescarbot mentions every flower and plant he can remember, every animal, every fish, every shellfish even to the humble clam (but not, strangely, the scallop and lobster for which this region is now famous). He predicts that the natural pastures of Port-Royal which the spring tides cover twice every lustration will feed a thousand cattle, support towns and cities "as a retreat from overcrowded France," and "change the manners of this savage nation."

There is no doubt that Lescarbot loved L'Acadie; but he too never returned.

VII

Quebec Founded and
Iroquois Attacked

THE third day of July 1608, when Champlain stepped ashore
at Quebec* and unfurled the fleur-de-lys, marks the birth
of that city and province, and indeed of Canada as a nation. One
cannot wholly separate Champlain the explorer from Champlain
the empire-builder, because the one served the other; but why did
he shift his efforts from L'Acadie to the St. Lawrence?

When he returned to Paris in October 1607, Champlain sought
out the Sieur de Monts and begged him to write off his Acadian
ventures as a loss, reorganize his company, and concentrate on
Quebec. There they would be hundreds of miles nearer the source
of peltries than in L'Acadie or Tadoussac, and at a strategic point
on the great axis of penetration of North America. De Monts
agreed, and he and Champlain persuaded the king to restore their
monopoly for one more year. De Monts then equipped three ships
for the season of 1608: one (name unknown) to operate in

---

* The name in its present form, Quebec, first appears on the Levasseur map of
1601. Champlain's earliest use of it is in *Des Sauvages* (1603, *Works* I 129):
"Nous vinsmes mouiller l'ancre à Québec qui est un destroit de ladicte rivière
de Canadas. . . ." H. H. Langton, footnoting this passage, states that the word,
in Micmac, is *Kĕbĕc*, and means simply the narrows of a river. The popular deri-
vation, from a French sailor exclaiming, "Quel bec!" when he first sighted Cape
Diamond, is a modern romantic invention.

L'Acadie; *Le Levrier*, commanded by Pont-Gravé, to trade at Tadoussac; and *Le Don de Dieu*, commanded by Champlain, to establish a permanent trading post at Quebec. She and *Levrier* carried workmen, supplies, trade goods, weapons, and a knocked-down pinnace and materials for a new habitation.

Don de Dieu sailed from Honfleur 13 April 1608 and raised Cape St. Mary's, Newfoundland, on 26 May, passed through Cabot Strait, made Tadoussac 3 June, and met Pont-Gravé, who had both sailed and arrived earlier. The tough Breton was practically a prisoner of some even tougher Basques, who laughed at de Monts's renewed monopoly and declared they would trade wherever they chose; they had fired on Pont-Gravé, wounded him, killed one of his men, and disarmed his ship. Champlain, who must have been a consummate diplomat, made peace with the Basque captain; and, while his pinnace was being assembled, took a trip in a shallop up the Saguenay as far as the Chicoutimi waterfall. He decided that this river had no possibilities for settlement, but he heard about Hudson Bay from the natives; they said it was a forty to fifty days' journey. "I have often wished to make this discovery," wrote Champlain in his 1613 *Voyages*, "but I couldn't do it without the savages, who don't want one or any of our people to go with them." This was the first of many frustrations experienced in Canada by Champlain. No Indian wished to show him any new country; all tried to keep him out, suspecting that to let the palefaces into the source of their peltries would be bad business. And of course they were right.

Resuming his course up the St. Lawrence on 30 June in the assembled pinnace, a 12-tunner, Champlain arrived off Cape Diamond and the Rock of Quebec on 3 July. Choosing "the point of Quebec," as the natives called it, he set men to work felling the butternut trees with which it was covered, laboriously sawing them into planks by the old sawpit method, digging a cellar and

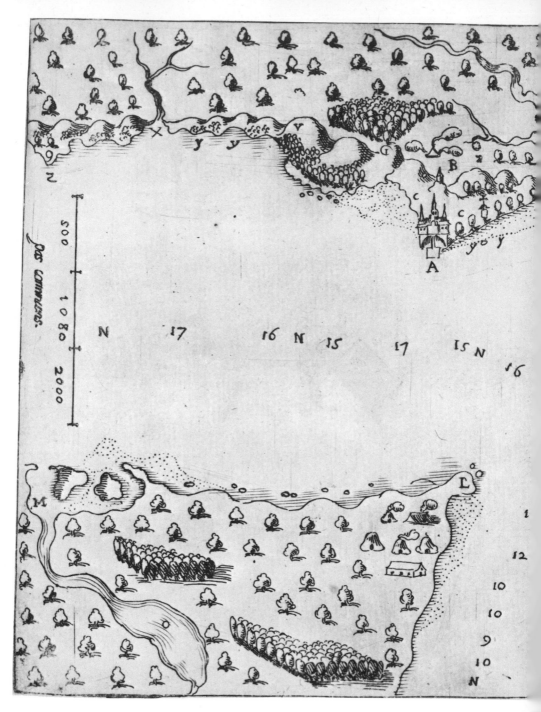

Champlain's chart of the St. Lawrence at Quebec. From Les Voyages *(1613).* KEY: *A. "Place where the habitation was built." B. "Cleared land where wheat and other grains are sown." C. "The Gardens." D. "Small stream" (now covered by the city). E. "River where Jacques Cartier wintered" (the St. Charles). The nets of which the Montagnais were expert weavers, were to catch fish. F. "Stream from the marshes" (now covered by the city). G. "Place where hay was collected for the cattle." H. "Great Falls of Montmorency" (out of place). I. "Tip of Ile d'Orléans." L. "Sharp Point on Shore to east of Quebec" (Pointe Lévis). M. "Boisterous river leading to the Etchemin" (River Etchemin, out of place). N. "Great*

*River St. Lawrence." O. "Lake Etchemin" (really 45 miles inland). P. The Lauren-
tians, seen from a distance. q. Lac de Neige (really 30 miles inland). R. "Ruisseau
de l'Ours" (Beauport River). S. "Rivière de Gendre" (son-in-law), now Mill
River, with eel trap at mouth. T. "Flats covered every tide." V. "Du Gua Mountain, very high on river bank" (now the Citadel). X. "Flowing stream, suitable for
all kinds of mills" (brook at Wolfe's Cove). y. "Gravel bank where one finds lots
of diamonds, better than those of Alençon" (the famous diamants de Canada).
Z. "Pointe aux Diamants." 9. "Places where the savages camp." Courtesy Harvard
College Library.*

building a storehouse to get all supplies under cover. The habitation, of which fortunately he left us a picture,* was on the site of the little eighteenth-century Church of Notre-Dame-des-Victoires. A too big and pretentious building of three stories, it had a gallery running around the outside. A quaint if useless embellishment was a dovecote, which only nobles were allowed to set up; de Monts, being a nobleman, rated this *colombier*. The whole structure had a moat running around it and a drawbridge before the main entrance, and "round about there are very good gardens." It is evident from Champlain's description that most of the building materials were prepared on the spot, but the handsome glazed windows and probably the doors had been brought from France in *Don de Dieu* and brought up-river from Tadoussac in several trips of the pinnace.

Before completing the habitation, Champlain had to deal with an incipient mutiny. Several workmen planned to murder their captain and sell out to the Basques. One conspirator blabbed, Champlain arrested the lot, and with the aid of Pont-Gravé, who sailed up from Tadoussac, tried five men by judicial procedure. The court found all guilty, hanged Jean Duval, the ringleader, and stuck up his head on a pike; the other conspirators were sent to France in chains. That was the last trouble Champlain ever had with his own people. But he had plenty of trouble with others, both white and red.

After 19 September, when Pont-Gravé left with the prisoners, work was resumed on the habitation, and ground cleared for planting winter wheat and rye. Everything was made snug before snow fell, but the first winter at Quebec was very severe; half the French died of scurvy. And it was even worse for the Montagnais who lived thereabout. They never made any provision for winter except to trap and smoke eels. When these gave out they

---

* See page 178.

went into the woods on snowshoes (which Champlain called *raquettes* as they reminded him of the courtly tennis rackets of France), to hunt beaver, deer and moose. That winter game was so scarce, and the snow so light, that on 20 February 1609 the hunters with their women and children appeared on Pointe Lévis across the river, shouting for help. When they tried to cross, ice floes roaring down the river crushed their frail canoes, and the survivors swam to a big floe which providentially grounded not far from Champlain's habitation. "They looked like skeletons," he wrote; most of them were unable to stand. He gave them bread and beans, but could not spare nearly as much as they wanted; and he also provided bark to cover a new set of lodges near the habitation. So famished were the Montagnais as to eat stinking carrion — a dead dog, cat and sow — which the French had earlier set out as fox bait. The stench this made when being half-cooked by the Indians was so overpowering that Frenchmen vomited when they approached the bark-covered cabins; and for people who were used to the odors of Paris at that era, this was saying a good deal. Finally, the spring shad run enabled the Montagnais to feed themselves. Champlain's compassion for these Indians was genuine. Especially he pitied the babies, who died of starvation when their mothers' milk gave out. These savages had their good points, but were "full of wickedness, revengeful, and great liars whom you can't trust." He wished that he could teach them to grow corn and cache it for winter use, as their neighbors did; and that they could be converted.

Champlain knew enough of the savages by that time to realize that feeding the hungry would not make them faithful allies; charity would soon be forgotten. What he must do was to help them, and their allies the up-river Algonkin and Huron, to make headway against the dreaded Iroquois, the Five Nations, in what is now New York State. He had earlier talked to the Indians he met in Maine about "reconciling them with their enemies," but those northern savages had no use for peace. Intermittent but perpetual warfare was their way of life. The Iroquois had forced the Huron out of the St. Lawrence valley, and they intended to raid that valley every year, as part of their life pattern. If the French, with gunfire, could aid the Montagnais-Huron-Algonkin alliance to defeat these raids, they might win their friendship and depend on them for trade. If not, and the French tried to remain neutral, Quebec would need a garrison of hundreds of trained soldiers to survive. It is folly, therefore, to criticize Champlain for what he did next.

When spring broke up the ice in April 1609, only eight of the twenty-four Frenchmen who wintered at Quebec were alive: half the survivors consisted of Champlain and his pilot and two boys, Etienne Brûlé and Nicolas Marsolet. The lads had well employed the long winter months by learning the Montagnais language and became valuable interpreters, but eventually turned traitor.

Champlain, reinforced by men from Pont-Gravé's ship (anchored at Tadoussac), now held a conference up-river with chiefs of the Huron, Algonkin and Montagnais. As a result, his fateful incursion against the Iroquois began on 28 June 1609. He and the Sieur de Marais (Pont-Gravé's son-in-law) traveled in two shallops with twenty men, three or four of them armed with the arquebus, a handgun fired by a slow-burning match. "The country becomes more and more beautiful as you advance," wrote Champlain. "The country is all covered with great and high forests." About forty-five miles above Quebec they reached a "very delightful" river that they named Sainte-Marie (now Sainte-Anne de la Perade); and, a little beyond, Champlain encountered a muster of two to three thousand Huron and Algonkin. With them he planned a campaign against the Iroquois, but

first had to invite them to Quebec for five days' dancing and feasting — indispensable preliminary to a warlike expedition. Pont-
Gravé arrived with more Frenchmen, but he did not join the war
party. On 3 July 1609 Champlain made a fresh start from Sainte-
Croix (now Pointe Platon) about thirty miles upstream from
Quebec. Passing Trois-Rivières at the mouth of the St. Maurice
River and "very fair and open forests," they reached the mouth
of the Richelieu River, which Champlain named after the Iroquois. There they tarried some time, feasting and haranguing, as a
result of which a good part of the Indians who had been clamor-
ing for war went home "with their wives and the wares they had
bartered."

Almost half the month of July was now spent. What was left of
the war party, about sixty Indian warriors in twenty-four canoes,
moved up the Richelieu. Balked by the rapids at Chambly,
Champlain decided to leave his heavy shallop behind and accept
canoe transportation. Completing the portage around the rapids on
12 July and after a seventy-five-mile journey from the Richelieu
River mouth, they reached the great lake which Champlain, with
pardonable pride, named after himself. The Adirondack Mountains, some still snow-topped, were seen afar off. The canoe flo-
tilla paddled south up the lake, their guides being certain that the
Iroquois would come that way. Nor were they mistaken.

The war party moved slowly and deliberately, camping every
night. Champlain described the Indians' tactics and organization
in forest warfare: separate groups of scouts, warriors, and hunters to supply the food. He criticized their practice of sleeping all
night without posting guards, exposing themselves to surprise;
but they answered, "We get so tired scouting and hunting in the
daytime we must sleep at night!" This time they were not sur-
prised.

After dark on 29 July they found a war party of the Mohawk

nation entrenched in a temporary camp behind a beach on a narrow meadow, which is now overlooked by the restored Fort Ticonderoga. All night Champlain's party remained in their canoes close to shore, exchanging boasts, threats and bawdy insults with the Mohawks "such as is usual at the siege of a city" in Europe, wrote Champlain.* At daybreak they landed unopposed. About two hundred Mohawks sortied from their barricade, "strong, robust men," wrote Champlain, who "came slowly to meet us with a gravity and calm which I admired; and at their head were three chiefs," distinguished by eagle feathers.

Champlain's allies ran some two hundred yards toward the Iroquois, then called on their leader to come forward and do his stuff. Clad in a plate corselet and wearing a steel helmet with a white plume like Henry of Navarre, he loaded his arquebus with four bullets, drew a bead on the three chiefs, and fired. All three fell, two dead and the third mortally wounded. Arrows then flew on both sides. One of the arquebusiers whom Champlain had cannily posted on the flank immediately fired; and that panicked the Mohawks. Running into the forest, they were hotly pursued, losing several more dead as well as ten prisoners. The allies lost nobody.

The accompanying view of the fight at Lake Champlain is the second attempt of the Captain, other than the pictures of West Indies plants and Spanish cities, to draw something superior to charts; his first attempt was on Cape Cod. One has to admit that he was not much of an artist, but we are grateful nonetheless for his efforts. He had no sense of perspective; but he had an eye for native forts, weapons, and artifacts. Both in this and in his later battle pictures, his greatest error was to depict the natives, both enemies and allies, as fighting stark naked, which they never did. Why did he do it? Because it was the fashion! Théodore de Bry,

---

* Romain Rolland *Colas Breugnon* has a classic description of one of these sieges.

in his earliest illustrated books on the New World, almost invariably depicts the savages naked, the more easily to distinguish them from Europeans. In any case the delineation of costumes was beyond Champlain's powers, and on his 1612 chart he employed an artist to present Montagnais and Huron in their accoutrements.

The canoes, too, are not well drawn; they look like French riverboats, and I expect that here, too, he was copying de Bry. And Champlain economized by dubbing in a couple of palm trees from his West Indian narrative!

On the day that this fight took place on the shores of Lake Champlain, Henry Hudson in the Dutch East India Company's *Half Moon* was sailing up the great river named after him. Upon reaching the site of Albany, *Half Moon* was boarded by a band of Indians. Hudson invited them below, plied them with bread and brandy, "which made them sweat awhile," and sent them ashore happily tipsy. One of the favorite stories in the early history of North America is the contrast between Hudson serving cocktails to the Mohawks (as his guests were assumed to be) and Champlain giving them hot lead. From these two incidents, we have often been told, stemmed the enmity of the Five Nations to the French, and their friendship toward the Dutch and their legatees the English. Alas, this is all nonsense. The natives who were given a shipboard dram by Captain Hudson were not Mohawks but the (not quite) last of the Mohicans destined to be rubbed out by the Mohawks within a few years; and the Five Nations' choice of friends was dictated by economic and political factors which long preceded European settlement. They had already driven back Huron and Algonkin from the St. Lawrence valley in the sixteenth century. And there was nothing decisive about this battle of 1609. Far from frightening the Iroquois into a passive policy, Champlain merely exacerbated a long-standing enmity, the North American Hundred Years' War. A compas-

Champlain's drawing of the battle on Lake Champlain, 1609. From Les Voyages *(1613).* KEY: *B. "The Enemies." C. "Thei canoes made of oak" (really of elm) "bark, each carrying 10 t 18 men." D and E. "Two chiefs killed and one wounded, fron one arquebus shot by the Sieur de Champlain" (shown in fu*

armor; see our frontispiece, where his figure is enlarged).
H. Indian allies. I. "Canoes of our savage allies, made of birch
bark." T. "Two arquebusiers" posted on the flank. Courtesy
Harvard College Library.

*Champlain's battleground, looking north (above)
and south, May 1971.*

Air view over Ticonderoga. Lake Champlain with Champlain's battleground at left. Lake George above. Richard K. Dean Photo. Courtesy Fort Ticonderoga.

sionate man, he may have doubted the wisdom of tangling in savage warfare when compelled to witness the torturing of Mohawk prisoners by his allies. All they would concede to his protest was to let him dispatch one poor wretch with a bullet in the head.

At the Chambly rapids the Huron and Algonkin parted to return home, and the Montagnais paddled themselves and their French leader down-river, a 120-mile journey in two days; so eager were they to exhibit scalps and perform a victory dance before the women.

Champlain, leaving Capitaine Pierre Chauvin of Dieppe in charge at Quebec, departed for France with Pont-Gravé on 5 September to support de Monts in a plan for extending his monopoly. They arrived at Le Conquêt, the little seaport behind Ushant, on 10 October. Henri IV received the partners graciously at Fontainebleau, expressed "pleasure and satisfaction" with Champlain's account of his adventures, and accepted his gifts of a Mohawk scalp, a belt of porcupine quills, the skull of a garfish, and two live scarlet tanagers. But he refused to do anything more for the company.

De Monts and Champlain decided nevertheless to carry on, as the fur trade at Quebec had proved profitable, and they might as well profit from their victory over the Mohawk. And Rouen merchants provided them with more money. Two ships were equipped: Champlain's carried eleven more workmen to Quebec, and supplies for the following winter. Embarking at Honfleur 7 March 1610, they were driven back by foul weather into three different French harbors, and did not really get going for another month. Champlain, suffering from *un fort grand maladie*, was set ashore at Honfleur for treatment part of this time. When they finally did sail on 8 April, a brave east wind gave Champlain's ship a record passage of eleven days to the Grand Bank. That seems to have cured him. Three days later, and only two weeks from France, they sighted Saint-Pierre, and on 26 April they made Tadoussac.

Arriving at Quebec in early May 1610, Champlain found the garrison in good shape after a phenomenally mild winter; no day had passed without fresh game to eat. "Which goes to show," wrote Champlain, "that you can't expect to have everything nice your first year, but that by doing without salt provisions and having fresh meat, one's health is as good there as in France." Captain Chauvin reported that "their greatest trouble was to amuse themselves" — they had nobody like Lescarbot to plan masques and feasts.

Some sixty Montagnais were at Quebec, eager to take the warpath against the Iroquois, whom they rightly guessed would be seeking revenge for the battle on Lake Champlain. What Champlain wanted of them was to be guided up the Saint-Maurice River to the great salt sea that they talked about, and to return by Lac Saint-Jean and the Saguenay. Had they accepted, Champlain might have found Hudson Bay before the English. But the northern Indians were always cagy about exploration; they instinctively objected to opening their country up to Europeans, whom they tolerated only as military allies and traders. Champlain could never get further than Lake Nipissing, and then only on the excuse of recruiting a war party.

On this occasion his Algonkin and Huron allies, instead of waiting for Champlain and the Montagnais, made a premature attack on the Iroquois' improvised fortress near the mouth of the Richelieu, and were beaten back. Champlain and his arquebusiers then arrived and turned the tide of battle. Arrows flew "thick as hailstones." Champlain was wounded in the ear by an arrow which split his ear lobe and stuck in his neck; he pulled it

Champlain's drawing of his 1610 battle at the Iroquois fort. From Les Voyages *(1613).* KEY: A. *"The fort of the Iroquois." B. "Iroquois trying to escape by the river, pursued by Montagnais and Algonkin" (represented by one figure) "to kill them." D. "The sieur de Champlain" (reloading his arquebus)*

"and his men." E. "Our savage allies." Their shields were of wood, covered with deerskin. F. "The Sieur des Prairies of Saint-Malo and his comrades." G. "Shallop of said Sieur des Prairies." H. "Big tree cut down to ruin the Iroquois fort." Courtesy Harvard College Library.

out himself. But he was more troubled by the swarms of mosquitoes, "so thick that they hardly let us draw breath," which worked their way inside his armor.

Seeing his powder running out, Champlain persuaded his Indian allies to take the fort by storm, and directed the assault himself. Indians shot arrows and the French poured a deadly fire into the fort. In the meantime one Sieur des Prairies of Saint-Malo, an independent trader, had come up-river in a shallop to help. Champlain sketched this fight and had it engraved for his *Voyages* of 1613. A group of his allies are advancing under cover of oak and deerskin shields to make a breach in the wall, and an Indian is helping them by cutting down a tall tree to crash on it. Champlain (shown reloading his arquebus) and five other arquebusiers are rendering fire support on the right, while the Sieur des Prairies (in plumed helmet) and friends do the same on the left. When the wall was breached, both French and Indians swarmed in and gave the defenders cold steel, killing all but a few who escaped by the river. Fifteen poor wretches were captured.

There can be no doubt from the way he tells this story that Champlain relished a good fight, but he was sickened by the torture of prisoners by the Montagnais women and children. "The wives and daughters," he wrote, "surpass the men in cruelty; for by their cunning they invent more cruel torments and it affords them great delight." He gives us the horrible details, which we are fain to omit.

This fight, on 19 June 1610, appeared to be more important than the one at Ticonderoga in 1609. The site on the Richelieu River, about a league above its mouth, became Cap de la Victoire, and is still so called. Of course it was not decisive; no battle or campaign in savage warfare could be, unless one side was exterminated.

Upon arriving at Quebec by canoe in the fast time of two days from the Richelieu, Champlain was deeply grieved to hear that his friend and supporter Henri IV had been assassinated. His nine-year-old son the dauphin became King Louis XIII under a regency held by his mother Marie de Medici, who cared little if anything for Canada. Yet fresh support must be sought for Quebec, especially as the fur trade had become a free-for-all. Illegal independent operators who took no part in the fighting, and shared no expenses of the habitation, were getting the best furs; and there was so much competition that the season of 1610 turned out disastrously for everyone. Accordingly Champlain left one du Parc in charge at Quebec, with sixteen men; he and Pont-Gravé sailed for home on 8 August 1610. Their ship arrived at Honfleur 27 September. En route they ran right over a whale, and Champlain took this opportunity to describe the methods of the Basque whale fishery in the Gulf of St. Lawrence. They harpooned the whale off shore, killed him when he rose to the surface, towed him ashore, flensed him, and rendered his oil in large cauldrons.

Here is another opportunity to discuss Champlain's appearance and personality. All alleged portraits of him in modern biographies are phonies. The only existing contemporary portraits of him are the sketches by himself, the best of which we have taken from his drawing of the battle on Lake Champlain (pp. 112–113) and reproduced as the frontispiece. He is wearing a steel helmet with a big white plume, as he doubtless remembered seeing Henri IV display in battle. Neck, chest and waist are protected by a steel corselet with an extension to cover his hips, and under it the then fashionable knee-length robe, worn with woolen breeches, woolen hose and leather shoes. He is taking a wide stance — for the arquebus had a terrific kick — and appears to be taller than the conventionalized Indian allies and enemies.

His features, except for eye and nose, are hidden by the butt of the arquebus; but like other sailors of the period he probably wore a beard. In the fight at the Onondaga fort in 1615, and the one on the Richelieu which we have just described, he is again distinguished by a white plume and is sketched in the act of reloading his arquebus.

Champlain exuded authority, whether on land or sea; but, as L'Ordre de Bon Temps proved, he could relax, sing, drink and make merry with his men. Both toward them and the Indians he was ever an upright and merciful judge. He had an inexhaustible store of energy, an iron digestion, became as inured as a savage to cold, hardship and hunger, and never complained of any physical ill. Uncompromisingly honest, he was severe toward the trickery of fur traders and the evasions of court politicians. Both before and during marriage he rejected his very many opportunities to prove his masculinity on the native girls. His loyalty to king and church never wavered; his frequent ejaculations of thanks to God were not conventional but genuine expressions of a profound faith, the faith in which he died.

VIII

Champlain Marries and
Returns to Canada

E VERYONE nowadays wants to know about the sex life of past
heroes, but there is nothing to tell about Champlain's. He was
a chaste and sober man; he never (to the Indians' astonishment)
frolicked with their frisky daughters. Nevertheless, after his many
displays of courage under fire and at sea, nobody dared hint that
he was lacking in virility. If there were critics and mischievous
whisperers, they had something else to talk about at Christmas-
tide 1610, when fortyish Champlain married a *fillette* aged
twelve!

Hélène Boullé was her name, a daughter of Nicolas Boullé,
secretary of the king's chamber, and sister of Eustache Boullé,
who had been at Port-Royal. She brought Champlain a dowry of
6000 livres (about $1200 in gold), 4500 of it down; and he con-
tributed 1800 livres annually toward her living expenses in
Paris during his absence. The marriage contract contained the
curious provision that "in consideration of the tender age" of the
bride, the bridegroom would not consummate his marriage for
two years, unless she and her parents and friends held a meeting
and agreed to an earlier *confection du dit mariage*. Their formal
union was celebrated 30 December 1610 in Saint-Germain l'Au-

xerrois, King Henri IV's own parish church; and the oddly matched couple set up housekeeping in the same quarter. As an index of the then cost of domestic service, Champlain contracted with a Paris bourgeois to employ a daughter as his wife's maid-servant at a salary of 30 livres tournois (about six dollars) per annum.

After what must have been a rather pallid honeymoon, Samuel de Champlain, *capitaine ordinaire de la marine,* as he is described in the marriage contract, left his child bride and sailed again to Canada. For de Monts and his partners had decided to try another year's trading at Tadoussac and Quebec rather than lose their investment in buildings and year-round salaries. He departed Honfleur 1 March 1611 in a ship (whose name we know not) commanded by Captain Pont-Gravé. After a long beat to windward, they encountered off the Grand Bank a heavy concentration of ice which all but closed them in; they had to come about every fifteen minutes to avoid crashing. Many a time "We thought we should not come out alive," wrote Champlain. "The whole night passed in toil and trouble, and never was the watch better kept, as nobody wanted to sleep. . . . The cold was so great that all the rigging froze . . . and you couldn't maneuver, or even stand on the quarterdeck." Daylight barely broke through the thick o' fog, they could not see beyond their bowsprit, so Pont-Gravé decided to lay the ship alongside a big berg and drift with it. This went on for four or five days, after which they rammed their way through an ice pack.

But that was not the end of their troubles. The ice that spring was as bad off Cape Race as the English had earlier found it off Baffin Island in July, and Champlain's account of dodging bergs is as vivid as those of Frobisher's shipmates in the far north. He referred to this experience with horror in his *Treatise on Seamanship.* Of all his twenty-three voyages across the North Atlantic, this was much the worst, and the longest — over ten weeks. Not until 13 May 1611 did the ship reach Tadoussac.

Several independent fur traders were already there, but doing little business; the Indians, having learned that "competition is the life of trade," were cunningly awaiting the arrival of more vessels to bid up prices. Pont-Gravé stayed at Tadoussac to see that his company got its share of the peltry, while Champlain took over the pinnace, which had been hauled out there all winter, and sailed upstream to carry out his summer plans.

Before we follow him there, suppose we take a look at La Traité (*the* Trade) as the French called the peltry trade in Canada. It was no longer a simple matter of swapping a few tools and trinkets for valuable fur. Those happy days for traders in the St. Lawrence were gone; the Montagnais and other tribes had become very choosy. If a trader wished to make a good deal, recorded Père Lalemant, he had to bring out caps and hats, nightcaps, shirts, sheets, coverlets, axes, iron arrowheads, knives and awls, swords, "tools for breaking the ice in winter," iron pots, dried prunes and raisins, maize, pease, *pain bisquit* (hardtack), and *petun* (tobacco). In return the traders bought moose and wolf skins, fox, otter, marten, fisher, wolverine, musquash, and the most sought after beaver. An average of 15,000 and as many as 22,000 beaver skins were imported into France annually. Costing the traders a couple of livres apiece in goods and selling at a tenfold to twentyfold markup, this was no bad deal.

Champlain's objectives were to meet his Indian allies beside the La Chine rapids, and there set up a new trading post and obtain native guides to explore the Ottawa River and the Laurentians. For, to insure a constant supply, he must have an independent peltry line from the country of friendly Huron and Algonkin.

At Quebec he found the French healthy and happy, caused the

habitation to be repaired, and set out some rose bushes he had brought from France. He then pushed on to the La Chine rapids, arriving 28 May. With an Indian boy whom he had taken charge of, baptized, and named Savignon, he explored the site of what General de Gaulle called "the world's second French city." With his sure eye for terrain, Champlain chose Pointe Callières, site of the present Canadian customs house, for a new habitation. The island facing it he named Saint-Hélène in honor of his child bride. Seeds were planted and a wall built with brick from local clay — but that was as far as the building went in his time. *Montréal* appears on Lescarbot's and Champlain's maps of 1609 and 1612; but the future city really began in 1642 with the first year-round settlement. In the meantime the shore around the La Chine rapids became the scene of the biggest annual peltry fair between traders and up-river Indians.

While waiting for his savage allies to appear, Champlain himself explored the St. Lambert River, which leads to the Chambly rapids, and allowed Savignon, with an adventurous young Frenchman named Louis and a Montagnais guide, to reconnoiter the La Chine rapids in a canoe. The lads made the mistake of trying to run the rapids instead of portaging, and both Louis and the Montagnais were drowned. Savignon, the survivor, showed the spot to Champlain, who said it "made his hair stand on end" to see such frightful white water, seven or eight falls of at least three feet in height tumbling from ledge to ledge, and a pool covered with thick foam like icing on a cake. But he was soon to run them himself.

The expected Huron and Algonkin turned up 13 June 1611 in company with Etienne Brûlé, now dressed Indian-fashion and speaking the Algonkin tongue better than French. With this assembly of two hundred or more natives Champlain held several parleys. About a dozen private traders, knowing that de Monts's

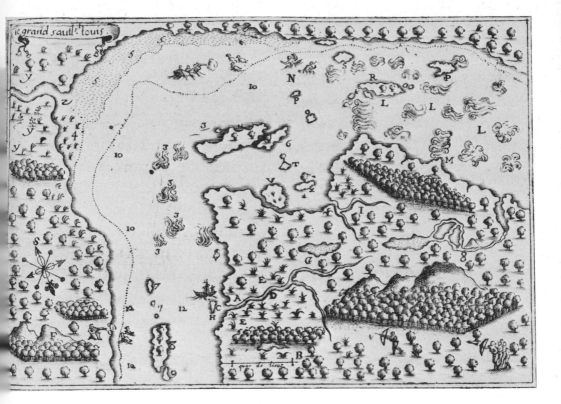

Champlain's chart of Le Grand Sault St. Louis (La Chine Rapids). From Les Voyages *(1613).* KEY: A. *"Little place which I had cleared" (site of Custom House Square, Montreal). C. "Islet where I had a stone wall built" (Market Gate Isle). D. "Little river where the boats are kept" (the St. Pierre). E. "Meadow where the savages camp when they come here." F. "Mountains seen in the distance" (Monts St. Bruno and St. Hilaire). L. "The Sault" (La Chine). M. "Spot where the savages portage their canoes along the north shore." N. "Spot where one of our people and a savage were drowned." O. "Small rocky islet." P. "Another islet where birds nest." R. "Heron Island." S, T, V. "Islets." X. "Another islet where there are a lot of wildfowl." Y. "Meadows." Z. "Small river" (St. Lambert).*

Here Champlain ran out of the alphabet, so continued his key with arabic numerals: 2 (looks like N). St. Paul's Island. 3. "Places uncovered at low water and where there are great whirlpools." 6, 7. "Little islands and rocks." 8. "Isle Ste. Hélène." 9. Ile Ronde. Courtesy Harvard College Library.

monopoly had expired, followed Champlain up-river to get a cut of the trade. The Captain and his interpreter (for he never really learned to speak any Indian language)* were at some pains to explain to the natives the beauties of a "free enterprise," in which he did not believe; nor did they like it any better. They wondered why the king of France, described to them as all-powerful, did not put a stop to it. Champlain wondered too. He and de Monts were very much provoked by having to suffer these chiselers, who had borne none of the risk and burden of exploration and would never send a man to fight with the Indians. "They expect people to hazard a thousand dangers, that they may take the spoils and others the labor." The Malouins, in particular, incurred his wrath because they argued that since Jacques Cartier came from their city, Bretons should have the monopoly. Well, wasn't Pont-Gravé, who hailed from Saint-Malo, a good Breton? The Malouins could have joined the de Monts company had they wished, but preferred to go it alone, for free.

At a night council with Huron, Algonkin and Montagnais chiefs, Champlain proposed that next year he bring out forty or fifty soldiers to go on an exploring expedition northwestward; and, if he found the country suitable, to establish a number of trading posts in the Ottawa region. The sagamores seemed to agree. When day broke at the conclusion of this conference, which took place just above La Chine, the Indians gave Champlain one of the greatest thrills of his life by running him down the rapids in a canoe, with an escort of seven other canoes. Imagine the howling and yelling as they just missed some big rock!

---

* Surprising as it may seem, all contemporaries agree on Champlain's inability to talk directly to the Huron, Algonkin and Montagnais. He learned only a sort of pidgin French that the traders used in dealing with the Montagnais. Another and less explicable lack on Champlain's part was swimming. He never learned to swim, even after crossing the ocean twenty-nine times. Possibly he shared the belief, prevalent along the Maine coast in my boyhood, that if you learned to swim you would take unnecessary risks and be drowned.

In order to obtain support for his ambitious enterprise of western exploration — and (we hope) to see Hélène — Champlain felt he must return to France. At Tadoussac he found a ship belonging to one Captain Thibaut of La Rochelle, and they made a very quick voyage, starting 11 August and arriving La Rochelle 10 September 1611. With a view to immediate profits for the company, he brought the peltry he had obtained at Montreal, and a quantity of split oak for wainscoting and window frames. Champlain never enjoyed a vacation; if not making improvements in New France, he was lobbying for the colony in Old France.

IX

First Western Explorations

C HAMPLAIN hastened to consult de Monts in his Château de
Pons in Saintonge, and thence went on his way to Paris. But
all the time saved by the quick ocean passage was lost, he said,
by "a wretched horse which fell upon me and nearly killed
me." Recuperation at an inn consumed several weeks, and Hélène did not see her husband until late in 1611. The two-year
embargo on her virginity did not expire until their second wed-
ding anniversary in December 1612. Possibly, however, her sea-
going husband invoked the family conclave envisaged by the
marriage contract and she was now allowed to yield her *puce-
lage* as a Christmas present to her fortyish lord and master.

However that may be, this child bride at the age of fifteen
made so much trouble that her parents went to the length of dis-
inheriting her. They alleged publicly on 10 January 1614 that
ever since her marriage, and especially since 1 October last, she
had distressed them by her *injures atroces*, and had now put
them to shame by fleeing from home, breaking her promise to
live in amity with and obedience to her husband. Neither he nor
they could locate her. Consequently they deprived her of all her
rights to inherit any part of her parents' real or personal estate.
She did in due course return to her husband, and the Boullé, in

the year of Champlain's death, restored their errant daughter's rights of inheritance.

The really important business Champlain executed in the next eighteen to twenty months in Paris was to publish one of his best books, *Les Voyages du Sieur de Champlain Xaintongeois, capitaine ordinaire pour le Roy, en la marine*. It bears the imprint of Jean Berjon *au cheval volant* in the rue St. Jean de Beauvais, and is dated 1613. This substantial volume includes thirteen harbor charts by the Captain himself, and a big folding map. It is dedicated to the young king and to his mother the Queen Regent. There are two long dedicatory poems, one of which predicts that "Glorious Champlain, with his high objectives and burning soul," will plant the French arms "at the ends of the Ocean"; and the other addresses Champlain as "bringing to the New World a courage blind to danger, fearing neither gales of wind nor monstrous whales." This poet, Motin by name, concludes:

Esprit plus grand que ta fortune,
Patient et laborieux,
Toujours soit propice Neptune
A tes voyages glorieux.
Puisses-tu d'age en age vivre,
Par l'heureux effort de ton livre:
    Et que la même éternité
    Donne tes chartes renommées
    D'huile de cèdres parfumées
    En garde à l'immortalité.

O Spirit greater than thy fortune,
Patient and laborious,
May great Neptune ever favor
Every voyage glorious,

> May'st thou live from age to age
> Through happy effort of thy book,
> And may the same eternity
> Preserve thy famous charts of sea
> In oil of cedar *parfumée*
> To guard their immortality.

Despite all rhetoric, Champlain's charts, even without being packed in perfumed cedar oil, will live as long as people care to read the story of exploring the oceans and the wilderness.

The folding map in this volume, entitled *Carte Géographique de la Nouvelle Franse* [sic] *faicte par le Sieur de Champlain . . . en 1612*, is the best map of Canada, L'Acadie and Norumbega* hitherto published, and none better appeared for many, many years. It covers everything west of Newfoundland and southern Labrador to and through Lake Ontario, together with a bit of Lake Erie; and from latitude 55° N to Long Island Sound. But the New England coast is less accurate on this than on the 1607 map. The land is adorned with pictures of native animals, and the ocean is studded not only with ships but fishes and whales. Champlain accurately depicts that antediluvian crustacean the horseshoe crab and, doubtless for fun, puts in a prominent place a sea cucumber, called by its vulgar French name *vit de mer*.

On the margin of this map Champlain caused to be engraved, from his own sketches, wild strawberries and cherries, raspberries, chestnuts, hazelnuts, and the wild plum or shadblow, whose white flowers greet one in those northern forests in earliest spring. As he could not draw human figures well, he hired one David Pelletier to add two pair of *sauvages*, Montagnais and Huron, in full accoutrements. Pelletier, like every other con-

---

* To be renamed New England by Captain John Smith in 1616.

[132]

temporary except Governor White of Virginia, could not manage the Indian face; his savages are undressed Europeans.

The map is up-to-date. Obsolete names from the Cartier era such as Hochelaga and Honguedo have been dropped, Montreal, Lac de Champlain, and many others added. One feature is all but unique in early American cartography. Along the north coast of the Gulf of St. Lawrence, which Cartier had discovered, is the legend *"l'auteur n'a point encorre recongru cette coste"* — the author has not yet seen this coast. Such an honest confession of ignorance was unprecedented. What immense trouble historians would have been spared had all Champlain's predecessors been equally frank about what they had or had not seen! But it must be admitted that he put parts of Hudson Bay and the Great Lakes on this map simply from what the savages told him; all his efforts to get there himself were frustrated.

The book contains a second *Carte géographique de la Nouvelle franse en son vray meridien,* meaning that compass variation had been taken into account. This, of smaller scale than the other, is of particular interest as including the northern discoveries by England — Davis Strait, Baffin Island, Hudson Strait and Hudson Bay, which he calls in English "The bay wher hudson did winter." That part, inscription and all, is copied from Henry Hudson's Map of 1612. Champlain explains how he ascertained compass variation and applied it to his maps; this is the map he recommends to be used for navigation. Earlier cartographers of North America had laid down the coast by "true" compass bearings, making the coast seem to trend much more east-west than it actually does.

Sieur de Monts now bought out his Rouen partners and took in fresh capital from La Rochelle, ceding the Quebec habitation with all fur trading rights to a group of merchants from that Protestant stronghold. It looked as if Quebec might even be aban-

Champlain's General Map of 1612. From W. F. Ganong's translation

In Champlain's key, A is Stage Harbor, Cape Cod; B, Cape Cod Bay; C, Boston Bay; D, Cape Ann; E, Cape Porpoise Harbor; F, Isle au Haut; G, Mount Desert Island; H, Great Wass Island; I, The Wolves; K, Cape Chignecto; L, Advocate Harbor; N, Cape Negro; R, Chebucto Bay; S, St. Margaret's Bay; and T, Jeddore. V. is in Mahone Bay (some Frenchmen had been killed there by Indians); X, isles in a row east of New Harbor, N.S.; Y, Whitehaven; and Z, Gut of Canso and Louisburg. Arabic numerals in Nova Scotia and New Brunswick

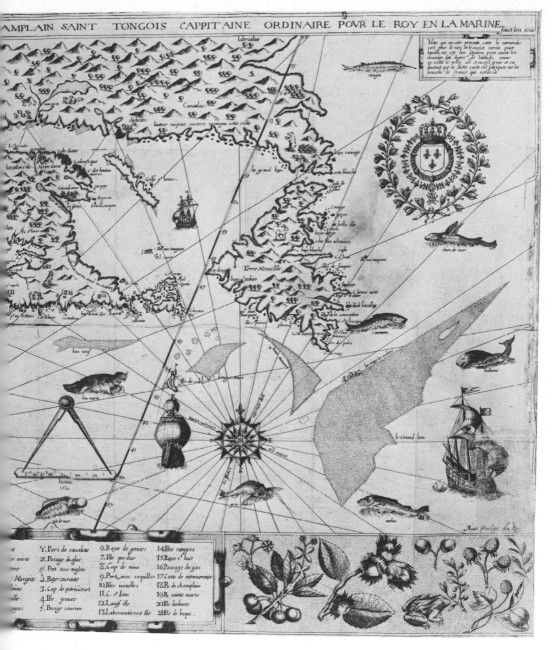

amplain Society Works. *Courtesy Harvard College Library.*

are 2, Lobster Bay; 3, Cape Split; 4, Whitehead Island, N.B.; 5, Grand Passage, N.S.; 6, Chignecto Bay; 8, Cape Spencer; 9, Head Harbor, Campobello; 10, Salkeld Islands, N.B.; and 11, southern entrance to St. John, N.B. (Number 7 is unidentified.) In Maine, 12 is Monhegan; 13, Heron or Schoodic Island; 14, Cross, Libby, Head Harbor and Great Wass; 15, Muscongus; 17, Muscle Ridge; 21 (over ou in Chouacoit, Saco), Richmond Island. On the St. Lawrence, 19 is R. Sainte Anne.

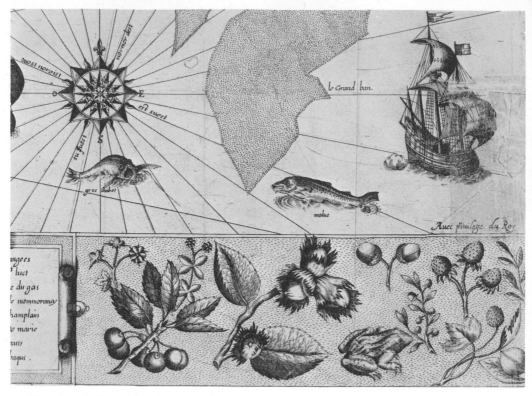

Details of Champlain's general map of 1612. Couresty Harvard College Library.

doned, since the strongest winds of French colonial enterprise were then blowing toward Brazil. The voyage of the Razilly brothers to Rio in 1612–13 brought home so rich a haul of logwood and spices that Brazil appeared to be another Cipangu or El Dorado. Fortunately for Canada, this enterprise ended in disaster in 1614; stout Portuguese threw out the French.

In the meantime, de Monts decided that what he needed to promote his and Champlain's plans was a figurehead — someone prominent to serve as titular head of the enterprise. After one false start, twenty-four-year-old Henri de Bourbon, Prince de Condé, Duc d'Enghien, cousin of the king and first peer of France, condescended to accept a royal appointment as Viceroy of New France. On 22 November 1612 he commissioned Champlain his "Lieutenant pour La Nouvelle France." Under Condé a new company was formed to enjoy the fur trading monopoly; any merchant could share the privileges if he paid a subscription. Before these arrangements could be completed a whole year had passed. This new commission and the company charter were bitterly opposed by independent merchants of Saint-Malo and Rouen. They even issued a diatribe against Champlain, describing him as a mere painter who went to Canada out of curiosity and had discovered nothing; to send him out again would only contribute to his own vainglory and drain the royal treasury. Finally Champlain had the essential documents published by the provincial parliaments which (he fondly thought) would make this new régime impregnable.

On 6 March 1613 Champlain departed Honfleur in Pont-Gravé's ship and commenced his sixth voyage to Canada. He now had more authority than before, as deputy to a viceroy and prince of the blood, but actually he enjoyed no more power than what he and his shipmates could exert on the spot. That did not trouble him for the moment, since his immediate object was western exploration. Nicolas de Vignau, a youth whom he had lent to the Algonkin in return for Savignon, and who returned to France with Pont-Gravé, assured Champlain that he had paddled up the Ottawa River to its source in a lake which had an outlet to the "Northern Sea"; that he had reached that sea (Hudson Bay) in seventeen days from the La Chine rapids, and had seen the wreck of an Englishman's ship and heard about an English boy who had joined the Indians. Champlain concluded that this was the wreck of the ship of Henry Hudson, who had wintered in James Bay in 1610–11, and he was eager to contest English possession of this country, with its northwest passage possibilities. Later he decided that Vignau was an "impudent liar" and had never been within hundreds of miles of the great salt sea. Vignau returned to Canada in *Le Soleil* of La Rochelle, whose owners had a permit from the Prince de Condé to trade. (Whenever Condé needed pocket money, he sold a fur-trading permit).

Pont-Gravé's ship sighted Cape Breton and Cape Ray, Newfoundland, on 21 April 1613, and on the 29th made Pointe aux Vaches near Tadoussac. There a crowd of Montagnais boarded her yelling "Where is Champlain?" The Captain had a little fun with them, keeping himself apart and pretending he had remained in France; but one old warrior identified him from the scar he had received on his ear in the second battle with the Iroquois, and all responded with whoops of joy. The Montagnais were so hungry after a bad winter as to eat the entrails of wild geese and hares that the French at Tadoussac brought on board, and even tallow scraped off the ship's topsides.

Champlain caused copies of the king's commission to Condé, and of his own as the prince's lieutenant, to be posted at Tadoussac, warning interlopers that this company was under royal protection. He then sailed in a shallop to Quebec, arriving 7 May, and found the people there in good health after a mild winter. Thence up to Montreal, where a small party of Algonkin consented to guide him up the Ottawa River, on his promise to lead them on the warpath the following year.

So, on 27 May 1613, the day after Whitsunday, Champlain started on his first western exploration. He had only two canoes, with one native guide and four French companions, including Vignau and an interpreter. They portaged past the La Chine rapids — Champlain remarking that it was "no small labor to those not used to it" — which every canoeist on his first trip will endorse. Two leagues further upstream they entered Lac Saint-Louis, confluence of the St. Lawrence, Châteauguay and Ottawa rivers. Choosing the last-named, they passed the Long Sault with some difficulty, detouring the worst falls. At some places there existed no portage trail through the thick woods; they had to "track" (tow) the canoes, stumbling over smooth wet boulders. In pulling his own canoe, Champlain got it broadside to a whirl-pool and almost lost both canoe and hand, around which he had wound the towline. "But Divine mercy preserved us all." One wonders whether he appreciated the beauty of white water. And how did he keep his gunpowder dry? Why did not the Indians use setting poles for upstream work?

Encountering a party of Algonkin paddling downstream in fifteen canoes, Champlain borrowed from them another native steersman and guide. They passed the superb site later selected for the city of Ottawa, where the Gatineau River flowing between "fine open woods and land fit for tillage" enters from the north, and the Rideau River from the south, and shortly thereafter a beautiful waterfall, the Chaudière, which now makes electric current for the city of Ottawa. This fall could be heard for miles, and in passing it by portage, the Indians performed propitiatory rites. One savage took up a collection of tobacco on a dish of birch bark, around which they danced and sang; he made a speech to the spirit of the waterfall, and then threw the tobacco into a boiling whirlpool at its foot. Do not imagine that these portages were as simple as those frequented by today's sportsmen. You had to carry the canoes on the first trip, and return twice for equipment, provisions and weapons. The country they passed through is all farmland now, with an escarpment of the Laurentians approaching the east bank; but in 1613 it was uninterrupted wilderness.

Entering Lac des Chats, the party spent a night and set up a cross. At the northern end, on the advice of their native guide, they portaged from a point now called Goulds Wharf near Portage du Fort to the thin chain of lakes and streams between the present Coldingham and Catherine lakes. This carry required an entire day and was very exhausting; Champlain himself toted three arquebuses, three paddles, his *capote*, and *"quelques petites bagatelles";* and the younger Frenchmen carried even more in weight. Even so, said he, we were "more bothered by the mosquitoes than by the burdens." But the portage was well worth the trouble, as it got them into a north-sloping watershed and saved them from a dozen or more carries around south-flowing rapids on the Ottawa.

At the northern end of little Green Lake the party had to portage through a windrow of fallen timber; and here either Champlain, or Père Lalemant on a later journey, lost the bronze mariner's astrolabe with which he took fairly accurate latitudes. Shortly after, at the south end of Muskrat Lake (a very pretty narrow one with wooded banks), the French met a friendly chief named Nibachis, who marveled that they had got that far and lent them two more canoes, with paddlers, to guide them through Muskrat and over the Stoqua portage into a big widening of the mainstream of the Ottawa now called Lower Allumette Lake. There

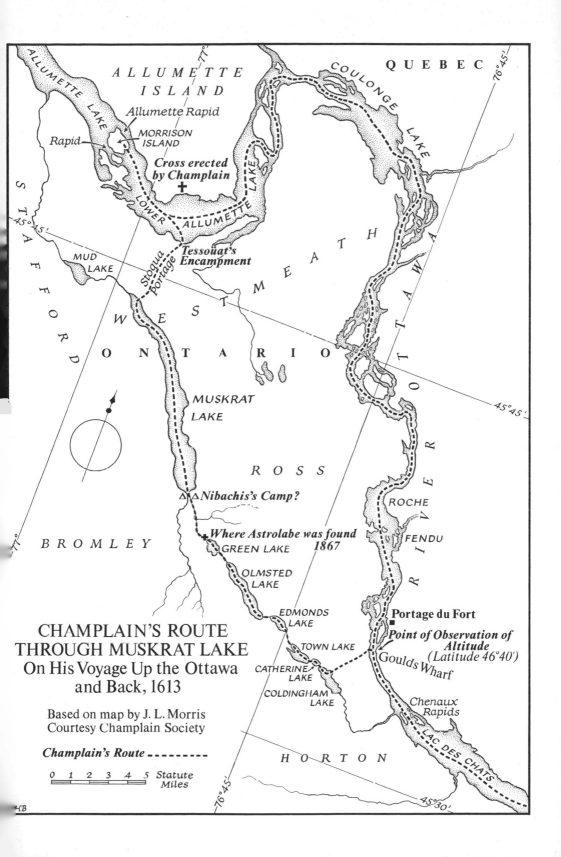

ALLUMETTE ISLAND

ALLUMETTE LAKE

Allumette Rapid

MORRISON ISLAND

Rapid

COULONGE LAKE

QUEBEC

77°

76°45'

Cross erected by Champlain

✝

LOWER ALLUMETTE LAKE

STAFFORD LAKE

45°15'

MUD LAKE

Tessouat's Encampment

Stoqua Portage

W E S T M E A T H

W E S T O N T A R I O

MUSKRAT LAKE

O T T A W A

R I V E R

45°45'

R O S S

△△*Nibachis's Camp?*

B R O M L E Y

77°

✝ *Where Astrolabe was found 1867*
GREEN LAKE

ROCHE

FENDU

OLMSTED LAKE

EDMONDS LAKE

Portage du Fort ■

Point of Observation of Altitude
(Latitude 46°40')

TOWN LAKE

Goulds Wharf

CATHERINE LAKE

COLDINGHAM LAKE

Chenaux Rapids

CHAMPLAIN'S ROUTE
THROUGH MUSKRAT LAKE
On His Voyage Up the Ottawa
and Back, 1613

Based on map by J. L. Morris
Courtesy Champlain Society

Champlain's Route - - - - - - -

0 1 2 3 4 5 Statute Miles

H O R T O N

LAC DES CHATS

76°45'

45°30'

JB

they were in the domain of Tessoüat, who had met Champlain at Tadoussac in 1603, and who found it difficult to believe that Frenchmen could have survived all those rapids. He accompanied Champlain's party to his headquarters in the center of his domain, a beautiful island in the river, now known as Morrison, bordered by rapids.

These people were an Algonkin tribe who lived in this region of poor soil for fear of the Iroquois but made a good thing of it, taking tribute from the Huron coming down-river with peltry. The chief declared that they would migrate down-river and camp near Montreal if Champlain would protect them there. That he promised to do, after participating courteously in a *tabagi* (feast) in his honor. Later comers agreed that Champlain was hood-winked at this point. Tessoüat's Algonkin, whom Père Sagard called the proudest and rudest Indians he had ever met, had no idea of giving up their strategic position, comparable to that of the medieval robber barons on the Rhine.

Champlain tried to persuade Tessoüat to lend him a few canoes to guide him to the Nebicerini (called the Wizard Nation because of their sorcerers) at Lake Nipissing, or even to Hudson Bay. He was particularly eager to reach the latter, having heard of the English wintering there, and in view of Vignau's tale that he had seen an English wreck and heard about a survivor who might have been John Hudson, Henry's son. Important officials in France, to whom Champlain had enlarged on the danger of Canada's being pinched by the English from the north as well as the south, had told him he should go there in person, and report. But his Indian hosts assured Champlain that Vignau had never left Tessoüat's village the previous winter; his tales were mere fabrications. The young man, confronted by hundreds of Indians yelling "Liar! Liar!" and threatening to tear his heart out, retracted, confessed that he had never been to any other lake. Knowing that these Indians had every reason to keep the French out of their country, one suspects that Vignau's original account was substantially true. He may not actually have reached Hudson Bay, but he had heard about it from the natives, who had met at least one survivor of Henry Hudson's expedition.

Now convinced that he could never reach Lake Nipissing or Hudson Bay that season, Champlain set up a cross of white cedar with the arms of France, on the north shore of Lower Allumette Lake, just behind a beautiful sand beach, a perfect canoe landing. He took leave of Tessoüat, whom he called *un bon vieux capitaine*, and started back to Montreal with a fleet of forty canoes, doubled en route by others joining. They followed the main channel of the Ottawa (now the provincial boundary between Quebec and Ontario), ran ten sets of rapids without mishap, and joined their up-river route on Lac des Chats. At the Chaudière falls the tobacco-tossing ritual was repeated. By 17 June they were back at the La Chine rapids, having made the round journey in three weeks, an amazing feat.

It is difficult today, even for a sportsman who loves white water and an easy portage and the savory evening meal of freshly caught trout, to imagine the hardships of those long canoe trips for Europeans. Champlain told of them in part, and later comers told more. Day and night, travelers were pursued by swarms of deer flies, black flies, mosquitoes, tiny gnats and other biting insects; to some Europeans these were so poisonous that you could hardly recognize their features, all bunged-up from the bites. The Indians repelled these pests by covering themselves with an aromatic grease which the French thought worse than being bitten. As a rule there was only one meal a day, in the evening; and food was both filthy and scarce. Each canoe carried its own cooking pot, but the Indians urinated in it while paddling. Their standard daily dish (the French called it *samagité*) was a sort of slumgullion with a base of

ABOVE: *Site of cross on Lower Allumette Lake.* BELOW: *Morrison Island, seat of Tessoüat.*

boiled parched corn; all kinds of flesh, fowl, and fish with the guts in, much of it putrid, were thrown in, but no salt. Champlain often managed, without offending his hosts, to catch and cook himself a fresh fish.

He was a man of action who could take anything, but this sort of traveling was hell for the religious. "Men steeped in antique learning, pale with the close breath of the cloister," as Parkman put it, were first tossed about at sea and then, with no time to harden their muscles, sent on one of these devastating journeys. Their wooden-soled sandals were the worst possible footwear for a rough portage or for wading over smooth rocks, their cassocks trailed sand and water into the canoes, which annoyed their native guides. They had to sleep on the ground with no better mattress and covering than hemlock boughs — or spruce boughs if there were no hemlock handy.

Père Le Jeune included in his *Jesuit Relation* for 1637 a "Guide to Good Manners" for the benefit of missionaries to Huronia or other savage nations. Never keep natives waiting to start a canoe journey, and debark nimbly when and where they tell you to. Bring a tinder box or burning glass to provide them with fire or to light their pipes; "these little services win their hearts." Pretend to like their "samagité or salmagundi" even if filthy and half cooked, for it's all you will get. Don't ask unnecessary questions or try to improve your vocabulary in the canoe; "Silence is then a good equipment." Try to keep a cheerful face, and thus prove that you joyfully endure the fatigues of the journey. Don't start anything, like paddling, that you can't finish. Bring a supply of awls, small knives, fishhooks and glass beads to buy fish from any savages you may meet en route. Go barefoot in the canoe, tuck up your cassock, and wear a small cap instead of your broad-brimmed hat, which annoys them — catching the wind and cutting off the view. Always carry something on a portage; the natives despise anyone who is not a good pack animal. All your philosophy and theology so painfully acquired in the seminary go for nothing in the wilderness; unpleasant things must be endured without complaint for the love of God. Some of the savages' manners will appall you; nevertheless, don't attempt to "civilize" them; concentrate on bringing lost souls to Christ. And you, "having found Jesus Christ in His Cross, will find roses among thorns, the sweet in the bitter, and all in nothing."

Below La Chine (which he always refers to as Le Sault Saint-Louis) Champlain was met by two French pinnaces. They gave him a cannon salute, "at which some of our savages were delighted, and others very startled, never having heard such music." The natives he met here had come to La Chine for the annual peltry fair. They agreed not to trade with anyone unless authorized by Champlain, but he had to issue a permit to one Sieur de Maisonneuve of Saint-Malo, who had arrived at Quebec with three ships and a permit to trade from the Prince de Condé.

At Quebec, as Champlain had ascertained, the little garrison had wintered well, and had found an outlet to their energy by shooting stag, wild pigeon, and catching various kinds of fish on which they had dined and supped daily. "Thus they were in better shape than I, attenuated by toil and moil, and having commonly eaten but one meal a day of badly cooked half-broiled fish." This is the first we have heard of the French at Quebec profiting from the multitude of fish in the river. Earlier, we are told, the only fish they had was salt cod from Newfoundland, re-exported from France.

Partly with the object of bringing the Malouin merchants into his company, Champlain returned with Maisonneuve to France. They made a slow passage, for this season of westerlies, leaving Tadoussac 8 August and Percé on the 18th, arriving Saint-Malo 26 September 1613.

X

Reorganization and
More Western Explorations

Iɴ France, Champlain lost no time in broadening the base of the
company. He persuaded prominent merchants of Saint-Malo,
Rouen and La Rochelle to join. To set forth what had already been
accomplished, he published *La Quatrième Voyage du Sr. de
Champlain,* including the trip up the Ottawa. It was printed at
Paris in 1614 with a 1613 imprint. A small map included in the
book covered very sketchily the country between the St. Lawrence and Hudson Bay. Champlain would get out a better one two
years later.

After much negotiation, a new society, La Compagnie de Canada, was formed on 20 November 1613 in the presence of Condé.
The subscribers were assured exclusive rights to the fur trade of
the St. Lawrence for eleven years; in return they made the Prince
the curious promise to present him annually with a horse valued
at a thousand écus — about $600 in gold. They promised to pay
Champlain an undetermined salary as Condé's lieutenant and, more
to the point, to take out six families to begin a permanent population of Canada. The Sieur de Monts remained a stockholder, but
was no longer an officer of the company. Badgered by lawsuits
connected with his Canadian ventures, Pierre du Gua went bank-

rupt and died about 1628, still a Protestant. As a founder of New France, de Monts was second only to Champlain in importance, and often Champlain's commander; but he has received precious little recognition from French Canadians, or anyone.

This new Compagnie de Canada was a pretentious but none the less feeble result of all the efforts by de Monts, Champlain and Pont-Gravé for the past ten years. None knew better than Champlain that it was high time something substantial was done, if France ever wanted a real establishment in North America. The English Virginia Company had been well seated at Jamestown since 1607, and in 1613 was strong enough to send Captain Argall to break up Madame de Guercheville's Jesuit colony at Mount Desert and to burn Poutrincourt's habitation at Port-Royal. English Puritans, in veritable hordes if you compare their numbers with the corporal's guard at Quebec, were about to descend on New England, which France claimed as part of L'Acadie. The Dutch were getting ready to establish the trading post of Fort Orange at the site of Albany. Could the Compagnie de Canada hold its own against this foreign competition, as well as that of the independent and disrespectful French traders?

One condition of permanency, Champlain well knew, was to take out a corps of missionaries to convert the Indians. He had tried to procure Jesuits in 1610, but they went to L'Acadie, no longer in his bailiwick. He now turned to L'Ordre des Récollets, reformed Franciscans who had a monastery in his native town of Brouage. They were willing to go to Canada, every one; four were chosen, and a small sum of money raised for their support. A ship of 350 tuns' burthen named *Saint-Etienne* was purchased by the company and commanded by the veteran Pont-Gravé. In her Champlain returned to Canada. With him were the Récollet friars Denis Jamet, Jean Dolbeau, Joseph Le Caron, and lay brother Pacifique du Plessis, each "moved by a holy zeal . . . to set up in these regions the standard of Jesus Christ." After confessing and receiving the sacrament, all sailed from Honfleur 24 April 1615. The six families of settlers are not mentioned, but possibly one or two did go out in *Don de Dieu* or *Loyal*, which sailed with *Saint-Etienne*.

This little fleet took only a month to reach Tadoussac. There her company fitted out shallops for the voyage up-river. Zealous Père Le Caron pressed on to Montreal; nothing would satisfy him but to join the savages without delay, and to spend a winter with them. Champlain and Père Jamet followed as far as La Chine, while Dolbeau and du Plessis stayed at Quebec to build a residence and chapel for their order.

Champlain had already ascertained that his two earlier campaigns against the Iroquois were not enough. His Huron, Algonkin and Montagnais allies expected him to support an annual invasion; so, to keep their loyalty and friendship, war became his most urgent business. After the Récollets had celebrated the first mass at Montreal on Midsummer Day 1615, the assembled allies, without waiting for Champlain to arrive, hit the warpath; but this expedition fizzled out and got nowhere. Since it had already been agreed that he visit Huronia to whip up their contribution to this hostile expedition, our middle-aged leader shoved off in two canoes, accompanied by two other Frenchmen, ten Indians, and a terrific lot of gear, which made the portages even more burdensome than usual. Champlain admired the birch bark canoe with white cedar ribs and thwarts as an ideal craft for river or sheltered coastal waters; it was light enough to be carried easily by one man, and could float the weight of a pipe of wine. The trouble came when you had to carry the freight around impassable rapids; and on the Ottawa not a day passed without portages.

This party paddled up the Ottawa and the Olmsted-Muskrat cutoff to Lower Allumette Lake, where Champlain had parleyed with Tessoüat two years earlier. There he was less than halfway to Huronia. Continuing for about seventy-five miles more up the Ottawa, he reached the mouth of the Mattawa River. That part of the Ottawa is now largely wilderness, with small wood-pulp mills at the rapids. At its confluence with the Mattawa River they turned up that stream, which still flows through a wilderness with scattered farms, and after passing at least ten rapids, reached on 26 July the site of North Bay on Le Lac des Nipisierinii, as he called Lake Nipissing. This valley of the Mattawa, wrote Champlain, is "very barren, sterile, and inhabited by only a few Algonkin," who subsist by hunting, fishing, and by drying for winter use the blueberries, raspberries and other small fruits which grow there in marvelous quantity. At the point where the Mattawa River enters the Ottawa, Champlain made so accurate a latitude observation — 46° N, only 18′ less than correct — as to lead one to conclude that he still carried the faithful astrolabe.

At Nipissing, which Champlain reported to be a fine lake full of fish, studded with pretty islands and bordered by fair meadows, he ran into a tribe of seven to eight hundred souls who "feasted us in several feasts . . . and took the trouble to fish and hunt in order to treat us as delicately as they could." After two days' entertainment, Champlain's party crossed the lake in their canoes and followed the French River, by which it discharges into Lake Huron. Champlain found this valley highly disagreeable, "all rocks and mountains with not ten *arpents* of arable land." Tastes change; we in 1971 found this river, with its wooded banks of mixed evergreen, birch and maple, utterly charming. It is still wilderness, not a house or even a pulp mill until one is close to Georgian Bay.

Before reaching that important part of Lake Huron, Champlain encountered three hundred warriors of an Algonkin tribe that he named Les Cheveux-Relevés because they arranged their hair in a

ABOVE: *French River between Lakes Nipissing and Huron.*
BELOW: *A few of the Thirty Thousand Islands, Georgian Bay.*

high brush; his picture of one (*Works* III 44) shows a hair-do resembling the Afro of 1971. They called themselves Outaouais, whence the name Ottawa. Champlain made friends with the chief, who drew a map for him in charcoal and said that his people came to this place to gather and dry blueberries for winter use.

The French now paddled along the easterly shore of the Georgian Bay of Lake Huron, threading their way among the well-named Thirty Thousand Islands. These are of glacier-ground smooth granite, reminding us of southern Labrador; some small as a big dinner table and perfectly bare, others of all sizes up to a hundred or more acres, with spruce trees and underbrush. It took the party four days to paddle the approximately one hundred miles to the Midland Peninsula, which divides Matchedash and Nottawasaga bays. They landed near the site of Penetanguishene.

Champlain was delighted to see La Mer Douce, as he called this great lake which he had been hearing about for over ten years. Penetanguishene is the gateway to Huronia, a section of the present Ontario Province only about twenty miles wide by forty long, lying between Lake Simcoe and Matchedash and Nottawasaga bays (both parts of Lake Huron). It was and is a land of fertile soil and tall trees; in the streams and lakes Champlain reported "monstrously great" trout up to four and a half feet long, and sturgeon from which the Canadians now extract a palatable fresh-water caviar. Here, favored by nature, lived an estimated ten thousand Huron.* Gathered into villages, some fortified, they lived fairly well owing to their strategic position for trade. Champlain walked from village to village to pick up contingents for the war party. "It is a pleasure to travel in this country," recorded Champlain, "so fair and fertile it is." And it was not the natives'

---

* Other estimates run as high as thirty thousand; but it is difficult to believe that even with a planting-hunting-trading economy, so many people could subsist in Huronia.

fault that he did not profit by the kindness of the young girls, one of whom evidently lay in wait for the handsome stranger when he bedded on the ground outside his host's cabin to escape a multitude of fleas within. "A shameless girl approached me with effrontery, offering to keep me company, for which I thanked her, sending her away with gentle remonstrances; and I passed the night with some savages" — and more fleas. Besides repelling boarders, sailor Champlain "took the sun" with his astrolabe and found the median latitude of Huronia to be 44°30″ N — correct.

At a palisaded village called Carhagoua, about two miles inland from Thunder Bay on the Midland Peninsula, Champlain caught up with Père Joseph Le Caron, who on 12 August 1615 celebrated a special mass for his benefit. The worthy father was not too happy; young Frenchmen who accompanied him were raising hell with the native girls, and he could not make head or tail out of the language. People told him a different word every time he pointed to an object like a stone or a tree. He was misled, too, by the Indian sense of humor, giving him dirty words for sacred things; so that when he tried to explain theology in their own language he uttered unwittingly the most horrible obscenities, which made his congregation roll on the ground with laughter.

The Huron around Lake Simcoe supposedly were hot to fight the Five Nations, but on 17 August 1615, when Champlain harangued a muster of many hundreds at the meeting spot in Cahiagué, a village near the present Hawkestone on Lake Simcoe, he had to use all his diplomacy and eloquence to persuade them to conclude their dancing and feasting and get going. He later learned that this was part of the war-making ritual, to appease the gods and whip up their own courage. The Huron were not difficult to move if you respected their conventions, and the bulk of the French allied force belonged to that nation.

ABOVE: *Thunder Bay, Georgian Bay, with ice, 14 May 1971.* BELOW: *Falls on Severn River between Georgian Bay and Lake Simcoe.*

Leaving Georgian Bay at the site of Port Severn on 1 September, the war party followed the line of the now canalized Severn River through Sparrow Lake to Lake Couchitching,* which Champlain calls *"un petit lac,"* and this little lake gave directly by a *détroit* — now the Narrows, where the natives netted a great store of fish to dry and cure for winter use — into *"un autre lac tout joignant"* — Lake Simcoe. Here the party picked up the Huron whom Champlain had harangued at Cahiagué,† and decided the strategy of this campaign. This was to make contact with the Andastes nation, who lived on the Susquehanna River just south of the present New York–Pennsylvania boundary, and persuade them to co-operate by simultaneous attack on a certain Iroquoian fortress. Consequently, two canoes with Etienne Brûlé as envoy and interpreter started from Lake Simcoe on 8 September 1615 to inform the Andastes that the Great White Father was coming on a certain date with plenty of firepower, and they had better go along for their own good, as the Five Nations were their enemies too. Timing, that persistent stumbling block to the success of combined operations, failed here as usual.

The main body left Lake Simcoe two days later, when there was *une forte gelée blanche;* or, as Parkman put it, "Champlain, shivering in his blanket, awoke to see the meadows sparkling with an early frost, soon to vanish under the bright autumnal sun." Parkman, who had been there too, remembered many such frosty mornings in the early autumn when the brightly colored leaves were still on the trees.

Champlain now had several hundred Huron, with perhaps

---

* A very beautiful lake, now lined with summer houses and the resort town of Orilla.

† In the 1632 *Voyages* (*Works* IV 245) Champlain states that he visited Lake Couchitching after the muster at Cahiagué, and one infers that he did not paddle along the Severn to get to Lake Simcoe but walked across Huronia from Thunder Bay, visiting villages en route.

[155]

twenty Frenchmen, including more arquebusiers who had paddled up the Ottawa after him and reported for duty in Huronia. They traveled a roundabout route across the Ontario peninsula. It is a tribute to the natives' sense of topography that the Canadian government in the last century built the Trent Canal from Lake Simcoe to Lake Ontario directly along this route, building chains of locks in many places where the natives used to portage.

Leaving Lake Simcoe, where the Trent Canal now begins, the full war party paddled upstream and through a chain of lakes to the big, oddly shaped Balsam Lake. This is the summit of the present canal system, 122 feet above Lake Simcoe and 600 feet above Lake Ontario. From Balsam the warriors portaged their canoes a good ten leagues* to avoid the Fénelon Falls. In Sturgeon Lake they found good paddling again. Continuing down the Trent and Otonabee rivers and passing through Pigeon, Buckhorn and Chemung lakes, they reached the site of Peterborough, Ontario. Thence they followed the Otonabee River, also part of the Trent Canal system, through Rice Lake and the Trent River itself, to the site of Trenton on the Bay of Quinte, an arm of Lake Ontario. By this winding bay they reached the eastern part of Lake Ontario between Amherst Island and Point Pleasant.

The country they passed through was one of rich soil and noble trees which the Huron had abandoned for fear of Iroquois raiders. Champlain, observing the tall butternut trees laced with wild grapevines, wrote, "One would think they had been planted for pleasure." Doubtless he looked forward to the distant day when this region would be carved into farms, as happened in the nine-

---

* According to Champlain (*Works* III 58). On the modern map, however, the overland distance between the two lakes is only five nautical miles, two of Champlain's leagues. Either he meant that it felt like a ten-league carry, or his guides went north of Cameron Lake, took a short hitch on water, and then carried around the Fénelon Falls. Or it may be a simple misprint, *dix* for *deux*.

teenth century. But the Trent Canal, with its well-kept locks, has been deserted in favor of the roads. We, flying over it in May 1971, did not see a single boat of any kind on the canal or the connecting lakes.

Champlain calculated that the distance from Lake Simcoe to Lake Ontario was about 160 nautical miles — assuming that he used the same league that he did at sea. The modern Trent Canal system measures 240 statute miles, but that includes the section between Georgian Bay and Lake Simcoe. The war party may have been slow starting, but it certainly made time — only twenty-five days from Lake Simcoe to the further shore of Lake Ontario.

On 5 October they crossed Lake Ontario (which Champlain named Lac Saint-Louis) by island-hopping, as Indians liked to do — the Ducks, the Galoos, Calf and Great Stoney — and landed at Stoney Point, which the French formerly called Pointe à la Traverse. There the savages hid their canoes in the forest and everyone walked south along the lake shore for four days. Champlain admired the country (now Oswego County, New York) "*un pays fort agréable et beau*," with many streams, ponds and meadows, and fine woods, especially the chestnut trees, which bore nuts "small but tasting good."

After crossing the outlet to Salmon River on 9 October 1615, the party continued its southward course through the forest to Lake Oneida. Near its outlet their scouts encountered a fishing party of eleven Iroquois, including women, young boys and a girl. A Huron chief, to begin a delightful bout of torture, chopped off a woman's finger. Champlain promptly reproved him for inhumanity and threatened to pull out the French forces "if he did not desist," which he did.

On 10 October, at about 3 P.M., the war party reached its objective — a stronghold of the Onondaga, one of the Five Nations, on a small pond south of Lake Oneida.* According to Champlain's own sketch it was a formidable hexagon thirty feet high, with galleries running around it, one side overlooking a brook and another the pond, scores of bark lodges inside, and gardens outside. Heaps of stones to hurl at attackers, and waterspouts to quench fires, were kept on the galleries. There was no sign of their Andastes allies, but the Huron chiefs insisted on attacking at once, and there was an inconclusive skirmish that very afternoon in which several on both sides were wounded and one Frenchman was killed.

Champlain, using siege tactics as old as Julius Caesar's, persuaded his allies to construct a cavalier, a platform high enough to overlook the palisades. They did this very promptly in the adjacent woods, and on 11 October two hundred Huron dragged it right up to the fort. Three or four arquebusiers were posted on top; and others, including Champlain himself, across the brook. (He is the figure in the lower left with plumed helmet, reloading his arquebus). When the battle opened, explosions from the arquebuses were drowned by hideous yelling on both sides; and the Onondaga, undismayed by the cavalier or by a fire kindled against the wrong (leeward) side of their wall, replied so briskly with stones and arrows that the French allies became disorganized and discouraged; and the Onondaga fire department put out all fires. Champlain, although badly wounded in the knee and leg, tried to shout down the vociferous natives and restore some semblance of order, but could do nothing. They had no sense of discipline, he said; it was everyone for himself. After three hours of battle, arrows flying "thick as hail," the attacking host retired to the nearby forest. Although only two of the native chiefs and fif-

---

* Local authorities differ as to exact location of the fort. The one sanctioned by the State of New York is a pond formerly called Nichols but now Atkins. It is just east of the village of Perryville, and you may also reach it by turning off the New York State Thruway at Oneida and running about ten miles due south. We easily identified it, now surrounded by farms, from the air.

teen others had been wounded, and none killed, the leaders insisted on waiting in an improvised fort at least four days for the Andastes allies to turn up before renewing the attack; and as the Andastes never did turn up, the attack was never renewed.

The leader, thoroughly disgusted with his allies, had never been "in such hellish torment" in his life. Unable to walk, he was carried, bound in a basket, on the back of a Huron warrior all the way to the lake shore where the canoes were hidden. And that took six days. Nothing would move the natives forward again; nor would they escort Champlain to Montreal. He perforce had to return with them to their own country and pass the winter

Atkins pond, site of the fort, in May 1971.

Champlain's drawing of his attack on the Onondaga fort. From his Voyages et Descouvertures *(1619). Champlain provided no key. On the right is the* cavalier, *with arquebusiers on top; it is shown as made of sawn timber, but must have been of logs. In the center, the fire, which the savages kindled on the wrong side. At left, more arquebusiers; Champlain is at lower left, reloading. The inside is filled with Iroquois longhouses, shown much too small. Courtesy John Carter Brown Library.*

there. After several days he was able to walk with difficulty, which he preferred to being carried even more painfully in a basket.

Etienne Brûlé's party had fared even worse. It reached the Andastes village, found them enthusiastic for war, but the chiefs insisted on spending several days in feasting and dancing before starting. Thus, by the time they reached the Onondaga fort, victory celebrations were under way and the Andastes ruefully returned home, Brûlé with them. During the winter, after exploring the Susquehanna River, Brûlé started back toward Huronia with Andastes guides. A party of Iroquois ambushed them, captured the French lad, bound him to a stake and began slow torture. Brûlé threatened them with the wrath of God, and a gathering thunderstorm made his threat so credible that the Iroquois released him; and, as one favored by the gods, he was even guided to Huronia. He attended the annual peltry fair at La Chine next year and there told his story to Champlain.

This defeat by the Onondaga was a serious setback for Champlain's Indian policy, for it proved that gunfire was not necessarily supreme, nor the French invincible. He had deeply involved French honor and prestige in a war that began, to be sure, long before his day but dragged on as long as the colonial period lasted. Not that Champlain did not try his best to conclude peace in these northern forests, scene of countless bloody conflicts; but northern Indians did not want peace. War parties were their way of life, their greatest pastime. And, forty years after this fight at the Onondaga fort, the Iroquois were masters of the Great Lakes.

Since winter set in early and the lakes and streams of the Trent system were soon frozen, the Huron decided to return by a sort of beeline cross-country, on foot, abandoning their big canoe fleet in the forest. First, however, they paddled from Lake Ontario up the Salmon River to a lake which Canadian historians have identified

as Lake Loughborough, arriving on 28 October. There the retreating war party made a long halt to fish and hunt. Every other
day for over a month they held a deer hunt. Champlain, who took
"a singular pleasure" in this *battue*, sketched the process for us;
the Indians, using wooden clappers to frighten the deer, drive
them into a V-shaped trap where they are slaughtered by spears
and arrows. Between 28 October and 4 December they killed 120
deer and saved most of the meat, tallow and hides for winter con-
sumption. During one of these hunts Champlain, pursuing a peculiar bird that tantalizingly hopped along the ground ahead of him,*
got lost in the forest. By following the courses of streams, he
found his friends again after three days and nights, and inciden-
tally learned a good lesson in woodcraft.

His native allies waited for a hard December frost to resume
their journey home. Packing the deer hides and meat on sledges
that they built in the forest, and walking on newly constructed
snowshoes, they went by frozen lakes and streams, dragging the
sledges. When they had to go through woods they abandoned
these crude vehicles, and each savage carried about a hundred
pounds' weight of venison and gear on his back. When they
reached another lake, new sledges were built. This went on for
nineteen days; then came a thaw, and for four days they had to
trudge through knee-deep slush and pick their way among wind-
rows of fallen trees.

This was Champlain's most difficult journey, one he never cared
to repeat. With all that venison the retreating war party had
plenty to eat, but they had to spend every night on the snow, with
no other bedding than hemlock or spruce boughs. Two days before

---

* He says it was the size of a hen, with a puffin-like beak, yellow body, red
head and blue wings, "which made short successive flights like a partridge." No
ornithologist has succeeded in identifying it! Parkman, who knew what it was to
be lost in the Canadian forest, has a vivid account of this episode in *Pioneers*
(1898), pp. 421–23.

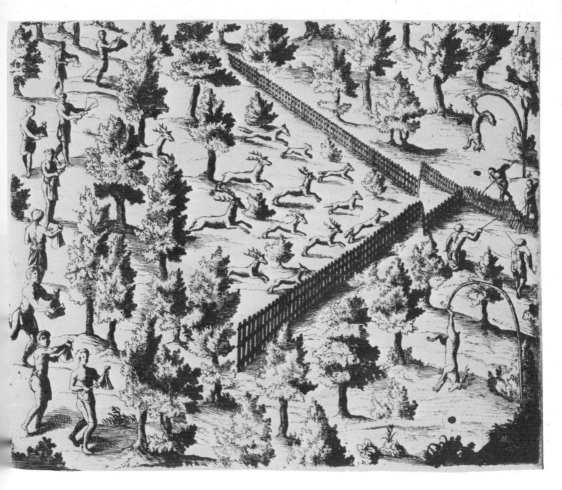

Champlain's drawing of the deer hunt. From Voyages ct Descouvertures *(1619). Again, no key. On the left, the savages
with wooden clappers are driving stags and does into a pound
where others are waiting to kill them with spears. At right, a
stag and a doe caught by a springe. Courtesy John Carter
Brown Library.*

Christmas they reached their first village, Cahiagué. Champlain, who had been carrying twenty pounds or more despite his lame leg, rested for the twelve days of Christmas 1615, then struck off for the village near Thunder Bay, Lake Huron, where he had left Père Joseph in the early fall. By mid-February 1616 he had sufficiently recovered to accompany the father on a visit to the Petun (Tobacco) Nation, who, more picturesquely, were also called the Tionontati. They lived south of Nottawasaga Bay, the southeastern bight of Georgian Bay.

The Tionontati were friendly and gave him "good cheer." Intrigued by some buffalo pelts which they had obtained by trade, he was preparing to make another northern exploration when he was called upon to mediate a dispute between Huron and Algonkin over a prisoner. The Huron had presented the Algonkin with an Iroquois captive taken in the Onondaga campaign, in order to give them the pleasure of torturing him. Instead, the Algonkin took a liking to the poor fellow and adopted him. This so enraged the donors that they sent a warrior to kill the prisoner, and that he did; but he in turn was rubbed out by the compassionate Algonkin. This was just the sort of thing to trigger an Indian war, which Champlain could not allow to happen between allies. All turned to him as mediator. So in mid-February 1616 Champlain met delegations from both tribes and patiently listened for two days to their harangues. He then addressed the assembly, "enlarged on the folly of fighting among themselves when the common enemy stood ready to devour them both," begged them to forget everything and make a fresh start. "And all returned to their lodges apparently satisfied," except the Algonkin. They were very sulky about his decision but made no more trouble.

Champlain spent at least four months of the winter of 1615–16 with the Huron, studying them and their country and collecting information about other Great Lakes. "Their life is wretched by comparison with ours," he wrote, "but happy for them because they have tasted none better and believe that there is none so good." He described their cookery, from which he so often had suffered; but he did like their bread made of corn meal and red beans, with blueberries and raspberries as plums; and he loved the roasted ears of green corn. "Dogs are in demand at their feasts," he wrote, and presumably he had to eat them too. Yet, he concluded, "With all their miseries I esteem them happy, since they have no other ambition than to live and support themselves, and they are more secure than those who wander through the forests like brute beasts. They also eat much *citroüilles* [squash or pumpkin] which they boil or roast in the ashes." He describes the dress of the women, their display of wampum and beads in ropes, and their heavy duties as gardeners, fishers and beasts of burden. "As for the men, they do nothing but hunt deer and other animals, fish, build lodges and go to war." Champlain tells how the parents fixed their babies to a board with a hole in it so they could urinate without soiling themselves, and their manner of child education. "The parents are too permissive," he says, "and never punish them, so they become so naughty and perverse that often they strike their mothers, and even their fathers!" They believe in no god, although they try to appease a devil called Oqui (equivalent to the Algonkin Manitou), with whom their medicine men (also called Oquis) are in league.

Champlain concluded that more than friars were needed to convert these savages to the French way of life. They needed a settled French population to demonstrate the virtues of civilization and *avec douceur* "wean them from their filthy habits, loose morals and rude license." He even quotes Huron chiefs admitting as much in conversation with him and Père Joseph. If this was not simply an example of that amiable trait of the North American natives to "yes" strangers, it was an amazing confession; for in general the last thing any Indian wanted was to have a European settlement nearby. Nevertheless, D'Arontal, the Huron chief who had been the Captain's particular host, confirmed these sentiments after accompanying him to Quebec.

As for courtship, they were completely promiscuous, and virginity disappeared early. Every evening the boys and girls ran from lodge to lodge, copulating as they pleased (as if in a 1972-style college dormitory), and it would not be unusual for a damsel to have had twenty different lovers before settling down to be a married drudge. The lads had to pay each girl they embraced in wampum or other native jewelry, so that a popular wench would acquire yards and yards of wampum belts as a dowry. Even after marriage she could have lovers if the appearance of fidelity was observed; and for that reason, all children's paternity was doubtful, and what little property the Indians had descended in the female line.

Champlain also describes the medicine men's favorite cure. As with other Eastern tribes, it consisted largely in raising a hullaballoo to frighten Oqui, and sweating out the disease with steam made by pouring water on hot stones. These methods, he says, killed more patients than they cured. He describes their mortuary methods, their masquerades and other amusements, their hunting, and fishing through the ice. In short, anyone who would study the manners and customs of the Huron in their primitive state could not do better than to read Champlain's *Voyages et Descouvertures* of 1619. It is certain that he liked the natives especially for their "jovial disposition," and that they respected and revered him.

On 20 May 1616, Champlain and the few other Frenchmen with him began their homeward journey to Montreal, guided by a party of his new Huron friends. They took it easy, spending forty days on the journey, and at the end of June reached the La Chine rapids. There they found Pont-Gravé, who had arrived from France with two vessels and more Récollet friars. Everyone was delighted to see Champlain, having given him up for lost. On 11 July he arrived at Quebec, where the friars held a service of thanksgiving for his safe arrival. He busied himself erecting some strong buildings with locally baked brick and slaked lime, to accommodate the still expected six families of settlers. During his absence the French had transplanted some trees from Normandy, given to them by the Sieur de Monts, together with seeds of various herbs and vegetables, "and all the gardens of the place were in admirable beauty, sowed with peas, beans and other vegetables, pumpkin, excellent roots of various sorts, cabbage, beets and other desirable herbs." Whilst Champlain appreciated the beauties of the Canadian wilderness, nothing pleased him more than a garden, with flowers, fruits and herbs from Old France.

Leaving Pères Dolbeau and du Plessis at Quebec, Champlain took Pères Jamet and Le Caron (who wished to drum up religious recruits in France) down-river to Tadoussac. Thence they set sail 3 August in one of Pont-Gravé's ships and "had so prosperous a wind that we arrived Honfleur in good health (thanks to God) on 10 September 1616."

I can see no evidence that Champlain's reputation suffered by the failure of his campaign against the Onondaga fort. On the contrary, his efforts, his wound, and his fortitude seem to have given him more credit than ever among the natives, even if they merely raised eyebrows at court. His last visit to Lake Huron, and his map of 1616 that followed, greatly extended French knowledge of the interior; and from information imparted by friendly Indians he now knew that the continent was a good deal wider, and the Pacific Ocean much further away, than anyone had supposed.

In any event, Champlain's forest rovings were now over. Already over forty-five years old, he had had enough fighting and laborious canoe journeys. The rest of his life would be devoted to nursing the puny colony of New France into growth and strength; and his only perils would be those of the ocean, and the Paris politicians.

XI

Madame Champlain
Comes to Quebec

U PON arrival at Honfleur in September 1616, Champlain was chagrined to hear that the head of his Compagnie de Canada, the Prince de Condé, had been arrested and put into the Bastille owing to dubious loyalty to the king. So the search for a noble figurehead had to be resumed. In October 1619 Condé, released from jail, sold his viceregal appointment for 11,000 écus to the Duc de Montmorency, another cousin of the king.

In the meantime, the company sent out a ship in 1617, returning Père Joseph and a second friar to Canada and also the Paris apothecary Louis Hébert, with his wife and daughters. Hébert had been with Champlain at Port-Royal during the merry winter of 1606–1607. His arrival at Quebec sets a milestone in Canadian history because he obtained a plot of ground, planted a garden, and really settled down. Since the company would not allow habitants to trade for fur, and required them to sell their garden produce at the same price as in France, for years nobody else could be persuaded to start a farm in Canada. The company's own employees were not allowed to do so. The Héberts were not only the first laymen to settle at Quebec, the pilgrim father and

Detail of Champlain's map of New France, 1616. From the original in the
John Carter Brown Library. KEY: 2. Lake Champlain. 4. Lac St. Pierre.
5. Rivière St. Maurice. 5. La Chine Rapids. 7. Lake Simcoe. 8, 8. Champlain's
route up the Ottawa. Courtesy John Carter Brown Library.
    Biferenis is Huronia; Mer Douce is Georgian Bay, Lake Huron; Lac St.
Louis is Lake Ontario; "Baye où ont hiverné les Anglois" is Hudson Bay.

mother, as it were, of the future colony; they stuck to the end
and lived out their lives under the shadow of the Rock.

Champlain went with them, but made a quick round trip, for
there is documentary evidence of his presence in Paris 22 July
1617. In the meantime he had brought out an engraved map of
La Nouvelle France dated 1616, which sold so well that later editions, with additions showing Boston, the Five Nations, Virginia, and a dotted route north of Hudson Bay *"tenu l'an 1665
pour aller au Japon et au Chine"* came out at intervals to 1677.
The central part of the first edition, which we have reproduced,
is amazingly accurate for the Ottawa River route to Lakes Nipissing and Huron. Champlain must have kept careful note of
courses and distances in his turbulent and laborious canoe journeys.

Early in 1618, when living in Paris with his now twenty-year-
old bride, Champlain drew up and presented to Louis XIII and
the Paris Chamber of Commerce two memoirs which, though
largely ignored by them, were of the deepest significance for the
future of Canada. In them he reminds the king of his labors for
New France for the past sixteen years. He warns him that if
France does not do something to strengthen her position in North
America, the English or Dutch may rub it out as they have the
settlements on Mount Desert Island and Port-Royal. A strong
French Canada will have many advantages for France; a domin-
ion "1800 leagues long" (a modest estimate indeed!), watered
by some of the world's fairest rivers and lakes, waters teeming
with fish, forests of valuable timber, thousands of acres of land
arable or fit for pasturage. He believes that a river entering Lake
Huron, or the St. Lawrence, may conduct boats to the Pacific
Ocean and the wealth of the Indies — that mirage which at-
tracted Cabot and Cartier and which men continued to envisage
in one form or another for centuries. Quebec is the key to it
all. The settlement there should be built up to a town the size of

Saint-Denis (the sepulcher of the old French kings), named Ludovica, with a beautiful church. "To obtain a solid footing" there should be forts at Quebec and at Tadoussac. Fifteen Récollet friars should be sent to Quebec to begin conversion of the savages, at least three hundred French families should be assisted to settle there, and a garrison of three hundred soldiers be provided by the crown. More domestic animals, too, should be brought out. Trading posts should be established at Trois-Rivières and the site of Montreal. This will cost 15,000 livres annually for fifteen years, after which Champlain promises to hand over land, jurisdiction, and the entire enterprise to the crown.

To the "Gentlemen of the Chamber of Commerce" Champlain is even more specific. The codfishery is already worth more than a million livres ($200,000 in gold) annually, and the salmon, sturgeon, whale and other fisheries are probably worth another million. Ships may be built of native timber, which is also in demand for wainscoting; these exports are conjecturally valued at 400,000 livres and otherwise useless wood may be burned to make naval stores and potash. Root crops (one of which produces a red dye like cochineal) and hemp for cordage will be worth another million. There are limitless possibilities of mineral wealth, especially iron, lead and silver (note that he makes no promise of gold). Vineyards are possible; and as for cattle, the Canadian climate is far more favorable than that of Peru,* where the Spaniards have done wonders in stock-raising. Finally (one would suppose that this would have been mentioned first) the peltry trade, including beaver and other fur, and deer, moose and buffalo skins, is already worth 400,000 livres a year. One is amazed to find that his estimate of the value of the fisheries is five-fold that of the peltry.

The Chamber of Commerce, obviously impressed, "humbly

---

* Probably an error for Mexico.

entreated" the king to grant funds to bring out three hundred families and three hundred soldiers, and to confirm "to the said Champlain and his associates the monopoly of the fur trade" for the fifteen years remaining of their charter, provided they take to Quebec at their own charge at least ten families a year.

Grandiloquent as these estimates must have seemed in 1618, in the light of history they were far from exaggerated. Canada now has everything that Champlain predicted; even the Northwest Passage. And it is clear what kind of colony he wished Canada to become: a source of primary products for France from fur trade, fisheries and forests, with enough farms to feed the inhabitants. No manufactories, of course; current doctrine prescribed that the home country have a monopoly of them in her colonies. But there must be a viable settlement with French families as a nucleus.

Champlain made another quick trip to Canada and back in 1618. Taking his eighteen year-old brother-in-law Eustache Boullé, he sailed from Honfleur in Pont-Gravé's ship on 24 May, and exactly a month later dropped anchor at Tadoussac. There his main business was to settle an Indian affair which threatened to break off good relations; he writes pages about it in his volume printed the next year. A French locksmith at Quebec beat up a Montagnais favored by the Sieur du Parc, Champlain's deputy commander. Nursing his wrath, the Indian murdered the locksmith when out fishing with a French sailor; and for good measure killed the sailor too. He bound the bodies together, weighted them with stones, and sank them midstream. But, as the old proverb says, "Murder will out!" The bodies rose to the surface and were identified, and the murderer's accomplice gave him away. Then, what a to-do! The Montagnais wished to punish the murderer merely by giving gifts to relatives of the victims, as they were accustomed to do among themselves; the French wished to execute them both, as a good example and as a deterrent. The affair was discussed by hundreds of Indians, the Récollets, and every Frenchman in Canada; nothing else was talked about in the colony for weeks. At one point a mob of Indians tried to rush the habitation to release the prisoner; Champlain raised the drawbridge, posted all his arquebusiers in front of the building, and the mob retired. Next, the murderer's father begged on his knees for his son's pardon. Finally, Champlain and his friends decided that since the father offered to go surety for his son's future good behavior, the fellow should go free. This, as it turned out, was a mistake. The man continued to be a bad actor.

Champlain on 27 June found the tiny settlement at Quebec on the verge of starvation after a hard winter, but Hébert's farm seemed to be flourishing, and his daughter Anne had been married by Père Joseph to a Frenchman — the first Christian marriage in New France. At Trois-Rivières Champlain met a great assembly of Huron who urged him to lead them again on the warpath, but he begged off. He had had enough of that. On 30 July he sailed from Tadoussac, enjoyed fair winds, and arrived at Honfleur 28 August 1618.

This time he spent a year and a half in France, writing his third printed book, *Voyages et Descouvertures faites en la Nouvelle France, depuis l'année 1615, jusques à la fin de l'année 1618. Par le Sieur de Champlain, cappitaine ordinaire pour le Roy en le Mer du Ponant* (Paris, chez Claude Collet, au Palais en la gallerie du Prisonniers, 1619). This covered his interior explorations and, very candidly, his unfortunate attack on the Onondaga fort.

In his most important business — to implement some, at least, of his plans for Canada — Champlain got nowhere. Not only was the court indifferent toward plans for overseas expansion; the very fur-trading merchants, even members of the company, were unfavorable or downright hostile. They were doing very well, thank you; they wanted neither a strong settlement-colony nor conversion of the heathen. The Captain's program might merely break a profitable pattern — savages bringing bundles of peltry to Montreal, Quebec and Tadoussac every spring and bartering them for axes, weapons and knickknacks. Moreover, a great many, perhaps more than half, of the fur-trading merchants in and outside the company were Protestants from La Rochelle; and although the exercise of the "pretended reformed religion" was prohibited in Canada by royal decree, the crews of Protestant-owned and -manned ships could not be restrained from holding service on board when in harbor. And, as singing metrical versions of the Psalms was an essential part of that service, "The Huguenots" (wrote Parkman) "set the prohibition at naught, roaring their heretical psalmody with such vigor from their ships in the river that the unhallowed strains polluted the ears of the Indians on shore." In France, a continual war of pamphlets and petitions against Champlain and his company attempted to undermine his and their reputation. When he went personally to La Rochelle to serve a writ in an action against an interloping merchant, the mayor of the city remarked, "I am showing you no little favor and courtesy in warning you to keep quiet and get the hell out. If the people knew you were here to execute the orders of the Royal Council, you would probably be drowned in the inner harbor, and I could do nothing about it." Rather like a Yankee trying to stir up the blacks in Mississippi in 1960. So it is no wonder that Champlain became embittered against the Huguenots.

He had plenty of trouble, too, with his Catholic associates. The Rouen merchants, said he, who "think nothing of their contracts and promises made under seal," demanded that Pont-Gravé be given supreme authority in Canada. Champlain personally went to Rouen and confronted them with his commission from "Monseigneur le Prince," which made him the sole representative of the viceroy's authority in Canada. "As for the Sieur du Pont," he wrote, "I was his friend and his age made me respect him as my father, but to consent that one give him what belonged to me by right and reason, that I would not suffer." He then produced a letter from the king to the merchants of Rouen, ordering them to cease their niggling demands and co-operate with him "in exploring, inhabiting, clearing, cultivating and planting the land." By dint of following the Council in its judicial tours of provincial France, Champlain finally obtained a royal decree affirming his right to command everyone in every part of Canada, as well as an injunction against Rouennais or other interference with his authority.

By the time he could flourish these documents under the noses of Rouennais and Rochelais, it was too late for Champlain to make a voyage to Quebec in 1619. The annual ship sailed without him. Thus, fortunately, he was in Paris when the Duc de Montmorency for thirty thousand livres bought the viceroyalty of New France from his brother-in-law Condé. Champlain promptly got the duke's ear and won him over at least partially to his colonial policy. All this made the Rouennais so angry that they even tried to stop the company's ship at Honfleur in the spring of 1620, and the king, to make them lay off, had to send Champlain a letter confirming his authority and assuring him of royal favor.

Finally the ship, the *Saint-Etienne*, cleared, and this time with lady passengers: Hélène Champlain, the wife of ten years, now a mature twenty-two-year-old (her husband now pushing fifty), three ladies-in-waiting, and the thirty-livres-a-year maid of all work, assuming she had not quit earlier. After a two months' crossing, they reached Tadoussac 7 July 1620 and there met Eustache Boullé, Hélène's brother. He told them that two Rochelais interlopers had been in the river, selling the savages guns and munitions. This is the first mention in Champlain's works of the natives getting firearms. A pinnace sailed the married couple and three newly arrived Récollets to Quebec, where the whole resident population (about sixty) and hundreds of visiting natives gave them a rousing welcome. Champlain took care to have the new viceroy's credentials, and his lieutenancy, formally proclaimed, and accented by a salute of cannon.

Poor Hélène! When her lord and master first showed her over the now twelve-year-old habitation, her heart must have sunk. He had probably described it to her as a transatlantic French château; but now it looked (he admitted) more like "some poor house abandoned in the fields after being used by soldiers." The colonists had built themselves small houses which were comparatively easy to heat, and the friars had their own convent overlooking the St. Charles, leaving the pretentious habitation, the only building at Quebec with dignity appropriate to a vice-regal lieutenant, to go to rack and ruin. The planking had shrunk, wind whistled through, and rain leaked in everywhere; the trash-filled courtyard was "dirty and disgusting." Champlain set everyone to work cleaning up and making repairs, and "in a short time it was ready for us to move in." Presumably he brought out beds, linen, hangings and furniture from France. How did Hélène manage to keep up this huge, barn-like structure? Did she train some Indian girls as house servants? Or did the sailors turn to and help? At any rate, the Champlains and their immediate family had it all to themselves, the workmen and artisans having moved to houses of their own; but there must have been a constant *va-et-vient* of traders bringing furs and workmen getting tools.

Here Hélène de Champlain passed four miserable years. She did her best to like Canada, but she hated the great forests, the long

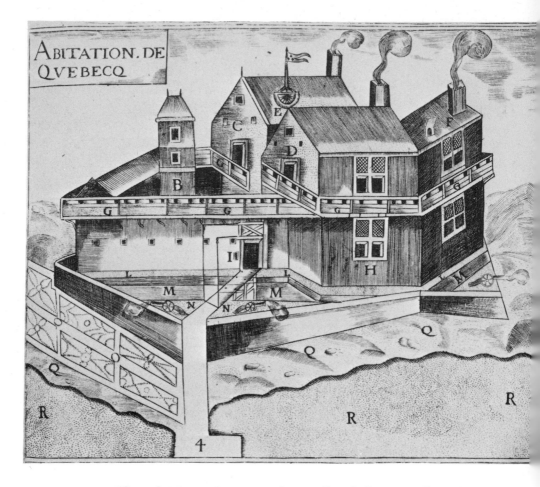

Champlain's rendering of the Quebec habitation. From Les Voyages (1613). (See also W. F. Ganong's rendering of this in the Champlain Society Works II 39.) KEY: A. "Storehouse" (above G). B. "Dovecote." C. "Building where we keep our arms, and the workmen live." D. "More lodgings for the workmen." E. "Sundial" surmounted by the fleur-de-lys banner. F. "Forge and artisans' lodgings." G. "Gallery all around the lodgings." H. "Lodging of the Sieur de Champlain," and presumably of Hélène when she accompanied him. I. "Gate of the habitation, with a drawbridge." L. "Promenade around the habitation, to the edge of the moat." M. "Moat the whole way round." N. "Platforms for cannon." O. "Sieur de Champlain's garden." P (building under letter G). "Kitchen." Q. "Space between the habitation and the river's edge." R. "The Great River of St. Lawrence." 4. The pier. Courtesy Harvard College Library.

winters, the desolate surroundings, the rough male society. She had nothing to do but attend mass or promenade on the gallery or beside the river; her husband must have walked with her to the Hébert farm or had her rowed across the river, but he certainly would not have let her walk alone in the woods. She had nobody of her own sex to talk to other than her three ladies-in-waiting (and they probably quit within a year), Madame Hébert and one daughter (the other having died in childbirth), the two Langlois girls married to Pierre Desportes, baker, and Abraham Martin, workman, and (during her last winter) the wife of Nicolas Pivert, the cowherd at Cape Tourmente. We do not know how Hélène got on with these women, but they were all the companions she had; and she became godmother to a Desportes daughter born in 1620.

A story told by the nuns of the Hôtel Dieu at Quebec later in the century shows Hélène to have been a gracious lady to the natives. Among her jewels was a tiny mirror hung from a necklace. The Indians loved to look into it, and when one squaw asked her why she could see her own face so near the lady's breast, Maddame answered, "Because you are always near my heart!" So we may conclude that she played her rôle tactfully and courageously; but we suspect that she prayed daily that her husband would retire to a neat little farm in France. After all, Jacques Cartier had done just that, as Pont-Gravé must have told her. But Champlain was made of different metal. As long as king and church needed him in Canada, and his health held out, he would carry on till death.

Not often did Hélène incur real danger, but during the summer of 1621 a roving party of Mohawk raiders suddenly descended on Quebec. They dared not make a frontal attack, for fear of French firepower, but diverted themselves by attacking the Récollets' convent. The friars had well fortified themselves and learned to shoot an arquebus (a sad surprise to the savages); and after a few of the attackers had been picked off, the rest retired.

Next year the Iroquois played a different tune, sending two Mohawks to Quebec to sue for peace with the Montagnais. These were the least important of Champlain's native allies, undependable, nomadic and relatively timid, but as the nearest tribe to Quebec it was desirable to keep the Iroquois off their necks. As the two envoys had no wampum-belt credentials from a tribal council, Champlain sent two Montagnais and two other Indians back to Iroquoia with these envoys, and they concluded a peace treaty in 1623. It may have spared Quebec a raid or two while Hélène was there, but it shared the fate of most European peace treaties; neither side respected it long. There was also talk of a peace treaty between Huron and Iroquois, but nothing came of it.

Champlain could never leave France without suffering from the fickle government. The viceroy, the Duc de Montmorency, now abolished the Compagnie de Canada, confiscated its property in Quebec, and conferred the monopoly and all assets and privileges on Guillaume de Caën of Dieppe and Emery de Caën, his nephew. One or both were Protestants. Louis XIII confirmed this flipflop on 12 January 1621. At the same time, inconsistently, the Duke confirmed Champlain's lieutenancy and doubled his modest salary. This news reached Champlain with the spring fleet of 1621. The Compagnie de Caën, as Montmorency's new organization was generally called, had a fur-trading monopoly for fifteen years, with the usual duty of taking six families to Canada, to support six Récollets, and build five houses. Nobody has yet explained this action on the part of Montmorency. One guesses that a big bribe, not necessarily to the viceroy, was responsible.

Champlain decided to make the best of the situation, complicated as it soon became; for the old company's merchants of Rouen and Saint-Malo refused to take this virtual confiscation lying down. As usual they sent to Canada their own ships, including a little one of 34 tuns named *Salamandre,* and the Caëns sent two of theirs, one commanded by Guillaume de Caën himself. Champlain, warned, prepared to defend Quebec against all and sundry; he strengthened Fort Saint-Louis which he had built on the Rock, and stationed arquebusiers in the habitation, which in his picturesque phrase would enable him to *parler à cheval,* speak from strength. On the last day of July he visited Tadoussac and succeeded in preventing Caën from seizing the *Salamandre.* The Récollets now sent home Père Georges Le Baillif to deliver a furious diatribe against the Caën heretics, and the king yielded to the extent of letting members of the old company join the Caëns'. Champlain, who would take orders from any legal superior if he judged it would help Canada, got on well enough with the Caëns, both Catholic and Protestant.

During those four years (July 1620–August 1624) at Quebec, Champlain caused the first road in Canada to be built, along the River Saint Charles, and followed that up by a *"petit chemin"* from the shore to Fort Saint-Louis on top of the Rock. And he did a great deal to strengthen that fort. In May 1624 he started work on a new habitation, with a foundation of stone, and caused his sawyers to make no fewer than 1500 planks to board in the building, and 35 beams to support the upper story. This second habitation got badly knocked about by the English during their occupation, and was never restored.

In this last spring that Hélène was with him at Quebec, Samuel kept a nature calendar, which reveals another side of him. He loved the quick unfolding of this northern spring, one of the most beautiful things in the world after a winter of deep snow.

8 May. Wild cherry shows its leaves, and the hepatica, "the primrose of these parts," springs from the soil.

9–10 May. Raspberries begin to bud, and "all kinds of herbs come out of the ground."

10th–11th. The *surean* (elder) unfolds its leaves.

12th. "White violets are seen in flower."

15th. "Trees all in bud, cherries leafed out, and wheat a span high. The raspberries put forth their leaves, the chevril is ready to cut; in the woods, sorrel two inches high may be seen."

18th. "The birches open their leaves, and the other trees follow them close; the oak buds swell and the apple trees transplanted from France and the wild plums" (the shad-bush) "bud out; cherry trees have quite large leaves, grapevines budding and flowering; sorrel ready to cut. . . . Violets white and yellow are in flower, maize being sown, wheat a little over a span high. Most of the plants and herbs are above ground; some days this month were very hot."

29th. "Strawberries begin to blossom, and the oaks to unfold their leaves."

30th. "All strawberries in flower, apple buds begin to break and their leaves to unfold, leaves of the oak about an inch long, plum and cherry trees in flower, and maize beginning to come up."

All this promised a fruitful autumn, but spring was a meager time for the little garrison at Quebec, owing to French essentials such as wine and wheat giving out, ships not arriving on time or bringing too few provisions. In early June, when flour and cider were about to give out, Champlain obtained supplies from a French ship at Tadoussac, and on 11 July two pinnaces of the Caëns' finally turned up at Quebec and did a big trade; but

Champlain, who had "had it" for the time being, decided to return to France with homesick Hélène.

The niggardliness or indifference of all these French companies toward their colony at Quebec is almost inconceivable. The historian Marcel Trudel has ascertained that in 1631 a beaver pelt sold for 1 livre 10 sols (30 cents in gold) to the trader, who sold it to the fur merchants in France for 14 to 15 livres ($3.00 in gold); that they collected 12,000 to 15,000 beaver skins annually, not to speak of other furs. After deducting the cost of shipping, wages, provisions, and Champlain's salary (now 1200 livres), the Caën company had a net profit of about 100,000 livres, of which one quarter went to the Rouen and Saint-Malo merchants and the rest was divided among the Caëns and their immediate associates. Yet they begrudged Quebec the barest necessities. Even at that, they did better than their predecessor, bringing out cattle and swine, and giving apothecary Hébert, who had been cheated abominably by the old company, a better break.

Louis Hébert had been trying for years to obtain from France, for his farm, one *charrue* (two-wheeled cart); no great commission, as dozens of them had been brought out by Roberval in 1541. The charrue — a "used" one — finally arrived, after Hébert's death. He was the only person to clear any land and plant it; two single men brought out especially for that purpose in 1619 were sent home by Champlain two years later because, as he wrote, "They have not cleared one bit of land, doing nothing but giving themselves a good time hunting, fishing, sleeping and getting drunk."

Another thing to the credit of the Caëns was their initiation of the seigneurial system, by which Canada eventually became peopled. This meant the granting of extensive feudal fiefs to individuals, who in return undertook to procure settlers; these paid rent or feudal dues to their seigneur. In 1624 the viceroy Montmorency granted to Guillaume de Caën the Seigneurie et Baronnie de Caën, comprising Cap Tourmente and L'Ile d'Orléans, and two years later the viceroy Vantadour gave Hébert title to the farm he had faithfully cultivated, together with a narrow seigneurie stretching miles back into the forest. The Jesuits got a much bigger one parallel to Hébert's. Champlain in July and August 1626 presided at the formal taking possession of these two fiefs.

He was disillusioned with all these companies. "It robs a man of courage," he wrote, "to serve people who pay no heed to those who are preserving their property, and killing themselves by the care and labor they bestow on the task." Had he known how the poor Pilgrim Fathers were getting along, with almost no help from England, and no wealth back of them, he would have had greater cause to blush.

Leaving Emery de Caën in charge at Quebec over a population now numbering only fifty-one, the Champlain couple dropped down-river to Tadoussac, and on 21 August 1624 sailed for France, apparently in one of the Caën ships, in a fleet of five. On 29 September they sighted Start Point in the English Channel, and two days later slipped into the harbor of Dieppe. Hélène, no doubt, fell on her knees for gratitude, and vowed never, never, never to return to cold, savage, unfriendly Canada.

XII

The English Conquest

Back again in Paris, Champlain bought a house on the rue de La Marche (now rue Saintonge) in the fashionable quartier du Temple, for himself and Hélène. And he lost no time in going to Saint-Germain to see the viceroy, Monseigneur de Montmorency, who presented him to the king and several members of the Royal Council. This gave the Captain an opportunity to tell his story in person.

Now came another overturn in the government of Canada. Montmorency, sick and tired of disputes, sold his viceroyalty for 100,000 livres to his nephew Henri de Lévy, Duc de Vantadour. This twenty-nine-year-old nobleman, having renounced the pomps and vanities of this world, had separated from his equally pious fourteen-year-old wife, intending to take holy orders. His only interest in Canada was to convert the heathen, and a Jesuit confessor convinced him that the famous Society of Jesus, long on zeal and rich in funds, would be the best means of doing it. Doubtless he was right; the Récollets were too few and feeble, as they admitted by asking for Jesuit assistance. The plea was granted; in June 1625 three members of the Jesuit order, Pères Charles Lalemant, Ennemond Massé and Jean de Brébeuf, arrived at Quebec and were received hospitably at the Récollets' convent. Two more soon came out, with twenty laborers. And in April 1625 the new viceroy forbade any exercise of the Protestant religion in Canada, whether on land or at sea.

Vantadour confirmed Champlain as his lieutenant in New France, and issued him a new commission on 15 February 1625, giving him practically full powers. Champlain returned to Canada without Hélène in the ship *Catherine* of 250 tuns, flagship to a fleet of four. The other three were a pinnace named *La Flèque*, *L'Alouette* of 80 tuns (carrying the Jesuits), and a vessel of 200 tuns. All four sailed in company from Dieppe on 24 April 1626. They reached soundings on the Grand Bank 5 June, made Cape Ray, Newfoundland, on the 12th, passed the Magdalens on the 17th, and anchored in the roadstead between Bonaventure Island and Ile Percée, where Emery de Caën awaited them.

An amusing incident of this encounter was Champlain's reading to Emery de Caën the viceregal edict that no more Protestant psalm-singing would be allowed in the Great River. The mariners, two-thirds of whom were Huguenots, grumbled and declared they should not be denied their rights. It was finally agreed that they could hold Protestant prayer meetings on board, but sing psalms only at sea where no pious Catholic ears would be offended! *"Ainsi d'une mauvais dette l'on en tire ce que l'on peut"* — from a bad debt you collect what you can, remarked Champlain cynically. As soon as Caën's back was turned, the sailors resumed bawling their psalms so loudly that Indians ashore could hear them. Why the singing of Clement Marot's excellent metrical version of the Psalms of David should be a red rag to the Catholics is not explained.

After working through a thick o' fog in the St. Lawrence, the fleet met a Frenchman in a shallop with news of another hard winter at Quebec. Pont-Gravé, there left in charge, had almost died of gout; and for provisions the colony was down to two bar-

Isle Percée. From an eighteenth-century engraving in William Inglis Morse Acadensia Nova.

rels of flour, which they were keeping for the sick. Everyone else was reduced to eating manganité, the Indian potpourri of maize, fish, game and what have you, which Champlain had found *mal odorante* and sickening. Mortified that people could starve at Quebec after seventeen years, he observed that life there would be precarious so long as the colonists were dependent on supplies from France. Ships brought in provisions only for one year, assuming that enough land would be cultivated to support so small a colony; but as nobody except the apothecary-turned-farmer did till the soil, French colonists starved if no ship came. He had warned of this repeatedly in France, but an injudicious economy at court prevented anything being done. No North American colony of any nation could endure without yearly support from home — witness Raleigh's two attempts on Roanoke Island; but it is equally true that, whilst powerful interests in England and Holland were behind Virginia and New Netherland, almost nobody in France cared a tinker's dam about making poor Canada anything but a string of summertime trading posts. English colonial effort in the early seventeenth century was central to the life of that nation, but Canada remained of remote and peripheral interest to France. Search the French literature of the reigns of Henri IV and Louis XIII and you will find very, very few references to Canada, and those mostly ironical; and even fewer to Champlain, one of the greatest Frenchmen of his age; and this is the more strange because he knew many people at court, and wrote eloquently of Canada and her needs. For the average well-educated Parisian, Canada in 1620 meant about as much as the Caroline Islands to a New Yorker of 1970.

Champlain reached Quebec on 5 July 1626. He found Pont-Gravé recovered but everything very slack; building materials he had caused to be wrought or brought there one or two years earlier were still in a heap, rotting. The population was now down to fifty-five, of whom twenty-four were laborers on the company's payroll. They had passed most of the winter lying about, smoking and drinking, and when spring came spent the long working days boating to Cape Tourmente to make hay from the salt meadows. Champlain put an end to that waste of time by causing a large cow barn and two houses to be built, Norman-fashion, at Cape Tourmente, and settling a few workmen there to mow the hay and tend the cattle. That done, he started work on a new and bigger fort to be built on the Rock of Quebec. He was delighted with the Jesuit fathers; they turned-to with the laymen and proved excellent workers.

The winter of 1626–27 began early; ice floated down the St. Lawrence on 22 November, and did not melt until the end of

April; snow fell to a depth of eight feet. Imported food, as usual, fell short, but the Indians furnished the garrison with plenty of moose meat. Emery de Caën returned in the spring of 1627 with a few cattle and a wheeled cart. But Louis Hébert, alas, who had been trying for years to get that cart from France, had died from a fall in January. He deserves to be bracketed with de Monts and Pont-Gravé as one of the most important founders of Canada after Champlain.

That spring Champlain had a fresh problem of Indian relations. Some of the natives close to Quebec had visited the site of Albany, where the Dutch suborned them to lead a war party against the Mohawk Nation, who were attempting to exterminate the mynheers' near neighbors, the Mohicans. Champlain, alarmed at this threat to his hard-won peace of 1623 with the Iroquois, sent his brother-in-law Eustache Boullé to address a great muster of savages up-river. He persuaded them not to fight the Iroquois, at least not then. But after Boullé had left, certain *"jeunesse folle"* insisted on taking the warpath. Their ignoble campaign resulted merely in capturing two Iroquois warriors on Lake Champlain and bringing them home to torture; Caën and Champlain arrived at Trois-Rivières just in time to save their lives. Champlain addressed the assembly, pointed out how heavily they stood to lose in a war with the Five Nations, and persuaded them to return one of the two captives (minus fingernails and hair) with propitiatory gifts. The other they kept as hostage; and, after hearing that the Iroquois had killed two of theirs, slowly tortured him to death by burning, chopping off his arms, and slicing cuts of his flesh to eat.

Fifty-five French men, women and children remained at Quebec for the winter of 1627–28.

The Caën company also sent out a vessel for whaling, but no more men to help make Quebec defensible. Champlain remarked that as the shareholders were making an average of 40 per cent annually on their investment, they might have given the tottering colony more people and more supplies. But, he wrote later, *"L'utilité demeure aux associés, et à nous le mal"* — profits for the shareholders, misery for us.

In October 1627 Champlain had another murder case on his hands. Two cowherds at Cape Tourmente had been stabbed, their heads bashed in, and the bodies thrown into the river. He had to proceed cautiously, for Quebec was short on munitions and unable to defend itself against any massed assault. After addressing a big meeting of Montagnais, who agreed that the murderers should be punished, Champlain took hostages while the savages undertook to find the guilty parties. Nothing more happened until January 1628, when a party of famished Montagnais came to Quebec, begged for food, and proposed to leave three more hostages, damsels of eleven, twelve and fifteen, to be brought up as Catholics. The girls appeared to be willing, and in return Champlain and Pont-Gravé (who growled over the deal) handed over a quantity of dried peas.

Champlain was a safe man to whom to entrust these young girls; for, as Père Gabriel Sagard wrote, "He was never suspected of any impropriety during all the years that he lived among these barbarous peoples; . . . he took care of them as his own daughters." They were baptized Foy, Espérance and Charité — Faith, Hope and Charity. Champlain drilled them in the catechism, and traced designs on canvas for them to embroider in wool. This business of converting the natives was infinitely slow and discouraging. Champlain admits that the only souls saved by the devoted Récollets were infants about to die, whom they baptized. And it was years before the Jesuits, who replaced the Récollets, did any better.

On 27 April 1628 Champlain had the pleasure of seeing land

at Quebec plowed by oxen for the first time. Hitherto, only an acre and a half, mostly the Hébert farm, had been brought under cultivation in the whole of Canada! Even the Pilgrim Fathers and the Dutch on the Hudson had done better than that; and in Virginia hundreds of acres were annually conquered from the forest. Virginia, of course, now had a valuable cash crop, tobacco; whilst Canada's cash crops came from the sea and the forest. And, as we have seen, there was no inducement to bring land under cultivation in Canada; quite the contrary.

On 18 June 1628 the Quebec garrison again went on short rations; its entire stock of provisions had fallen to four or five casks of moldy hardtack and some peas and beans; no ships from France were yet reported. Caën had left no pinnace, no naval stores, and no sailors at Quebec except Champlain himself. The garrison obtained pitch from spruce trees, killed an ox at Cape Tourmente for his tallow, made oakum from old rope, and with the help of a former shipwright — Hébert's son-in-law — made an old shallop fit for river navigation, to seek aid at Tadoussac.

Before this shallop could be launched, news came from an Indian that six strange ships had been seen in the river. The savages' stories sounded fishy; but Champlain soon learned the truth from refugees from Cape Tourmente. England and France were at war, the ships were English, and the sailors had wantonly destroyed everything at Cape Tourmente, even burning cattle alive in the new barn. This was just what Champlain had always feared, an attack by *les Anglais mécréants* on his beloved, almost indefensible Quebec.

The Scottish family of Kirke had seized this opportunity to make a fortune. They were Gervase "Querc" (as Champlain spelled the name), who had lived in Dieppe and married a Frenchwoman, and their sons David, Louis and Thomas Kirke, of London. The Kirkes took out letters of marque from Charles I, and their three armed ships were manned in part by Huguenot refugees from La Rochelle, then being besieged by Louis XIII as a Protestant stronghold. In command of the English ships was one Captain Jacques Michel, a furious Protestant Rochelais, burning for revenge.

Now opened the most trying period of Champlain's life. He at once set men to work strengthening the fort on the Rock, which had never been completed. On 10 July a boat appeared off Quebec, manned by Basques whom the Kirkes had captured at Tadoussac. They were now using these Basques as messengers to serve Champlain with a summons to surrender. Very courteous in form, as befitted that age when gentlemen made war, it informed "Monsieur de Champlain, commandant à Quebec," that "General Kirke" had eighteen armed ships under his command, and had blockaded the St. Lawrence so that Quebec was completely cut off from French succor. So he had better surrender. Signed 8 July on board the ship *Vicaille*, "Your affectionate servant David Kirke."

Champlain quickly consulted with Pont-Gravé and other leading men of the settlement. Despite their penury in food and munitions, they decided to hold out. For there was no telling whether France might not send a relief fleet to drive off the English, or that they might get tired and go away as they had after their occupation of the Ile de Rhé off La Rochelle. So he sent a bluff but valiant reply to Kirke by the Basques — Quebec still had plenty of food, and his duty to God and the king was to fight to the death. It closed, *"Je demeurai, Monsieur, votre affectioné serviteur, Champlain."* This letter, he imagined, convinced Kirke that they were not too badly off. Actually, Quebec had on hand only fifty pounds of gunpowder and, of imported food, only seven ounces of peas daily per man. Of course they had corn, fish and game; but Frenchmen, like other European pioneers in

America, always felt starved if they had no food, wine or cider from home. And Quebec's wine cellars had long since run dry.

It was now early August. A shallop arrived with eleven Frenchmen, bearing the news that the French relief fleet, under the Sieur de Roquemont, had arrived at Gaspé; there had been a battle between them and the Kirke fleet, but the French in the shallop had run away and knew not the result! Actually, the English fleet won and, noted Champlain, "These eleven men meant just so many additional mouths to feed." In order to splice out the peas, he had them ground into meal to make soup. When the eel-fishing season arrived, the local Indians sold the French ten eels for one beaver pelt — an outrageous price. Hébert's farm brought a disappointingly small harvest, which enabled Champlain to distribute only a daily ration of nine and one-half ounces of barley, corn and peas.

A very wretched winter followed, that of 1628–29. Firewood had to be brought from the forest over a mile away. Some of the men went moose-hunting with the Indians, but when they made a kill they devoured the moose on the spot, saving only a few venison steaks for the colony. Vegetables were exhausted by spring, "in spite of all the economy I could practice," wrote Champlain. So he decided that if no succor arrived by June, he would have to make the best arrangements he could with the English. Two desperate expedients that he discussed and rejected were to go on the warpath against the Iroquois to get corn, or try to get some from friendly Indians along the Kennebec.

Faced by a real famine at the end of May, when he was down to seven ounces of pease meal a day per person, with almost a hundred mouths to feed, Champlain sent the shallop downriver with letters to any French vessel she might encounter, begging for provisions. He then made another shallop ready for sea, hoping to take thirty persons to Gaspé, shift them to a French fisherman going home, and bring back cured codfish to Quebec. It was deplorable, he said, to see little children crying with hunger; and all this suffering could have been prevented if the company had given their employees land to cultivate. Both the Virginia Company and the Pilgrim Fathers learned that lesson early. Even the Hébert family, the one exception, had been so badgered and bullied by the company that they kept most of their garden produce for themselves.

Without awaiting the shallops' return, Champlain and Pont-Gravé decided to send their pinnace down-river to try to get some of the settlers onto vessels bound for France. Stout old Pont-Gravé, now over seventy years old, was relieved from his gout by this *misère* (says Père Sagard), since gout attacks only those who eat and drink to excess; "the necessity of the country" forced him to go without wine, bread, salt and butter. Frequently "this good old man, naturally jovial," would toss down a full cup of undiluted wine, and subsequently scream for help from his pain! He dreaded an ocean voyage at that juncture more than he did the English, especially as the pinnace was very meagerly provisioned; the crew apparently were expected to catch fish and live on what they could beg from French fishermen at Ile Percée. Champlain tried to persuade him that nothing could be worse than awaiting the worst at Quebec; but even that did not move him. Without Pont-Gravé, and with Eustache Boullé in command, the pinnace sailed from Quebec 26 June 1629.

The remaining garrison spent most of its time in the forest grubbing up ground-nuts and other edible roots; those of the Solomon's seal and of a wild lily* appear to have been favorites. Père Brébeuf, the future martyr, returned from Huronia bringing some two hundred pounds of corn meal. The usual flock of In-

---

* Either *Lilium Canadense* or *Clintonia borealis*.

dians came to trade peltry, but one couldn't eat that; Champlain was at his wits' end.

The 19th of July 1629 opened with a thunderclap. Most of the Frenchmen were out fishing, and the rest, as well as the native girls Espérance and Charité, were in the woods searching for roots, when a native came on the run, crying out to Champlain, alone in the fort, that English vessels had been sighted behind Pointe Lévis. The Récollets came in for consultation, and with them Champlain decided that in their half-starved, defenseless situation the French must capitulate. In due course a boat put out from the English flagship, carrying a white flag. Champlain raised another over the fort and came down to the water's edge. There an "English gentleman" stepped ashore and handed him a letter from Louis and Thomas Kirke, calling on him to surrender and assuring him of "the best treatment" and favorable articles of capitulation. Champlain accepted, and lost no time in drafting a very favorable surrender document, to which the Kirkes agreed. They promised to repatriate the entire garrison, lay and religious — allowing the French to keep their personal arms and baggage — and to furnish them with sea stores in return for peltry. The English fleet (a flyboat of 100 tuns and 10 guns, two *pataches* of 40 tuns and 6 guns each) moved up to take possession.

Among the landing force Champlain was mortified to recognize Etienne Brûlé and Nicolas Marsolet, who had gone over to the enemy. There were about 4000 pelts in the warehouse, property of the Caën company, and these the English gleefully annexed. On 22 July the fleur-de-lys came down for the first — but not the last — time over the fortress of Quebec, and the royal ensign of Great Britain ran up, to the sound of salutes from the ships' guns and volleys of musketry from the English soldiers. The several French renegades did plenty of looting, but

"We had every kind of courtesy from the English," wrote Champlain. Louis Kirke, said he, was so "French in disposition" as to invite the Hébert family and other habitants to remain and cultivate farms, and on Champlain's advice most of them did.

Two days later, Champlain and his "family" started downriver in Thomas Kirke's flagship to Tadoussac. Off Murray Bay they had a successful board-to-board battle with a ship of Emery de Caën, which Champlain would have enjoyed had not he and the girls, as "enemies," been confined below decks with the hatches nailed down. At Tadoussac they found the main English fleet, under Jacques Michel the renegade.

While awaiting a ship to take him home, Champlain engaged in a protracted negotiation with David Kirke over the two Indian girls — Charité (twelve years old) and Espérance (fourteen), whom he wished to take to France; partly because he had become greatly attached to them himself, and partly to give his wife Hélène the daughters she lacked. Unfortunately Nicolas Marsolet had conceived a great passion for the elder girl. She repelled all his efforts to seduce her, and in a confrontation before Champlain called him a traitor, a lecherous monster, and every other insult she could think up. Marsolet, out of face, turned to Charité saying, "Haven't *you* something nice to say to me?" To which she replied, "No. I support everything my sister said, and I'd like nothing better than to tear out your heart and eat it!" Marsolet hit upon a means of getting Espérance out of Champlain's hands and into his own. He convinced Louis Kirke that a great assembly of Montagnais had demanded the girls' return and threatened to make war on the English if they did not get them. Nonsense! said Champlain; he well knew that natives, once having parted with children, had no further use for them. The poor damsels wept and pled, but nothing could move Kirke. So, making the best of it, Champlain sent them back to Quebec in care of the Couillards (Hébert's granddaughter and her husband), who promised to treat them as their own. Without their beloved adopted father the little girls moped and languished, and finally, like their elder sister Foy, returned to their own people and were lost to the faith and the French.

At Tadoussac, Champlain had a certain grim satisfaction over the death of the traitor Jacques Michel, who cursed the Jesuits and Saint-Malo and the Kirkes, and uttered all manner of blasphemies. "Good God!" said Champlain to him. "How you do swear for a Protestant!" "True," said Jacques, "but I am so full of passion and anger with those dogs of Malouins, and I wish I had struck the Jesuit who gave me the lie." That was Père Brébeuf, to whom he had declared that the Jesuits came to Canada "not to convert the savages, but to convert the beavers"; and Brébeuf had replied, "That's false!" Michel retorted, "It is only out of respect for the General" (Kirke) "that I don't slap your face!" Shortly after that peppery conversation he died, cursing God. The English gave him a proper military funeral, but "Never was there such rejoicing, especially on board his own ship," wrote Champlain. The local Indians despised him so that they dug up his body and threw it to the dogs.

David Kirke did send supplies to Quebec, and then set sail for England. Champlain, who accompanied him, was furious with the English; for, as he wrote, "We never disturbed them in Virginia, which Verrazzano discovered for France; why couldn't they have let us be in Quebec?" But he got along well with individual Englishmen, and in his *Treatise on Seamanship* gives them credit for teaching him John Davis's new method of keeping a sea journal.

The aged and ailing Pont-Gravé sailed to England in the same or another English ship. Champlain, who resented two attempts of the tough old Malouin to usurp his authority, says nothing more about him in his 1632 *Voyages,* from which one may infer almost anything — that he died on the voyage home, or in England, or was still living at Saint-Malo. Pont-Gravé, who went out to Canada as shipmaster even before Champlain did, and whom Champlain in an earlier book said he revered as a father, deserved a few lines of praise, or an epitaph, from the Father of New France, but nobody has been able to find out what eventually became of him.

On 18 October 1629 the English flagship sighted the Scilly Islands and on the 20th ran into Plymouth. There they heard that England and France had concluded an armistice. The war was over, "which greatly angered the said Kirke," as he was making a fortune out of his Canadian venture. Champlain sought the French ambassador at London and told his story. He was not treated as a prisoner of war, moved about freely, remained in London five weeks working on the return of Canada to France, and crossed the Channel to Dieppe late in November.

The Treaty of Saint-Germain-en-Laye (29 March 1632), which formally concluded this war, provided for the return of Canada and Acadia to France, in return for payment by Louis XIII of a long overdue debt of 600,000 écus, dowry of his sister Henrietta Maria when she married Charles I. This, amounting to about $36,000 in gold, we may call the French ransom for the Kirke conquest.

Who got the best of the bargain? This may be argued in light of the many later English attempts on Canada that were repulsed, the conquest and cession of 1759–63, and the astonishing persistence of French nationalism. No French Canadian can doubt that Louis XIII got a bargain — buying back Canada by paying a bad debt. If England had retained Canada, it is possible that both countries would have been saved a lot of blood, sweat and tears, but it is not probable that France, with sea power inferior to England's, could ever have won it back.

During the two and a half years of diplomatic squabbling preceding the signing of the treaty, the English were "making hay" in Canada. Two English ships returned to London in 1629 carrying 300,000 livres' worth of peltry. But they had lost ninety lives, mainly by scurvy, during the winter. Most of the French, except those who chose to stick it out at Quebec and Tadoussac, reached home safely. An exception was the ship that was supposed to take home the Jesuit fathers Lalemant, Noirot, and several others. She struck a rock off Canso on 24 August 1629, and only ten out of the twenty-four men on board survived. The Jesuits swam or drifted to a small island, where they were rescued by a fishing vessel from Saint-Jean-de-Luz. The master tarried six weeks on the coast of L'Acadie to complete his fare, so they did not start home until 8 October. After a very rough passage of forty days, the Basque ship ran aground near San Sebastián. She "broke into a thousand pieces and all the cod was lost"; but the indestructible Jesuits got ashore in a shallop and proceeded to Bordeaux; and at the first opportunity returned to Canada.

XIII

The Hundred Associates

EVEN before the English attack on Quebec, Champlain received news of a colonial reorganization which promised great things for his beloved Canada. Cardinal Richelieu, now the king's first minister and counselor, had himself appointed to a newly created office, "Grand Maistre, Chef et Surintendant général de la Navigation et Commerce." He canceled the monopoly of the existing company, confiscated the property of the Caëns, and organized a new and more powerful company, the Cens Associés (Hundred Associates) under his personal direction. Champlain retained his former position as the company's and the king's lieutenant in Canada. Richelieu, although he hailed from inland Poitou, was the first French statesman to look for the future glory and power of France overseas; but the East Indies, where the Portuguese were amassing fortunes, and the West Indies, with fabulous profits from sugar cane, interested him far more than Canada. As early as 1619 Ezechiel de Caën of Dieppe organized L'Association pour la Navigation aux Indes Orientales, and sent thither three ships commanded by Robert, son of François Pont-Gravé, in 1626. Richelieu organized La Compagnie des Isles d'Amérique, with the right to conquer Guadeloupe and Martinique from the Caribs.

The account of the Cens Associés in volume XIV of *Le*

Mercure françois (the earliest French periodical), written or at least edited by the Cardinal's right-hand man Père Joseph, states that Richelieu aimed at a powerful colony. The Associates were incorporated 29 April 1627 as La Compagnie de la Nouvelle France, and granted "in perpetuity" all North American territory between Spanish Florida and the Arctic Circle, and from Newfoundland to La Mer Douce (Lake Huron) and beyond (if there were a beyond), with a monopoly of the fur trade. They must send out at least four thousand colonists in fifteen years, including neither Protestants nor foreigners. For the first time settlers would have the right to buy furs from the Indians — but they must sell them to the company. Canadian products would be exempt from French customs for fifteen years. Seigneuries must be set up and titles of nobility from duke down could be granted. One hundred shares were issued at 3000 livres ($600 in gold) each. Shareholders met annually to choose a board of directors for a two-year term, the Cardinal to be perpetual head of the company. This organization resembled in some respects that of the first Virginia Company of London in 1606, but differed essentially from the second Virginia Company in being directly under royal control, and in allowing no vestige of local self-government in the colony.

This promising effort of the Cens Associés proved to be as disappointing as all preceding, for several reasons. Its first expedition to Canada in 1628, captured in part and the rest chased off by Kirke, cost the company more than half its capital; and Richelieu insisted on reimbursing the Caëns for their losses, which left the company with almost no working capital. There is no doubt that the Cardinal wished Canada well; but he paid very little attention to his northern domain and made bad decisions. Thus New France languished (Quebec had about two hundred inhabitants at Champlain's death) while the English and Dutch colonies in North

America were being built up to the thousands. According to French historian Jean H. Mariéjol, the main cause of Canada's slow growth was neither incompetent management nor lack of government support, but the nature of the French people. They "had a savings-bank mentality, modest in their tastes, stay-at-homes. They preferred to live in a petty way on the income of some office than to try their fortunes in the colonies or abroad." French capital, too, was timid. If the Cens Associés had been wholly subscribed, which they were not, their total capital would have amounted to only 300,000 livres ($60,000 in gold). "How," asks this historian, "with these miserable resources, could they support an establishment, unproductive years, maintaining an army and a fleet for transporting and provisioning the colonists?" But, one asks, why were these resources so miserable? France then had many times the population and wealth of England.

It seems to me that lack of encouragement had a lot to do with it. The Cardinal himself was shocked to find that emigrants to Canada (of which there had been only eighteen families to 1627) had been charged 36 livres each on leaving France. The seigneurial system, beginning under the Caën régime and further developed under Richelieu, offered the first real inducement to French peasants and artisans to settle in Canada. And colonial propaganda was almost wholly lacking in France. Where Canada had only Champlain, Lescarbot and Sagard as literary promoters of colonization, Virginia and New England had Hakluyt, Gilbert, Raleigh, Peckham, Captain John Smith, Michael Drayton, and a host of lesser writers. In England hundreds of ballads were printed, exhorting Englishmen to settle in Virginia or New England:

> Who knowes not England once was like
>   a Wildernesse and savage place,
> Till government and use of men,

that wildnesse did deface;
And so Virginia may in time
be made like England now,
Where long-lovd peace and plenty both
sits smiling on her brow.

But for France we have only two lines in a prefatory poem by an obscure poet named de la Franchise, to Champlain's *Des Sauvages*:

Fi des lâches poltrons qui ne bougent d'un licu
Leur vie sans mentir me paraît trop mesquine.

Fie, cowardly slobs, who never leave their station,
Their life truly seems too petty to mention.

The real difference is that Elizabethan and Jacobean England were bubbling over with energy and enterprise, while France merely simmered, or aimed at defeating Spain and suppressing religious dissent. Richelieu might have built up Canada by encouraging thousands of Protestants to emigrate thither, instead of killing them off at La Rochelle, but the thought never occurred to him; it would have seemed blasphemous.

A long delay elapsed after signing the treaty, and a great deal of hanky-panky went on about delivering Quebec back to France. For Champlain this meant lobbying at court to have a king's ship sent to take over, as the Kirkes were still doing business in the St. Lawrence with powerful armed ships. It also meant that he was able to see through the press his longest and most ambitious work: *Les Voyages de la Nouvelle France Occidentale,* * *dicte Canada, faits par le Sr de Champlain, Xainctongeois . . .* [dédié] *à Mon-*

---

* Note the *occidentale*, which I suspect to have been dictated by Richelieu, as he had other *nouvelles Frances* in mind — the so-called *antarctique* in Brazil, the East India Company's *nouvelle France orientale*, and the West Indies.

seigneur le Cardinal Duc de Richelieu (Paris : Chez Claude Collet au Palais, en la Gallerie des Prisonniers, à l'Etoille d'Or). The first edition, of 1632, is in two parts, usually bound separately; each contains 318 pages, and the second part adds the *Traitté de la Marine* by Champlain himself, a *Doctrine Chrestienne* by Père Ladesme, S.J., with Huron translation by Père Brébeuf, and an *Oraison Dominicale* (Sunday Prayer) translated into Montagnais by Père Massé, S.J. It is meagerly illustrated, but contains a big folding chart of the whole of Canada, Acadia, and New England. Corneille wrote a comedy, *La Galerie du Palais*, which appeared in 1634; he and several other writers indicated that these galleries alongside the law courts had become fashionable promenades for gallants and their ladies and their dogs, a place for rendezvous, flirtation, and gossip. One of Corneille's characters, Le Libraire, tries to sell books *de la mode*, but Champlain's works are not among them.

Through the kindness of the Bibliothèque Nationale we have reproduced (pp. 206–207) a contemporary engraving by Abraham Bosse of one of these galleries, including a bookstall, a boutique for gloves and fans, and one for lace. Champlain's name does not appear on the bookstall, which belongs to Augustin Courbe, the king's printer. The book being sold over the counter is the *Marianne* of Tristan l'Hermite, and other writers featured are Cicero, Seneca, and Francesco Guicciardini. The last stanza of Bosse's ironical verses below the picture tells us that if a *lingère* finds her linen selling indifferently, she blames it on the pettifoggers who take up so much room in the gallery discussing their cases that eager buyers cannot get near her boutique.

One may conjecture that bookseller Claude Collet, who had already published *Les Voyages* of 1619, talked to Champlain in this wise: "Your last book was too small, and so had too little notice. Now, M. de Champlain, write a big fat one which will impress the public, and make more money for you and me. Monseigneur the Cardinal's interest in colonies will make La Nouvelle France almost fashionable. But no more of those expensive illustrations; unless, of course, you care to pay for them yourself!" Anyway, the 1632 *Voyages* is a fluffed-up book. Champlain opened with a surprisingly accurate summary of earlier French efforts in the New World and of his own voyages to 1619, and added chapters on Newfoundland, L'Acadie, and the manners and customs of the Huron. There are three appendixes; two to show how well the Jesuits were getting on with native languages, and the third his own *Treatise on Seamanship*. Of this I think so highly as to make it an appendix to this book.

That the 1632 *Voyages* was a mild success is shown by the fact that Collet brought out a second edition in 1640. But it did not cause the author to be admitted to any Parisian literary group. Neither Morris Bishop, who appended a chapter "The Awareness of Canada in Seventeenth-Century France" to his biography of Champlain, nor Canadian scholars who have combed French literature looking for notices of Champlain, have found any substantial reference to the Father of New France in the general literature of that era. An exception may be made of *Le Mercure françois*. There are short notices of Canada in volumes XIII, XIV and XVIII, and one of over a hundred pages in volume XIX (1636). This was after Richelieu had made his famous shadow, Père Joseph, the editor. Père Joseph reprints the *Jesuit Relation* of 1634 by Père Le Jeune, and a useful account of Champlain's last voyage to Canada by an "honest person" unnamed, a layman who accompanied him. It appears that the sophisticated French, unlike their counterparts in England, Italy and the Low Countries, had slight use for true narratives of travels in North America. Their chief interest, insofar as they cared for anything overseas, lay in the Middle East and the Levant. *Les Voyages du Seigneur de Villa-*

La Galerie du Palais.
This was the Palais du Justice
on the Ile de la Cité.

LA GALERIE DV PALAIS

Caualiers les plus aduantureux   Jcy faisant semblant d'acheter deuant tous   Jcy quelque Lingere a faute de succez
les Romans s'animent a combatre ;   Des gands, des Euantails, du ruban, des danteles ; A vendre abondamment, de colere se picque
r passion les Amans langoureux   Les adroits Courtisans se donnent rendez-vous,   Contre des Chicaneurs qui parlant de procez
les mouuemens par des vers deTheatre.Et pour se faire aimer, galantisent les Belles.   Empeschent les Chalands d'aborder sa Boutique.

le Blond le jeune excud Auec Priuilege du Roy.

mont, a sprightly account of travels in Turkey, Syria and Egypt, was printed thirteen times between 1595 and 1600. The contemporary historian Jacques-Auguste de Thou devoted only about seven pages in two thick volumes of his *Histoire Universelle* to de Monts and Champlain, and carried their story only to 1609.

Champlain himself never received any personal recognition, title, or even compliment from Richelieu or the monarchy. In a document of 1630 he is referred to as *"gentilhomme de la Chambre du Roy"*; but this means nothing more than that he had been presented to the king, probably by his father-in-law, who was a minor official of the king's chamber. Nor was this paladin of God's kingdom ever made a Knight of Malta or elected to a French order of chivalry such as the Saint-Esprit. Louis XIII even had the meanness to cancel his modest pension of six hundred livres granted by Henri IV; and Champlain had to petition for its restoration — one of the most eloquent products of his pen. Thus Champlain had no distinctions to show on title pages except that of captain in the merchant marine, and *Xaintongeois,* his provincial origin.

This indifference to Canada and neglect of a great Frenchman is in strong contrast to the interest taken by the English people and their sovereigns in colonial pioneers and promoters such as Sir Humfry Gilbert, Sir Walter Raleigh, Sir Thomas Smythe, Sir Edwin Sandys, and Lord Baltimore. Even the humble and inconspicuous Pilgrim Fathers enjoyed more publicity in England than all Canada and L'Acadie obtained in France. This helps to explain the bitterness of French Canadian nationalists toward Mother France, who neglected their ancestors when they were few, poor and needy, and "abandoned" them to the English after they had formed a viable society. The third Republic honored (?) Champlain by naming a second-class cruiser after him in 1874, and a store ship in 1919.

Louis XIII, King of France and of Navarre.
From frontispiece to Mercure François, *tome XIII.*
Courtesy Harvard College Library.

All Champlain's later books were prefaced by dedicatory poems by minor poets; these could always be procured by the publisher. For the 1632 *Les Voyages* he obtained a very mediocre ode composed by Pierre Trichet, lawyer of Bordeaux, author of several Latin poems and tragedies and a treatise on musical instruments. As Bordeaux was the seat of Richelieu's Cens Associés, Trichet may have owned a share. The poem begins:

> Veux-tu, voyageur hazardeux,
> Vers Canada tenter fortune?
> Veux-tu sur les flots escumeux
> Reçevoir l'ordre de Neptune?

> Dost thou wish, traveler brave,
> Toward Canada try thy fortune?
> Wishest thou on foamy wave
> To receive the Order of Neptune?

If so (continues Maître Trichet), be governed by this book of the Sieur de Champlain. He learned his elegant language from Pithon, his skill from Thetis; and he will render thy ship secure from furious winds and sea monsters, as if he were the son of Tiphys, pilot of the Argonauts! All aboard!

XIV

Last Phase

DURING the three years and four months which Champlain spent in France, he lived with Hélène in Paris. They still occupied the house he had bought for her in the rue de La Marche, quartier du Temple, then a fashionable part of the city. We know absolutely nothing about their social life or their circle of friends; and their marriage, by the little data we have, seems to have been unfortunate. After returning from Canada in 1624 and before Champlain went out again, Hélène proposed to go into a convent — the only kind of divorce open to a good Catholic. Samuel dissuaded her, agreeing that in future they sleep separately and live as brother and sister. Thus their reunion in Paris in 1629 cannot have been very passionate. If Champlain had only been able to bring Espérance and Charité home, they might have been a bond between the childless couple; but they might also have been horrible little pests. In any case, before his next voyage to Canada, he settled on Hélène all his property in France, suggesting that he expected never to return; and on his deathbed he dictated a will giving evidence of his affection and esteem for the only woman he is known to have loved.

During most of this time Champlain was playing the self-chosen rôle of lobbyist for Canada, traveling about France trying to get

Cardinal Richelieu.
Courtesy Boston Museum of Fine Arts.

the ear of king and cardinal, and conferring with the directors of the Cens Associés at Paris or Bordeaux. The Treaty of Saint-Germain-en-Laye, signed 29 March 1632, formally restored Canada to France. Some time elapsed before it could be implemented. Richelieu, having annulled the Récollet fathers' mission in Canada (without a word of thanks for their pioneer efforts), and given the Society of Jesus exclusive spiritual authority in New France, sent out Paul Le Jeune (the future martyr) and two other priests in the spring of 1632 along with forty male settlers and Emery de Caën, who had now become a Catholic to protect his interests. On 3 June they entered what Le Jeune called *"l'un des plus beaux fleuves du monde,"* the St. Lawrence; landing at Gaspé, they found snow still on the ground. They called on 18 June at Tadoussac, finding the Saguenay *"aussi beau que la Seine"* — a remarkable understatement; spent three weeks anchored at a spot called L'Echaffaut aux Basques because the Basque fishermen dried cod there; and after losing two anchors in a furious squall at the Ile d'Orléans, anchored off the fort at Quebec on 5 July. Thomas Kirke, obeying orders from his king and respecting the text of the treaty, made no objection to surrender. On 13 July 1632 the Cross of St. George came down and *Vexillum Regis*, the fleur-de-lys banner, went up; this time to stay for a century and a quarter. Emery de Caën and his lieutenant the Sieur du Plessis Bochart took over the command of Quebec, pending Champlain's return.

They found everything at sixes and sevens. The English had burned down the already rickety habitation. The Indians, having been sold alcohol by the English, were indulging in murderous drunken brawls every other night. The Héberts feared for their lives; Espérance and Charité had slipped off to join their own nation in the forest. But the hospitable Héberts had a new pet, a little black boy from Madagascar abandoned by the English. The

Jesuits taught him his letters along with their few Indian catechumens; but we do not know what became of him. After the English cleared out, the supply of alcohol was cut off and the Montagnais sobered up; the French forbade selling *eau-de-vie* to the natives under pain of confiscating trading licenses, and the cat o' nine tails.

Champlain himself set sail 23 March 1633 on his last voyage to Canada. Although, as we have seen, he still had no title of honor, he enjoyed enhanced power and prestige as lieutenant for Cardinal Richelieu and as commodore over three ships outfitted by the Hundred Associates. These were: (1) *Saint-Pierre*, Captain Pierre Gregoire, 150 tuns, 12 guns, and 82 people including crew and intended colonists. Pères Massé and Brébeuf sailed in her, and among the colonists were one woman and two little girls. (2) *Saint-Jean*, Captain Pierre de Nesle, 160 tuns, 10 guns, and 75 men including crew, workmen and artisans for Quebec. (3) *Don de Dieu*, Captain Michel Morieu, 80 to 90 tuns, 10 guns, and 40 people including the crew. The most reverend principal of the Society of Jesus made a special trip to Dieppe to bless the fleet.

All three vessels departed Dieppe 23 March 1633. Every night each ship lighted flares in an iron cresset aft, so that the three could stay together. They enjoyed fair winds as far as Tor Bay, England. Foul weather and contrary winds, accompanied by rain, hail, thunder and lightning, set in on 12 April, and the ships had to close-haul, but they were only passing through a "front"; next day opened fair and they were able to carry full sail. In a thick fog on 26 April they sounded and found 45 fathom; Champlain knew the Bank so intimately as to declare that they were well into it, at latitude 45° 30′, and to shape the correct course for Cabot Strait. It was lucky that he knew his way, because it took them a week to get out of the fog-mull. On 2 May they raised Cape St. Lawrence, Cape Breton Island; and after bucking strong west-northwest winds without making much progress, decided to put in at Sainte-Anne, a Jesuit mission recently established on the shores of Cape Breton. Only two of the ships anchored there, *Don de Dieu* having separated; she showed up at Tadoussac later in the summer.

The Jesuits at Sainte-Anne had a good habitation with a frost-proof wine cellar; but their fur trading had not amounted to much, since Basques and independent Frenchmen had earlier established relations with the nearby Souriquois and got the cream of the trade. And one concludes from negative evidence that they had not done much for God. During Champlain's lifetime, French priests, Récollet or Jesuit, had baptized only about a dozen natives: babies or young children who were about to die.

On Sunday 7 May, *Saint-Pierre* and *Saint-Jean* weighed from Sainte-Anne, passed Brion Island with a fair wind, and on the 9th were off Gaspé, where a northwest wind compelled them to spend a few days in the familiar roadstead between Ile Percée and Bonaventure Island. Thence they made for Tadoussac, which Champlain had orders to repossess. The English, in spite of the treaty, had continued to trade there.

Arriving Tadoussac 17 May, the two French ships found an armed Englishman in the harbor, and Champlain politely ordered her to get out and go home. There ensued an amusing game of bluff. The English captain stalled, although outgunned by the French, because it was so calm in the roadstead that they could not sail within cannon shot of him. Then, while everyone was waiting for a break, two English armed ships under one Captain Smith, each with 38 guns, sailed into the roadstead. That shifted the balance of power from the fleur-de-lys to the Cross of St. George. Champlain, knowing that he would have a poor chance if he elected to fight, parleyed with Captain Smith and, finding that the English ships were already so well charged with fish and peltry that they were eager to return to England, wisely decided to let them go with a warning not to return.

Champlain now sent a shallop up-river to warn the French commander at Quebec of his approach, and to forbid all natives to descend the St. Lawrence below Quebec, or to trade with any English they might encounter. The shallop reached Quebec 23 May 1633, only one hour ahead of the fleet, so favorable had been the wind. Since the Rock was already in French possession, Champlain merely exchanged the traditional three-gun salute and went ashore, preceded by pikemen and musketeers, with a roll of drums, to receive the keys to the fort from du Plessis.

Since the habitation was in ruins, the Jesuits entertained the Cardinal's lieutenant at their hostel overlooking the St. Charles River, and returned his visit on board *Saint-Pierre*, bringing a choir of seven Indian boys who sang *Pater noster qui es in caelis* in their own tongue; the captain of the ship rewarded them with biscuits and cheese. All hands were put to work clearing the site of the ruined habitation and building a chapel dedicated to the Virgin, Notre-Dame de la Recouvrance, Our Lady of the Recovery. This little church, replaced by the cathedral later in the century. was ready by autumn for the Jesuits to sing high mass every Sunday.

Another Catholic foundation, equally dear to Champlain, was the Jesuit school. The native boys who sang the *Pater Noster* belonged to the school for savages which had been opened by Père Le Jeune shortly after taking over from the English. At least as early as August 1635 this ambitious Jesuit was also teaching the catechism and the first elements of letters to the children of French habitants. In the year that Champlain died, the Jesuits opened a seminary at Quebec to prepare young savages for holy orders, but that did not last long; it was no more successful than parallel efforts at Harvard and in Virginia to make Protestant ministers out of young Indians. The Quebec College, as it was called, began instructing French boys in Latin about 1637, and prospered, attaining university standards a quarter-century later.

If Champlain now expected to enjoy a sinecure or a tranquil old age, he was soon disabused. Only a day or two after his arrival, eighteen canoes of the up-river Algonkin arrived at Quebec. Champlain made them an eloquent speech to dissuade them from continuing downstream to trade with the English, recalling all that he and the French had done to protect them from the Iroquois, and promising that all their needs in trade (tactfully not including "firewater") could be satisfied at Quebec. Capitanal, chief of the local Montagnais (who were there in even greater numbers), warmly replied that he would obey, and his people wished to follow French example, even to cultivating grain, which hitherto they had absolutely refused to do. Champlain, encouraged, made a magnificent prophecy: the union of both races under the aegis of the risen Christ: "Our sons shall wed your daughters and henceforth we shall be one people." This made the Indians laugh, as an example of Champlain's always saying something nice to please them. Yet to a great extent this prophecy was fulfilled by intermarriage of the races in Canada proper.

The Iroquois menace, alas, was worse than ever. One of their raids killed two Frenchmen and wounded four on 2 June, not far from Quebec. A big trading party from Huronia that summer warned Champlain that they must have more protection. The Lieutenant, as we should now style him, made a long speech promising to do his best, and wrote to king and cardinal begging for a modest military garrison of 120 men. Even with so few, he predicted, the Five Nations could be brought under control and a *pax gallica* imposed on war-torn North America. And although Champlain was now about sixty-three years old, he proposed to lead this war-and-peace party himself into the heart of the Iroquois country. Never receiving an answer to his letter, Champlain must have thought bitterly, *Plus ça change, plus c'est la même chose.* And so it would be until 1664, when Louis XIV assumed direct control of Canada and sent out the soldiers that Champlain had asked for in 1633. It was then too late to save the Huron. The French army under Louis XIV gave Canada peace and stability for thirty years, but these might have been better secured thirty years earlier, before the Five Nations acquired firearms.

For immediate protection, Champlain built a trading post on Richelieu Island above Quebec and mounted cannon there. Another strongpoint he set up in 1634 at Trois-Rivières on a table-land overlooking both the St. Maurice and the St. Lawrence rivers. Champlain was never idle. If anything within his resources was needed to protect Canada and improve the quality of life there, he saw that it was done.

The Cardinal's Lieutenant promptly occupied himself with re-building the habitation and the houses at Quebec which the English had damaged, and adding a big storehouse for peltry and supplies, with gun platforms where cannon could be mounted to command the river. He also established a third trading post on an island just below the La Chine rapids, which he named Sainte-Croix. The purpose of this move was to place the center of *la traite* at a point convenient for Huron and Algonkin, and easy to defend against Iroquois raids; but he also wanted to prevent up-river Indians from disturbing the perpetual sabbath that the Jesuit fathers maintained around the Rock. Employees of the Cens Associés traveled up-river to trade at Montreal, and there were enough Montagnais along the lower river to feed the trade at Quebec and Tadoussac.

Champlain soon had another problem, the murder of an un-armed Frenchman who was peacefully engaged in washing his clothes near Quebec, by a supposedly friendly Indian. It was the fifth case of that sort. This murderer was an adult warrior, who defended himself by asserting that he had to kill someone to avenge an uncle killed by the Iroquois. This seemed perfectly logical to the Indians but inexplicable to the French. All earlier murderers had been pardoned by Champlain, but he now concluded that his mercy had been misplaced. The murderer's tribe tried to buy him off with a present of two little girls like Espérance and Charité; but the Cardinal's Lieutenant was adamant. Our honest man of *Le Mercure françois* reports Champlain's reply: "These innocent children cannot carry the guilt of the murderer. I desire no further hostage than the guilty one, in my hands, a perfidious traitor, with no more courage or friendship than a tiger, forgetful of the good treatment he received from the Sieur du Plessis, who only last winter cured him of a wound. . . . How will we obtain security if we do not punish the wicked who deserve death? If he had had courage, would he have made so cowardly an assassination? This is the fifth of our people that you savages have killed!" Champlain exchanged long harangues with the murderer's father, and with the chief men of his and other tribes, to no avail. There could be no meeting of minds on the subject.

During these discussions there was much talk about the native *jeunesse folle* getting out of hand. Their chiefs could not restrain them from killing anyone they pleased. Evidently "permissiveness" in the native scheme of education had the same results as in modern society. Youth could do no wrong; at least no wrong that could not be requited by a few belts of wampum. Finally, on Père Le Jeune's plea that to execute the murderer would precipitate a bloody vengeance by the prisoner's relatives on the missionaries in Huronia, and that he had been warned that they were already lying in wait along the river to snipe at him and Père de Noüe on their way thither, Champlain consented to imprison the culprit pending advice from France. Long before that arrived, the fellow solved the problem by escaping, and the Jesuits set up their mission to Huronia in 1634.

Shortly after this affair there came up a question of punishment which showed another side of native justice. A big booby white boy was practicing on a drum, throwing his arms about and flinging up the drumsticks in the manner approved by French army drummers. An inquisitive Indian visiting Quebec approached too near and received a smart clout on the head from one of the boy's drumsticks. The wound was not serious, although it did draw blood; so Champlain, to demonstrate that he was the natives' brother and protector, ordered the young lout to be stripped to the waist and flogged. All friends of the wounded native rallied around and protested; one even flung his fur robe over the lad and presented his own bare back to the Frenchman who wielded the cat o' nine tails, crying, "Whip me if you will, but not him!" Thus the boy got off. The idea of inflicting corporal punishment on a youngster, especially for an accident, seemed monstrous to the natives — utterly repugnant to their principles of justice. The proper way to assuage guilt, for them, was to give presents to the wounded person, or to the relatives of one who had been murdered.

The Jesuit missionaries showed admirable patience. Père Le Jeune reported to his provincial that the expected harvest of human souls was worth it. He wished that every Frenchman "could see in one of the grand streets of Paris what I saw three days ago near the great river St. Lawrence, five or six hundred Huron clothed *à la sauvage*, some in bearskin, others in beaver, others in deerskin, all well-made men of fine figures, tall, strong, good-natured, able-bodied . . . asking help and uttering in their language the words of that Macedonian to St. Paul: 'Come over into Macedonia, and help us' " (*Acts* xvi, 9).

French workmen at Quebec made more trouble than the Indians. Men engaged as sailors, gardeners and bricklayers objected to doing common labor such as tilling the soil and cutting firewood, and in their common dormitory they were continually squabbling. Père Le Jeune suggested that lay brothers of his order be sent out to do the difficult and dirty work.

The most important event of Champlain's last years, for the future of Canada, was a resumption of the seigneurial system tentatively begun under the Caëns. A surgeon named Robert Giffard, who had already been to Canada and loved the country, arrived with an order from the Cardinal entitling him to a seigneurie running back from the St. Lawrence at its confluence with the Rivière de Beauport. He recruited colonists in his native Perche, that little *pays* between Maine and Paris so famous for draft horses, and brought out some forty two-legged Percherons in June 1634. Each family received about a thousand acres on very favorable terms. Giffard lost no time building his *manoir* and settling his people, some of whom founded first families of Quebec. One, the Sieur des Châtelets, obtained in 1635 a seigneurial grant of his own at Cap Rouge above Quebec. This seigneurial system became the most successful feudal land settlement scheme in all North America, not excepting the patroonships in New York and the manors of Maryland.

Monastic sobriety marked the atmosphere around the Rock of Quebec during the last years of Champlain's life. Père Le Jeune praised his "wisdom and prudence"; he said that the fort, where the Cardinal's Lieutenant had his apartments, was like a well-regulated academy. Edifying books such as *Lives of the Saints* and "a good historian" (unfortunately not named) were read aloud at his table by one of the black-robed guests, and evening prayers were recited after dinner. The Angelus sounded from Notre-Dame de la Recouvrance thrice daily to remind all hands to cross themselves and pray. During Lent, abstinence and fasting were faithfully observed. Some artisans caught the ghostly infection, and whipped each other to do penance for their sins; but they were in the minority. In early summer, when the ships arrived from France, there was a certain amount of drunkenness, but nothing to compare with the debauchery of the English régime. For, to man their ships, the Cens Associés engaged only *matelots* certified to be sober and God-fearing. Naturally a few bad actors slipped through, to the scandal of the Jesuits and joy of the Indians at Tadoussac and Quebec.

Thus the atmosphere of Quebec became more "pure" than that of the Puritan colonies of New England. The Jesuits somewhat overdid it. After the paternal and humane authority of Champlain had been removed, the priests posted on a column before the church a list of severe punishments for blasphemy, drunkenness and absence from mass, and attached two instruments of torture to the pillar as a hint of what malefactors might expect. The soldiers replied by going on a rampage and pillaging the chapel.

In the meantime the fur trade prospered, and supplies from France arrived in abundance, the Cens Associés having at last realized that their Canadian employees must have enough to eat and drink during the winter and the long, discouraging spring. But the hunting in Champlain's last winter, 1634–35, was poor; cannibalism broke out among the forest Montagnais.

In 1635, for the last time, Samuel de Champlain witnessed the superb Canadian Indian summer. The leaves turned scarlet, russet and gold, and fluttered to the ground and the river, stippling the dark waters with their brilliant colors. The first snow fell, and promptly melted. Savages offered him their autumnal delicacy of smoked eel, but he had no stomach for it. In October he suffered a paralytic stroke and never again rose from his bed. His last will and testament was dictated and on 17 November signed, with Père Lalemant as chief witness.

This document was somewhat incoherent, as one would expect from a dying man. Remembering that Champlain had already bestowed all his French property on his wife, it is understandable that in this will he leaves her only his papers, his *Agnus Dei*, a gray fox skin and other pelts, and a gold ring mounted with *"une espèce de diamant."* This must have been one of those famous quartz crystals found near Quebec, ironically called *"diamants de Canada."* As residuary legatee, Champlain named his cousin Marie Cameret, wife of Jacques Hersaut or Hersan, *"piquer de chiens à la chambre du Roy"* — chief whip of the royal kennels.

The rest of the will helps us to understand Champlain's character. His chief legatee in Canada is the Blessed Virgin as represented by Notre-Dame de la Recouvrance, to which he left 500 livres to be used to buy proper altar furniture, and 400 livres for saying masses for the repose of his soul. To the Jesuit mission at Quebec he left 3900 livres ($780 in gold) which he had already deposited with them. And there were pious legacies in Paris: 100 livres to L'Eglise de Saint-Esprit vers la Grève — apparently Hélène's parish church — to pay for thirty masses for his soul; 400 livres to the Charity Hospital in the Faubourg Saint-Germain and the same amount to the Hospitaliers de Paix near the Place Royale. And 600 livres more for that same hospice to distribute to *les pauvres honteaux*, those ashamed to beg. There were several personal legacies to the little community at Quebec, numbering at his death no more than two hundred souls. Madame Giffard received a painting of the Blessed Virgin, and Père Lalemant a painting of Our Lord Crucified which hung over the Lieutenant's bed. Suits of clothes went to his valet Poisson, to a mason named Marin, and to his godson Bonaventure. To Madame Hébert, widow of the pioneer apothecary, he left a pair of white fustian *brassières* (which then meant short vests or bodices); these probably had been left behind by Madame Champlain. To his goddaughter Pivert, pins and silk aiguillettes; to Père Lalemant, his compass and the copper astrolabe which had already traveled to Lake Nipissing and back, and which the legatee, a wide-roving priest, would find useful by land and by sea.

To Marguerite Martin, Champlain left 600 livres "to help her to marry a man of Canada," and half that sum to Marguerite Couillard, his goddaughter (Hébert's granddaughter), with no string to it. Hélène Desportes, Madame Champlain's goddaughter, received 300 livres. Most interesting is a legacy of 600 livres to Abraham Martin, to be spent for clearing land, always one of Champlain's chief concerns. This particular clearing may well have been the Plains of Abraham, where the decisive battle in which both Wolfe and Montcalm fell was fought in 1759; for it is known that Abraham Martin once owned this famous plain.

Slowly the Father of New France sank to his death. He heard the boom of cannon ushering in Christmas Day, when *Te Deum laudamus* was sung at the midnight mass in Notre-Dame de la Recouvrance. He received the last rites of his church, and on Christmas Day 1635 gave up the ghost. The little community at the Rock sincerely mourned Champlain, as did all the Indians with whom he had been in friendly contact. At next spring's peltry fair, the natives of Huronia brought a collection of wampum belts for the French habitants of Quebec, "to help wipe away their tears."

"We gave him a highly honorable funeral procession," wrote Père Le Jeune, "of people, soldiers, captains and priests. Père Lalemant officiated, and I gave the funeral oration, for which I lacked not materials." He was buried under the church, and a chapel erected over the tomb. When Notre-Dame de la Recouvrance was replaced by a greater church, no one could recall exactly where Champlain's remains had been laid; and the monument, if one there was, disappeared. Exactly what happened to the remains of Columbus! Canadians are still arguing as to the present location of all that is mortal of the father of their country.

Dying when he did, Champlain was spared the pain of learning that he had been replaced as the Cardinal's Lieutenant by Charles de Montmagny, a Knight of Malta. He was a good man; but what a perfect example of the ingratitude of princes! Arriving at Quebec in the spring of 1636, Montmagny brought not even a word of thanks from king or cardinal to his predecessor, news of whose death had not reached Paris when he sailed. And he was given the title of Governor of New France, which the Father of New France had never enjoyed.

Père Lalemant, returning to France in the spring of 1636, broke the news of her husband's death to Hélène. She could have claimed widow's rights over his Canadian property, but she amiably signed the will when it was probated in Paris. The residuary legatee Marie Cameret raised difficulties and managed to lay her hands on Champlain's share in the Cens Associés, par value 600 livres, and on some of his pious legacies in Quebec.

Widow Hélène was fairly well to do. Her husband had accumulated a goodly sum from the fur trade and left it to her in Paris. She realized her middle-age ambition by entering an Ursuline convent in the Faubourg Saint-Jacques, and years later, in 1648, with a gift of 20,000 livres she took the initiative in founding a new convent of that order at the ancient city of Meaux, southeast of Paris. As foundress, Sister Hélène was dispensed from rising at four in the morning, and enjoyed a fire in her chamber, and a special maid. There, assisting the teaching sisters, she finished her life in pious tranquillity, dying in 1654. If, as we may assume, she kept her husband's manuscripts, his unpublished drawings of Canada and other little legacies, they were destroyed when the convent was suppressed at the time of the French Revolution. Not one article belonging to Champlain, except his astrolabe, has survived the changes and chances of three centuries.

Père Lalemant, in the *Jesuit Relation* of 1640, wrote: "The reputation of M. de Champlain, who stayed here [in Huronia] some twenty-two years ago, still lives in the minds of these barbarous people, who honor, even after the lapse of so many years, the many lovable virtues that they admired in him, and particularly his chastity and continence. Would God that all the French, who were the first to come into these regions, had been like him!"

Perhaps more important for Canada in the long run than Champlain's example of the New Testament life was his policy of making friends with the Indians, respecting their customs and prejudices, and treating them with wisdom and justice. What a contrast to Spanish and Portuguese America, where the native population had to choose between slavery and extermination; or Anglo-Dutch America, where (with the best of intentions) the colonists deprived natives of their hunting grounds and radically altered their way of life. As a result of Champlain's policy, French Canada grew and developed behind a hedge of friendly natives and kept at bay the savage hordes of the Five Nations which might have overrun and destroyed her. Perpetual war with the Iroquois continued; but Canada, unlike Virginia and New England, never suffered a backlash from local Indians.

Many, many years elapsed before either France or Canada fully appreciated the character and exploits of Samuel de Champlain. Not until the nineteenth century did anyone in authority call him the Father of New France, a highly appropriate posthumous title. For he had devoted the last thirty-two years of his life to Canada. He wrote four important books relating her early history and describing her native people and resources; books in which innate humility prevented him from blowing his own trumpet. He compiled the best maps hitherto made of North America, and the earliest harbor charts; and for posterity depicted Indian fights and fortresses, and the fish, fauna and flora of New France. He had faced almost incredible hardships and repeatedly risked his life to explore routes to Canada's western wilderness. He not only fought for her, but pled, begged and intrigued for her in France, crossing the North Atlantic no fewer than twenty-three times. Champlain, with the aid of a few devoted priests like Père Le Jeune and laymen like Pont-Gravé, nursed struggling Quebec to sturdy life, and anticipated the noble future of Canada. No other European colony in America is so much the lengthened shadow of one man as Canada is of the valiant, wise and virtuous Samuel de Champlain, Xaintongeois.

FINIS

APPENDIX I

Champlain's Itinerary

		Chapter
	24 May–30 July. Round trip to Canada.	
1619	*Les Voyages et Descouvertures du Sieur de Champlain* published.	
1620	May. Sails for Canada with Hélène.	
1621	Compagnie de Caën succeeds Compagnie de Canada.	
1624	21 August. Returns to France with Hélène.	
1626	24 April. Sails to Quebec with Jesuits.	XII
1627	29 April. Richelieu organizes Compagnie des Cens Associés.	XIII
1628	July. Refuses Kirke's demand to surrender.	XII
1629	19 July. Surrenders Quebec to the Kirkes. September. Sails to England in English ship. 30 November. Arrives in France.	
1632	29 March. Treaty of St. Germain-en-Laye. Publishes *Les Voyages de la Nouvelle France Occidentale.*	
1633	23 March. Last voyage to Canada. Builds Notre-Dame-de-la-Recouvrance at Quebec.	XIV
1634	Builds armed trading posts at Richelieu Island and Trois-Rivières.	
1635	25 December. Dies at Quebec.	

Including three round voyages to the West Indies, Champlain crossed the Atlantic 29 times; 23 of these were between France and Canada.

APPENDIX II

Traitté de la Marine, et du Devoir d'un bon Marinier

(Treatise on Seamanship and the Duty of a Good Seaman)

T HE *Treatise* appeared as an appendix to Champlain's longest
work, *Les Voyages* of 1632, and is reprinted in his *Works*,
Champlain Society edition VI 252–346, with an English translation by W. D. LeSueur and H. H. Langton (Toronto 1936). The
French text had earlier been reprinted in the C. H. Laverdière
edition *Oeuvres de Champlain* (1865 and 1870).

In my teaching days I found this so fascinating to young sailors
that I made a partial translation of it for their use, and this is it,
with later corrections. There is nothing else in French on the handling and navigation of ships at this period; and in English we have
only John Davis *The Seaman's Secrets* (1594) and Captain John
Smith *A Sea Grammar . . . Accidence for Young Sea-Men*
(London 1627) which will be found in most of the Arber editions
of Smith's works. Comparing Smith with Champlain, I do not
think that either borrowed from the other.

Contemporary captains who read Champlain's *Treatise* must
have thrown up their hands in despair over the author's counsel of
perfection. Very few, if any, followed his suggestions to take
drawing lessons so they could provide a pictorial record; but his
other principles of "a good mariner" were eminently practical.
When he wrote this, Champlain had crossed the South Atlantic six
times and the North Atlantic, from France to Canada and back,
twenty times; and he would cross it thrice more before he died.
He had known many captains — Spanish, French and English —
and had himself commanded ships and pinnaces. Nobody in the
western world as capable as he could have been found to write a
treatise on seamanship; and it is fortunate for us that he did.

Many thousand mariners have made long voyages with less

equipment than Champlain stated to be the minimum. Captain Joshua Slocum, for instance, in his memorable voyage around the world in the *Spray*, had nothing but a dollar alarm clock, an old sextant (better, probably, than Champlain's astrolabe), an *Old Farmer's Almanac*, and a Bowditch. I wish to emphasize, and Alan Villiers will bear me out, that a *feel* for the sea is even more important than technical navigation; and Champlain proves again and again that he had that *feel* to a high degree.

I have not translated the entire *Treatise*, but omitted the sections "How to use the marine chart" (*Works* VI 285–92), "How to keep a daily sea journal" (VI 315–22) and most of "How to prick the chart" (VI 323–26 and 329–46). This last includes directions for the traverse table, and the earliest known engraving of a chip log, complete with line, reel and glass, often reproduced since. These sections are very detailed, somewhat obscure (even to this ancient mariner) and mainly of interest to specialists in the history of cartography and navigation. Some member of that craft should write a monograph on Champlain as navigator and mapmaker. As such he has never been properly appreciated.

So many times, in rereading the *Treatise*, I find myself exclaiming, "How right you are!" Or, "It happened to me, more than three centuries later!" Take, for instance, his injunction to correct your mistakes on the chart when safely in port. In the 1920's, crossing from Cape Cod to Nova Scotia in schooner *Black Duck*, a "dungeon fog" thwarted our celestial navigators, but Dr. Alexander Forbes (the best Corinthian navigator I have ever known) insisted on frequent soundings, all timed. We were aiming at Halifax but made St. Margaret's Bay — so named by Champlain. Once safely anchored, Dr. Forbes insisted on backtracking on the chart and finding just where and how we had gone wrong. It was most instructive!

Treatise on Seamanship and the Duty of a Good Seaman

By the SIEUR de CHAMPLAIN

FRIEND READER: After having spent thirty-eight years of my life in making many sea voyages, and run through many dangers (from which God hath preserved me), and having always been eager to travel into distant and foreign regions, wherein I have had much pleasure, chiefly in what pertaineth to navigation, learning as much by experience as by instruction I have had from many good navigators, as well as through the simple pleasure that I have had from reading books on this subject; that hath prompted me, at the end of my discoveries in New France Occidental, to compose for my own satisfaction a small but intelligible treatise, profitable to those willing to make use of it to learn what is necessary for a good and perfect navigator, and notably in the matter of dead reckoning, and how to proceed in constructing sea charts by the aid of the mariner's compass; for as regards other branches of navigation many good authors have written very particularly about them, and this prevents me from saying more about them. Begging thee to look with favor on this little treatise, and if it is not in accordance with thy notions, pray excuse its author; for it is what he judged to be necessary for those who shall have the curiosity to learn more particularly that which I have not seen described elsewhere — I remain, friend reader,

YOUR SERVANT.

OF NAVIGATION IN GENERAL

It hath appeared to me not out of order to do a little treatise on what is necessary to be a good and finished navigator, and on the qualifications that he should have. He should above all be a good man, fearing God and not allowing on his ship His holy name to be blasphemed, for fear (being often in peril) lest His Divine Majesty chastise him; and being careful night and morning above all else to have prayers said; and if the navigator can find means, I advise him to take with him a competent and qualified churchman or religious to exhort from time to time the soldiers and mariners, so as to keep them always in the fear of God, and likewise to help them and confess them when they are sick, or in other ways to comfort them during the dangers which are encountered in the hazards of the ocean.

He should not be dainty about eating or drinking, adapting himself to the localities in which he finds himself; if he be dainty or of weak constitution, being exposed to changes of air and diet, he will be subject to many ailments, changing from good to coarse food, such as is eaten at sea, which produces a condition of the blood contrary to his temperament; and such persons should be especially apprehensive of scurvy, even more than of other diseases peculiar to long voyages; and there should be some provision of drugs proper for those so afflicted.

He should be robust, alert, with good sea-legs,* inured to hardships and toil, so that whatever betide he may manage to keep the deck, and in a strong voice command everybody what to do. Sometimes he should not be above lending a hand to the work himself, in order to make the mariners more prompt in their attention and to prevent confusion. He should be the only one to

---

* "Avoir le pied marin."

speak, lest contradictory orders, especially in doubtful situations, cause one maneuver to be mistaken for another.

He should be pleasant and affable in his conversation, absolute in his orders, not communicating too readily with his shipmates, unless with those who share the command. Otherwise, not doing so in time might engender a feeling of contempt for him. He should also punish evildoers severely, and make much of the good men, being kind to them, and at times gratifying them with a friendly pat on the back, praising them but not despising the others, so as not to give occasion for envy, which is often the source of bad feeling, like a gangrene which little by little corrupts and destroys the body; and want of early attention to this sometimes leads to conspiracies, divisions, or factions, which frequently spoil the most fair enterprises.

If rich and lawful prizes are captured, he should not defraud the Admiral of his rights, nor those with him, nor his shipmates whether soldiers or sailors, in any way. If possible nothing should be wasted, so that he may render a faithful account of all on his return. He should be liberal according to his opportunities and courteous to the vanquished, favoring them according to the laws of war, and, above all, keeping his word if he has made some agreement, for anyone who does not keep his word is looked upon as a coward, and forfeits his honor and reputation, however valiant he may be, and no trust is ever reposed in him. He should never use cruelty or vengeance like those who are accustomed to barbarities, and thereby show themselves to be more barbarians than Christians; but if on the contrary he useth victory with courtesy and moderation, he will be esteemed by all, even the enemy, who will pay him all honor and respect.

He should not allow himself to be overcome by wine; for when a captain or a mariner is a heavy drinker it is not well to entrust him with command or control, owing to the accidents which may happen while he is sleeping like a pig; or he loseth all judgment and sense, becoming insolent in his drunkenness just when it is most urgent to escape from danger; for should he happen to be in that condition, he will be unable to know his course or to con those at the helm if they do well or ill, which maketh him lose his reckoning. He is also often the cause of a vessel's loss, abdicating his authority to the ignorance of one whom he supposes to be a good seaman, as many instances have shown.

The wise and cautious mariner ought not to trust too fully to his own judgment, when the pressing need is to take some important step or to deviate from a dangerous course. Let him take counsel with those whom he knoweth as the most sagacious, and particularly with ancient navigators who had most experience of the fortunes of the sea and have escaped from dangers and perils; and let him weigh well the reasons they may advance, for it is not often that one head holds everything, and, as they say, "Experience surpasseth knowledge."

He should be wary and cautious, without being too bold, in making landfall, particularly in foggy weather, when he will sail parallel to the coast, according to the place, or stand off-and-on according to the position of the ship, inasmuch as in fog or darkness there is no pilot.* He must not carry too much sail with the idea of making headway; this often splits the sails and unmasts the ship, or, if she be crank and is not as well ballasted as she should be, it bringeth her bottom-up.

He should make the day his night and watch the greater part of the latter; always sleep clothed so as to be promptly on hand for accidents that may happen; keep his own private compass and often look at it to know if the course is being properly kept; and see that every member of the watch is doing his duty. He should

---

* "En ce temps de brune ou obscur il n'y a point de pilote," meaning that under such conditions no pilot is any use.

have a list of the watch, and distribute properly the men who understand navigation, so that they may have an eye to the helmsmen and see that she always keeps on her course and that the sailors keep good watch. If there are enough soldiers on board, one should be a sentinel forward, another aft, and a third at the mainmast, with a lighted lantern hanging between decks, so as to see and hasten to help if something unexpected happens.

He must not be ignorant, but know everything that concerns ship handling, everything at least that is necessary for putting to sea and for mooring in readiness to make sail, as well as all other matters needful for the safety of the ship.

Of Ship Husbandry

He should take good care to have good food and drink for his voyage and such as will keep; to have good dry bins in which to store the bread or biscuit, and, especially on long voyages, to have too much rather than too little; for sea voyages have to be made in fair weather or foul and in all kinds of winds. He must be a good steward in issuing rations, giving each man what he reasonably needeth; doing it otherwise engendereth dissatisfaction between sailors and soldiers who claim to be ill-treated, and who on occasion are capable of doing more harm than good. He should entrust the issuing of rations to a good and loyal dispenser, no drunkard, but a good manager; for a careful man in an office of this kind cannot be too highly valued.

He should be particularly careful to see that everything is in good order on his ship, both to make her strong enough to carry the weight of the guns she may mount, and to improve her appearance, so that he may take pride in her when entering and leaving port, and may give pleasure to those who see him on board, just as an architect is pleased after having adorned the structure of a splendid building which he hath designed. Everything on a ship should be very neat and clean, after the fashion of the Flemings, who by common consent take first place in this respect over all seafaring nations.

He should take great pains when there are both sailors and soldiers on board to make them keep as clean as possible, and fix it so that the soldiers be separate from the sailors, so that there may be no confusion on board, and he should often have the space between decks cleansed of the filth that accumulates there; for it frequently causes a stench and even fatal diseases, as if it were a pestilence and contagion.

Before embarking he must have everything requisite for giving first aid to the people, with one or two good surgeons, not ignorant, like most of those who go to sea.

If possible, he should know his ship and have sailed her, or he must learn about her to know the best ballast for her, and what speed she can make in twenty-four hours according to the strength of the winds, and what leeway she makes with the wind abeam, or when close-hauled with only the topsail or mainsail to steady her so that she doth not labor, and to keep closer to the wind.

On Dangers and Precautions

He must be in readiness for ordinary dangers, be they fortuitous or through ignorance or rashness, getting you involved, as running before the wind onto a coast, doggedly trying to double a cape, or pursuing a hazardous course by night among banks, tidal flats, shoals, isles, rocks, or ice. But when misfortune bringeth you to such a pass, that is where you must display manly courage, mock at death though it confront you, and in a steady voice and with cheery resolution urge all to take courage and do what can be done to escape the danger, and thus dispel fear from the most cowardly bosoms; for when they find themselves in a hazardous situation, everyone looks to the man who is thought to have experience, and if he is seen to blanch and giveth orders in a trembling and uncertain voice, all the rest lose courage. Often one hath seen ships lost in situations from which they might have got clear had the men seen their captain undaunted and resolute, giving orders boldly and with authority.

He should be careful to take soundings off all coasts, roadsteads, ports, harbors, reefs, banks, rocks and flats, so as to recognize the bottom, the dangers, the anchorages if in need, or to be able to shape his course if by chance no altitude had been taken or sight of land, of which one should keep reckoning in one's paper sea-journal.

He should have a good memory for recognizing landfalls, capes, mountains, and the bearing of the coast, tidal currents and their bearing, wherever he shall have been.

He should never cast anchor except on a good bottom, or else he may be forced to buoy his cables by means of can-buoys, puncheons, or other devices, so as not to have them, with lapse of time, cut themselves on a bottom of rock, shingle, or coarse shell; and should hold that position as short a time as possible if not so compelled; and should keckle the cables at the hawse-holes, for fear of having them part, since, if the cable faileth, one will be in danger of losing his life. Therefore it is necessary to take care to have good cables, anchors, grapnel, and hawsers; and above all to pay out plenty of scope if you have it, especially in foul weather, to ease the ship and not to have her labor or drag her anchor.

He should not be dilatory in striking sail when he sees a big wind gathering on the horizon.

He must take care, also, when a storm arrives and the ship is lying-to, to take down the lesser masts, to house the yards and secure them, as well as all other rigging, to dismount the guns if need be so that in a rough sea they will not work and break their tackle and other things too; if you don't dismount them, lash them well. There are some ships which do not labor so much with the mainsail set as when it is not; experience will tell you what is best in this particular.

He must know how properly to moor his vessel when she is in harbor so that no damage be done to her; also he must not allow any fire to be carried within her except in a lantern, especially in the powder magazine; he must prevent the men from smoking between decks, because a mere spark of fire is enough to burn everything, as often occurs by accident.

To be careful to have good gunners, expert in the use of fireballs and other things needful in a fight, and have everything suitable, well arranged and handy in their cabins, as well as all else pertaining to the guns.

He should not (if he can help it) be ignorant of anything required not only to build a ship, but he must know the measurements and proportions requisite to make her of the burden or size desired; in a word, he must be ignorant of nothing, so that he may discuss these matters to good purpose when need be.

He should be careful to keep the ship's reckoning, to know her point of departure, destination, position, where the land lies in relation to her, on what point of the wind; he should know what leeway she makes, and what she makes good on her course. He must never grow slack in these matters, which are a main source of errors; that is why, in all changes of wind and course, he should take great care to ascertain his position as near as possible, for sometimes good pilots are found to be well lacking in their reckonings.

On Celestial Navigation

He should be a good celestial navigator, skilled in taking the altitude either with the cross-staff or the astrolabe, know the right ascension of the sun and its daily declination, in order to add or subtract [from the altitude], to take the altitude of the pole star with the cross-staff, take the bearing of the Guards,* and add to or subtract [from the altitude] the degrees they are above or below the pole star, according to the locality.

He should be able to recognize the Southern Cross when in south latitudes, add or subtract the degrees, recognize on occasion other stars if possible, so as to take their altitude when he loses sight of the former, or when he has not been able to take the sun's altitude owing to not seeing it precisely at noon.

He should know if the instruments he uses are accurate and properly made, and, in case of necessity, be able to construct others for his use.

He should be experienced in pricking the chart correctly, to know if it is accurate according to the meridian where he is, if he can rely upon it, [and] how many leagues for each rhumb of the wind he must reckon for every higher degree. He should know the currents and tides and where they are to be met with, to properly enter the harbors and other places where he will have business, whether by day or night; and, if need be, he should be provided with good compasses and rutters for that object, and have seamen on the ship who know [those places], if by chance he has not himself been there; for sometimes the lives of the whole ship's

---

* The outer stars of the Little Bear or Dipper, whose angle with Polaris helped in a simple calculation of latitude. The navigational methods just before Champlain's time are amply discussed and illustrated in S. E. Morison *The European Discovery of America: The Northern Voyages* A.D. *500–1600* (1971), and nothing indicates that Champlain used any seventeenth-century improvements.

company are saved by making use of these [currents and tides] in due time and place.

He should always be provided with a number of good compasses, especially for long voyages; and for these he should have compass cards which give easterly and westerly variation of the meridian line* besides others giving north and south; and have a number of sand-clocks† and other instruments to the purpose.

He must know how to estimate the variations of the magnetic needle, in order to make allowance for them at the proper time and place, [how] to ascertain if the needles are properly magnetized and well balanced on the pivot, the pivot itself straight, the gimbals free; and if all is not right, to make it so; and for this purpose he should have a good loadstone, no matter what it may cost, and remove all iron from near the compass and binnacle; for that is very harmful.

He must be able to find the pole of the loadstone not merely with the same compass needles, if you don't know that they are properly magnetized; but there are other easy means, certain and foolproof, for there are some needles which when magnetized point northeast or northwest of the pole of the loadstone by two or three degrees; and these sometimes engender grave errors in navigation, especially on long voyages.

Never forget often to ascertain variations of the compass needle in all localities, that is, to know how much it varies from the meridian toward the east or west, which is useful in determining longitudes if one has observations for them; and when you return to the same place where you took them, and find the same variation, you would know whereabouts you are, whether it be in the hemi-

---

* In *Les Voyages* of 1613 (*Works* II 222–30) Champlain explains how to adjust compass cards for variation.

† *Orloges de sables,* half-hour or hour glasses, the only method used for keeping time on board unless the captain owned a very fine watch. One is shown in Champlain's picture of log and line, below.

sphere of Asia or that of Peru; and of this you should not be neglectful. It is also useful for finding the longitude of the locality, and for checking the wind directions according to the position of the ship, that is to say, all the names of the points of the mariner's compass.*

To know how to make charts, so as to be able to recognize accurately the lie of the coast, entrances to ports, havens, roadsteads, rocks, shoals, reefs, islands, anchorages, capes, tidal currents, inlets, rivers, and streams with their heights and depths, the sea-marks and beacons on the edges of shoals, and to describe the richness and fertility of the lands, what they are fit for and what to expect of them; who are the inhabitants of these places, their laws and customs; and to depict the birds, animals, fish, plants, fruits, roots, trees and everything unusual that is seen; for this a little drawing is very necessary, and the art should be practiced.

To know the difference of longitude between two places, not only along one parallel [of latitude] but along all; and even those which lie on different degrees of latitude, like Rome and the Straits of Gibraltar, and so for all other places in the world.

To know the Golden Number, the concurrent days of the year, the solar cycle, the dominical letter for each year, whether it is bissextile or not, the days on which the moon is in conjunction; on what day the months begin, how many days there are in each; the difference between the lunar and the solar year; the moon's age, how many degrees it traverses every day; what are the constellations of each month; how many leagues make a degree, north and south; how long the days are for each parallel of latitude, and how

---

* How Champlain expected to find longitude by this means is beyond my comprehension. Neither he nor any other navigator of the seventeenth century could calculate longitude except by dead reckoning, but they were always trying to find out. From the above paragraph it would seem that he subscribed to an erroneous theory as old as Columbus — that the lines of compass variation ran due north and south so that if you found your local variation you would know what longitude you were at.

much shorter or longer they become every day; what are the hours of sunset and sunrise; what is the sun's daily declination, whether in the northern or the southern hemisphere; and to know on what days the movable feasts begin.

To know what is meant by a sphere, and its axis, the horizon, the meridian, the altitude, the equinoctial line, the tropics, the zodiac, parallels, longitude, latitude, zenith, center, the circles arctic and antarctic, the poles, the northern and southern hemispheres, and other matters pertaining to the sphere; the names of the signs of the zodiac and of the planets, and their motions.

To know something about regions, kingdoms, towns, cities, countries, islands, seas, and peculiarities of the land, something about the latitudes, longitudes and declinations if he can, and chiefly along the coasts where navigation is conducted; and when he knows as much by practice as well as by science, I'll say he may be classed among first-rate navigators.

ON BATTLES AT SEA

Besides what is related above, a good sea captain should not forget anything necessary in a sea fight, in which he may often be involved. He should be brave, foreseeing, prudent, governed by good sound judgment, taking every advantage he can think of, whether for attack or defense, and if possible keep the weather gauge on his enemy. For everyone knows how useful it is to have this advantage, whether for boarding or not; for the smoke of gunfire or of the fire-balls sometimes obscures the enemy so as to throw him into disorder, preventing him from seeing what he should do; this is often the case in sea fights.

The Captain should see in advance that all the cannon, swivel guns, cannon balls, fire-balls, powder and other weapons needed for a fight or for protection are in good condition, handled and managed by men of sense and experience, to avoid accidents, and particularly in respect of the powder and fire-balls. He should not put them in charge of any but discreet and sensible men, who know how to distribute them and make use of them to good purpose. He should see that such rules are applied to all these matters and that every man obeys orders, whether it be for beating to quarters or for handling the rigging of the ship, so that each man is in his place, and does not leave it except by order of the commander, or of someone on his authority; and to this end all the sailors and mariners should be in readiness and so disposed as to have an eye to the rigging and sails, and to make them fast both aloft and alow. The pilots should also be careful about matters connected with the helm and with the men on that station. So also all the carpenters and caulkers, with their tools, must be ready to repair damage that the enemy may do in a fight. The ship must not be encumbered, so that they may go below freely and repair the damage that the guns may inflict below the waterline. There should be pots ready, filled with water to extinguish fire, in case some accident should happen, whether by effect of powder or fire-balls, or other things.

He must see that the wounded are attended to promptly by those appointed for the purpose, and that the surgeons and some assistants are in readiness and provided with all necessary instruments, as well as with medicaments and dressings, with fire in an iron brazier for cauterizing, or for anything else when necessity requireth.

The commander must be always on the alert, sometimes in one place, sometimes in another, so as to encourage everyone in doing his duty, and to make such dispositions that there be no confusion, since that is the cause of great harm, especially in a sea fight. The wise and vigilant captain should take into consideration everything that makes for his advantage, and get the advice of the most experienced people, so as to execute orders with the means he judges to be necessary and advantageous. He should not be a novice in encounters and their consequences, but have had experience in the ordering of battles, which are fought in various modes of attack and assault, and in other matters which, experience shows, may be more advantageous to one side or the other.

On Charts for Navigation

Nothing is so helpful to navigation as the marine chart, inasmuch as it represents all parts of the world, with the coasts, roadsteads, ports, rivers, capes, promontories, bays, beaches, rocks, reefs, islands, banks, mud flats, harbor entrances, sea-marks and beacons, and their depths; anchorages according to their situation, and the dangers which may be encountered; the elevations, distances, and compass bearings by which one sails. On the same charts are also noted the streams, channels and double lands,* those seen inland and along the coasts; and by these I mean charts made exactly and without error, with reductions for distances from the spherical to the plane surface as accurate as possible; and although there is some difficulty in this, yet it can be done, to be of service and to navigate well. The points of the compass card must be accurately and finely drawn, all the degrees must be absolutely equal, the scale of places must correspond to the degrees of latitude, and all in proper relief. And to this end one must know how to draw, in order to be able to make an accurate chart, on which it is sometimes necessary to depict many particulars in the countries or regions, such as representing mountains, the appearance of two coastal outlines, as seen by one sailing along the coast. Also there might be shown the birds, animals, fishes, trees, plants, roots, medic-

---

* He means adjacent lands which are similar and so likely to be mistaken for each other.

inal herbs, fruits, dress of the peoples of all the foreign countries, and everything worthy of remark that may be seen or met with. Thus, it is very difficult to navigate without a chart; that is why all seamen should have good ones, with all the instruments and other accessories to navigation, and they should be accurate with the degrees properly marked. Also it is necessary to have good compasses, according to the localities to which one intends to sail.

* * * * *

On Accidents Which Occur Owing to Mistaken Reckonings

The dead reckoning that should be kept on sea voyages is very essential to navigation, although it can never be altogether accurate; and this results in many errors, especially where the seamen have not had much experience, not knowing accurately the speed of the ship in which they sail, or mistaking one meridian for another through not knowing the variation of the compass in the locality where they are sailing, or trying to take one direction instead of another, contrary to their [intended] course, or sometimes having bad helmsmen, who let the vessel drift down-wind. All these faults partly arise from not observing longitude as well as latitude, and I believe that, in order to approximate these, one must take frequent note of the variations of the magnetic needle, which shows the true meridian of one's locality, as I have said above. Also one meets with tidal currents which, if you don't take care, deflect the vessel from her course, besides the violence of storms which drive the vessel before the wind, taking the wrong course. An infinite number of other accidents occur, preventing an accurate dead reckoning from being kept, and this is the cause of countless ships being lost, and the death of many men, and all on account of the obstinacy of certain navigators, who think they will lose face if held to be out in their reckoning, and are unwilling to communicate with anybody for fear their mistakes may be discovered,* wishing thereby to make one believe that they have some infallible method. Such navigators often make bad voyages, to their own ruin and to that of those under their charge.

One thing in dead reckoning should never be forgotten — to overestimate rather than underestimate the distance traversed; for instance, if the vessel seems to make two leagues an hour, give her one-eighth or more in addition, according to the distance covered by the reckoning and the length of the voyage; for it is better to be twenty leagues behind than too soon ahead, in which case one might find oneself ashore or in danger of shipwreck. This has happened to many vessels through lack of care, who, supposing themselves to be some distance from land, and carrying sail in a dark night or in fog, or during a great storm when they cannot see, are amazed to find themselves ashore. If soundings are to be had off one's destination, one should begin to heave the lead a day earlier rather than later; and if having done so, one expects to find bottom, keep on heaving it every watch during the night or in fog. This is the way to avoid danger, for one cannot be too apprehensive of what one would not like to see, particularly since you cannot make that mistake twice. Also, if you have to double a cape or island at night or in fog, always set your course half a point more to seaward, to avoid the land; or if the tide is running toward it, set it rather one whole point. The judgment of the seaman in this respect should be governed more or less by the force of the tides, and if you are sailing in seas where there is apt to be ice and you suspect its presence, watch for it all day, and have sailors at the crow's-nest to sight it. And if you do not sight it during the day or night, shorten sail, and if it is foggy or dark in a doubtful situation, come about on the other tack or strike all sail, waiting until the air

---

* Champlain was probably thinking of Champdoré. See Chapter V.

be clear and serene; and if you do see ice, proceed carefully and do not get involved in the midst of it. During the night lay-to in order to avoid danger until you are clear of it, and do not be obstinate in proceeding inconsiderately among these risks. Once I found myself hemmed in by ice for seventeen days,* and without the help of God we would have been lost, like others whom we saw wrecked through their rashness. This is why the wise mariner should fear all the difficulties which may occur (like that of his reckoning) in which the oldest navigators are the most expert. On this account I shall discuss different ways of reckoning later.

DIVINE PROVIDENCE

God the all-wise, all-merciful, all-powerful, foresaw that men who sail the waters of this vast ocean would run a thousand perils and shipwrecks if He did not aid them with instructions which might preserve them from death and the loss of their vessels. Since man hath no certain knowledge in his voyages of longitudes, and no one in this life should wear out himself on that subject since it would be in vain (as many have found by experience in our time), there have been plenty of arguments and treatises without any solid or fixed results. But God, the author of all things, since it hath not pleased Him to grant us this knowledge, hath given us another lesson whereby seamen may correct their reckoning, avoiding the dangers they might incur far more than they do but for Divine Providence. It is certain that the observations of latitude taken, whether by the sun or by the pole star or others, give the accurate information from the point of departure up to that of destination, and one's latitude, which puts the seaman right. But they do not give the length of the course, which can only be done

* See page 124.

by guesswork; quite apart from one's position north-south,* one has to reckon the distance between two positions, of neither of which one is quite certain! Were the navigator certain of his course he would not have to guess, but would know for sure the position of his ship whenever he pricketh the chart.

Using another manner of speaking; when the reckoning proves to be no good, one must correct it, and how? That's what I have never been able to learn from any mariners with whom I have talked, except that it be done by fanciful rules, all different, some better than others; hence you have to be very cautious in navigating. This is why the most experienced and ancient navigators have a better judgment about reckonings and other things that occur at sea than others who often pretend to know more than they do. Now, as before said, there are sure indications for navigation which guard against the dangers one may encounter, and so certain that, when he recognizeth them, the mariner rejoiceth along with his shipmates as if he had already reached the haven where he would be, relieved of all his cares and past reckonings, recognizing the mistakes he made, such as being too far ahead or behind his dead reckoning; and by this means he is guided, and corrects his reckoning again, and pricks his chart well and good. Little by little, and by constant practice, you may become more certain in navigation.

Sailing Directions for New France, and Home

Now let us see what these sea-marks and means of learning are; let us begin with those of Nouvelle France Occidentale. Between

---

* I.e., one's latitude. You might conclude from this paragraph that Champlain originated the expression "navigating by guess and by God," common a century ago. It is evident that he was bothered by lack of any method to determine longitude by celestial navigation; nor was any found prior to the "lunars" of the eighteenth century.

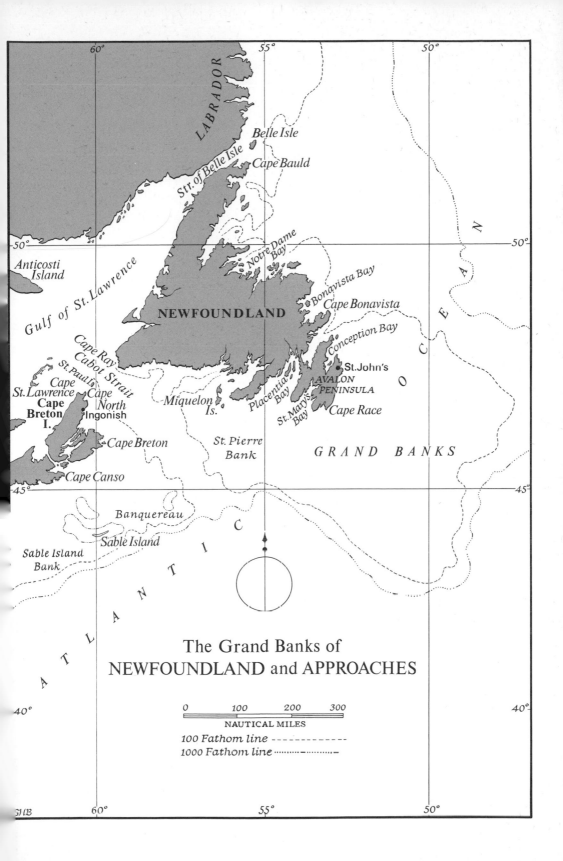

The Grand Banks of
NEWFOUNDLAND and APPROACHES

```
0        100       200       300
NAUTICAL MILES
```

100 Fathom line - - - - - - - - - -
1000 Fathom line ········ — ········ —

that country and ourselves there is the Grand Bank, where numbers of vessels, both French and foreign, fish for cod, as they do on the mainland and the island adjacent: which fish is caught in parts of these places at all seasons, a manna of inestimable value both for France and for other kingdoms and countries, with which there is a very great and important trade therein. This Grand Bank extends from the 41st to the 51st degree of latitude, being 90 leagues from northeast to southwest, as reported by navigators by means of soundings, since no other method is possible; and its width in places — for instance, between latitudes 44 and 46 — amounts to 50, 60, and 70 leagues, more or less according to the latitude.* From this width it narrows gradually as you go north; and from the 42nd to the 44th degree it is shaped almost like an oval, at the extremity of which there is quite a narrow point. Thus it is drawn by all former seamen, from the innumerable soundings taken by them, which by degrees have made known the shape, both of this Bank and of others which are to the west and west-northwest such as Green Bank and the Banquereau; and others not far from Sable Island, which you hit 25 to 30 leagues out to sea before reaching this Grand Bank.† Flocks of certain birds are seen, called gannets, and this gives the pilot warning that he is not far from the edge of the bank which forms its side; then one readies the lead for taking soundings until this edge is reached, to recognize which when one is nearing the Grand Bank, one heaves the lead every six, four, or two hours, according

---

* Reference to a modern chart of the Grand Bank shows that both here and on his general charts, Champlain knew it pretty well but was not infallible. The Grand Bank extends from above 42°30′ N to 49° N, and Champlain's NE-SW measurement is good only if you include the Banquereau, St. Pierre and other smaller banks off southern Newfoundland and Cape Breton. Extreme width, if you include these, is a little over 300 nautical miles. The "narrow point" is not there today. Note on our chart how the 100-fathom curve drops off to hundreds and even thousands of fathoms.

† An error; for "before reaching" read "after passing."

as the pilot thinks he is near or some way off. Now, he recognizes that he is at the edge by the depth, which will be 90, 80, 70, 65, 60 and 50 fathom, more or less, according to the latitude he is in; and when on the said Bank he will find 45, 40, 35 and 30 fathom, more or less according to latitude. Where other data are unavailable, the lead tells the initiated where he may be; and it is certain that before sighting land he must cross this Bank, which tells him the length of the course he has to run and assures him as to what he has run, even though his dead reckoning be out. This Bank is 25 leagues distant from the nearest land, which is Cape Race, in latitude 46½ degrees, and belonging to the island of Newfoundland; and between the Bank and the land there is great depth, which gives information that one has passed over the west-northwest edge of the Bank. Moreover, on this Grand Bank one sees sure indications in the infinite number of birds such as fulmars, sea-mews, loons, gulls, gannets, great auks or eider-ducks, and several others, which mostly follow the fishing vessels, which take cod, in order to feed on the head and entrails of the fish which they throw into the sea. All this, as has been said, gives information as to where one is, to everybody's great content. The seaman, having taken his latitude (which on no account should be omitted or, if he gets no good latitude, let him fall back upon his dead reckoning of where he thinks he is, or from the soundings data), will shape his course for the place whither he wishes to go; and the navigator, foreseeing by the reckoning that he is nearly "debanking," heaves the lead until he gets no bottom, or at least a great depth such as 100, 130 or 140 fathom. After some little distance, say 10 to 12 leagues, the Green Bank is reached, and soundings on this continue until you are through the St. Pierre islands, which are 5 to 6 leagues distant from the island of Newfoundland; or else you will pass other banks called Banquereau, which give complete information together with the latitude in which you are; and thus with certainty the course is run from the aforesaid Grand Bank.*

But if the latitude is only ascertained by dead reckoning on the Bank, one tries as best one can to get in sight of land, in order to set the course with certainty; land such as Cape Race, Cape St. Mary's, the St. Pierre islands, or other capes belonging to this island of Newfoundland, or by certain shoals that some recognize by soundings, and by the fish caught there, and so seek a sure spot to get right and make certain of the course; and one must check these landfalls, except in foggy weather or at night. One should proceed with judgment and discretion, keeping a good lookout, and watch the tide currents, according to the locality where one is. Of those who leave the Bank behind, many who have taken a good latitude observation proceed until they sight the St. Pierre Islands or Cape Ray, belonging to the island of Newfoundland, [and pass] between St. Paul Island and Cape St. Lawrence on the island of Cape Breton, in order to enter the Gulf of St. Lawrence, according to the course each wishes to make.

And if one chooseth to go to the coast of Acadia, the Souriquois, the Etchimins and the Almouchiquois, one may make for Cape Breton or the islands of Canso, Wedge Island, Sambro, La Have, Cape Sable, Grand Manan, Long Island and Mount Desert Island, or Cape Cod near the Malabarre, where 20 or 25 leagues off-shore there are soundings of 50 fathom, with a soft bottom as one goes toward the land, a sign given by God to navigators so that they may not be lost — provided they are neither lazy nor negligent in sounding.

All these coasts and capes above mentioned are not far from the

---

* These directions for crossing the Grand Bank into Cabot Strait en route to the Gulf of St. Lawrence are accurate; Champlain must have had, in addition to his own experience, information from hundreds of French fishermen.

Grand Bank; Cape Breton only 100, Canso 120 leagues; between these two is Sable Island, in latitude 43°30′, 25 to 30 leagues from Cape Breton on a north and south line, very dangerous and shoal, and one should beware of it. The flood tide runs toward it from the north and north-northwest.

Thus, navigation in these regions is fairly safe, without many risks, even if the dead reckoning is not quite accurate; one knows where one is and can begin a new reckoning as if one were leaving a harbor. A seaman who has passed this way once or twice would indeed be ignorant if, in the 125 leagues from the Grand Bank to the coasts of La Nouvelle France, he made so many mistakes in his dead reckoning that he could not take care to avoid the land, which might often happen but for the knowledge of the Grand Bank. This is the cause of so many vessels not being lost, as they would have been if the Bank were not there, since it enables the seaman to correct his reckoning.

And for voyages taken from La Nouvelle France Occidentale to the coasts of France, England and Ireland, there are indications and signs in the sea from soundings taken from 35 and 30 to 25 leagues out to sea from these places, according to the latitude where one is; these give information as to one's position, the distance one has to go, and the course to shape so as to establish a new basis of dead reckoning; and if the latitude is only by guess, the old navigators by long practice, both past and present, recognize the bottom where soundings are taken, whether it is rock, fine sand, or mud, clay, shell, or tiny shell, chips of rock, gravel, and other names given to distinguish bottoms. Along with this the depth in fathoms causes them to recognize the place where they are and the course they ought to shape to reach the coasts whether of France, England, or Scotland. If they are not mariners well acquainted with these soundings, it may happen that instead of entering the English Channel they get into St. George's Channel, very dangerous if one is not acquainted, which lies north of the Scillies and the coasts of England, and which is to be dreaded like the coast of Brittany. But if the weather be fair there is nothing to fear; and if in so short a distance as 35, 30, or 25 leagues so bad a reckoning is kept that they are like to run on shore, the seaman must be quite fresh and ignorant in navigation; and in this is seen the providence of God and the teaching He gives to seamen in order to preserve their lives and correct their dead reckonings.

There is another thing which gives great relief to the seaman, and this is the fact that on the Spanish coasts the water is very deep, and the land for the most part very lofty, so that it can be seen by sailors far off, and on account of this one approaches as near as the navigator chooses; only fog or night could bring him to harm, and I will add that in foggy weather one may come very near and yet avoid danger and put out to sea again, on account of the coast being sheer. This could not so easily be done off a low coast, where one would be ashore before being able to guard against it; and this happens because of the reckoning of the pilot, who sets it too far behind: on the contrary one must always set the reckoning ahead. But however that may be, one gets information before reaching land, whether by soundings, coasts, land birds, seaweed such as is met with in some waters, fishes, change of weather or climate, and many other marks known to navigators, which greatly relieve the pilot's dependence on his dead reckoning and afford great comfort. Indeed, if there were not these marks and signs at sea, navigation would be much more perilous and subject to risks than it is; for in a good ship there is nothing to fear except a lee shore and fire; that is why, when surrounded by land and near shore, one must be particularly careful to get one's sleep more by day than at night, and be on guard against tidal currents, in order to avoid the places whither they might carry one, so that when you shall arrive in a snug harbor you may render thanks to God.

* * * * *

There is no doubt, when the mariner is certain of sailing along a particular rhumb without making leeway, and on taking a good latitude observation, finds it agreeing with his dead reckoning, he will be satisfied with his course whether in north or south seas.

This difficulty being settled, another more troublesome and difficult presents itself . . . to ascertain how many leagues one has fallen off the course one has been following against contrary winds. . . . With a head wind from the west, absolutely contrary to her course, the ship is unable to do more than beat up on one tack then on the other, south-southwest and north-north-west,* so as not to wander from her course, keeping the same latitude as best she can. With these head winds she cannot fail to make leeway northerly or southerly, and she might drift southeast or northeast if the force of the wind is great enough, and make sternway instead of advancing. In order not to lose way you might be forced to strike all sail, put the helm down and lash the tiller to leeward, secure all the rigging that causes the ship to strain, house all topmasts and secure the yards, sometimes tauten the shrouds when they become slack, and secure the guns, which must be kept in good order to prevent confusion.

There are ships which cannot keep up to the wind without a great press of sail; the mariner will know in this respect what is best for his ship. After some days in this wretched state, buffeted by the wind, with rain, fog and other annoying obstacles to navigation, the wind will moderate, the furious sea will go down, the weather clear; and, free from clouds and squalls, the vessel is eased, sails are set to the wind, the course is resumed, the sails do

---

* This indicates that Champlain did not expect a ship of his day to sail nearer the wind than 7 points (79 degrees).

not split and the running rigging is not stiff, the ship sails on her course quietly, with very little leeway, the reckoning is easily made, nobody is anxious, as when the ship was being tossed about, and everyone rejoiceth without thinking again of the past. The mariner should mark on his chart all the courses taken, of which he should have kept strict account, as well as how far he drifted on one or another tack, and having done so he should prick the chart to know where he is.

* * * * *

Description of the Chip Log, which he says
he had seen practiced among certain
good English navigators*

You must have a board 3 feet by 15 inches, divided lengthwise into 13 divisions and across into five divisions. In the first space [of the first set of divisions] mark "Time," and in the following spaces [give the hours by twos] up to 12, and beginning again at 2, proceed [by twos] for another twelve [hours], which will make twenty-four hours in the twelve divisions, as you may see in the accompanying figure. In the second set of divisions next following will be noted the number of knots per hour; in the third, the fathoms; and in the fourth and fifth [the course and] the rhumbs on which you sail. You must have a line — not too thick, so that it may run out more quickly — at the end of which you must put a little flat piece of oak about one foot by 6 inches, loaded with a small strip of lead at the back, with a small wooden tube tied by a piece of cord to both sides of the [lower] end of the little board, and another small piece of wood like a peg which goes quite easily into the tube. It is this that keeps the little board al-

---

* For the chip log (the only means of measuring a ship's speed until the invention of the rotating log, registering knots on a dial) see my *European Discovery of America: Northern Voyages*, pp. 610–11.

Heures.	Nœuds.	Braſſes.	Routes. Rumbs.
2	3	2	Cap au Nort $\frac{1}{4}$ du Nordeſt.
4	2	4	Cap au Nort-nordeſt.
6	4	2	Cap au Nor-deſt.
8	5	3	Cap au Nor-deſt.
10	2	3 $\frac{1}{2}$	Cap au Nort $\frac{1}{4}$ du Nordeſt.
12	3	5	Cap au Nort-nordeſt.
2	2	3	Cap au Nordeſt $\frac{1}{4}$ de l'Eſt.
4	2	4	Cap au Nor-deſt.
6	6	1	Cap au Nort.
8	6	3	Cap au Nordeſt $\frac{1}{4}$ du Nordeſt.
10	6	2	Cap au Nort $\frac{1}{4}$ du Nordeſt.
12	3	4	Cap au Nort-nordeſt.

Champlain's picture of log, line and hourglass, with table for their use. From the Champlain Society Works VI.

ways upright behind the ship when in the water, and only comes out when the board is being drawn up out of the water.

The line fastened to the little board must have some 8 or 10 fathoms' length before the first knot is reached, . . . until the little board is in the sea and the line runs out as far as the first knot. One man should hold the line, and another a little sand-glass containing the amount of sand that will run through in half a minute, which may be the interval required to count up to 28 without hurrying. At the moment when the first knot passes the hands of the man who throws the line, allowing it to run out freely according to the speed of the ship, have another turn the little glass in your presence until the sand has run out. Immediately when that happens the first man must hold back the line and not allow it to run out or slip through any farther. Then, hauling it in, see how many fathoms there are from his hand which pulls the line to the first knot; then count all the knots that have slipped off into the sea while the glass was running. . . .

For instance, to show how you ought to make this count, I find that in 24 hours' sailing the line has been streamed every two hours; and, since the ship travels more or less fast according to the force of the winds or currents, if it makes leeway too, there will be more or fewer knots run according to the speed of the ship. To figure how far the ship has sailed, add all the numbers of knots set down in the twelve squares of the little table, and it will be seen that these make up 44 knots and over 36½ fathom, which at 7 fathom to the knot make 5. Adding all together, 44 knots plus 5 make 49 knots, multiplied by two will give 98 miles at 2 miles per knot; reducing these to leagues, they will come to 32¾ leagues and a little more at 3 miles per league, which is what the ship will have run in twenty-four hours. One must not forget to take the latitude at every opportunity, to correct the distance or the course, and note it on the daily log-book. By this means one finds out what distance the ship has gone and the amount of leeway, and whereabouts it is, and in what direction lies the place to which one expects to go, and what course must be taken to get there; and I will say that of eight ships which were in company for 500 leagues I foretold within about an hour and a half when they would be on soundings, and this was found to be true.

* * * * *

In matters of this kind, and in all others dependent on navigation, great care and constant practice do a great deal for the safety both of the ship and of those who sail in her. That is why good and truly experienced navigators and pilots should be sought out and encouraged by good pay, to afford them the more encouragement to do well in this art of navigation. This should be prized highly by every nation of the world, on account of the great benefits and advantages that kingdoms and countries receive therefrom, however near or far removed they may be.

THE END

Bibliography

1. SOURCES

There is, unfortunately, no corpus of Champlain's letters and other manuscripts, but he described his travels and tribulations vividly in his own writings. Of these, by far the best edition is *The Works of Samuel de Champlain in Six Volumes*, published by the Champlain Society of Toronto, with a running English translation, under the general editorship of the late eminent Canadian authority H. P. Biggar. Here are the contents of the six volumes.

Vol. I, 1599–1607, Toronto 1922

Brief Discours . . . aux Indes Occidentalles, from the manuscript in the John Carter Brown Library, Brown University. Translated and edited by H. H. Langton.
Des Sauvages, ou Voyage de Samuel Champlain, de Brouage, fait en la France nouvelle, l'an mil six cens trois, from the Paris 1603 edition. Only 36 pages. Translated and edited by H. H. Langton.
Les Voyages du Sieur de Champlain Xaintongeois, Book I, Paris 1613, from a copy of the original edition; translated with valuable notes and introduction (pp. 194–202) by W. F. Ganong.

Vol. II, 1608–1613, Toronto 1925

Les Voyages (*1613*), Book II: *Les Voyages faits au Grand Fleuve Sainct-Laurens, par le sieur de Champlain, depuis l'année 1608 jusques en 1612.* Six contemporary documents relating to Champlain. Translated and edited by John Squair.

Vol. III, 1615–1618, Toronto 1929

Voyages et Descouvertures faites en la Nouvelle France, depuis l'année 1615 jusques à la fin de l'année 1618. Par le Sieur de Champlain Cappitaine ordinaire pour le Roy en la Mer du Ponant. Paris 1619. The rarest of Champlain's books. Translated and edited by H. H. Langton.

[269]

Les Voyages de la Nouvelle France Occidentale, dicte Canada, faits par le Sr de Champlain Xainctongeois . . . & toutes les Descouvertes qu'il a faites en ce païs depuis l'an 1603, jusques en l'an 1629. Paris 1632. Books I and II, through 1607. This, the most ambitious of his books, dedicated to Cardinal Richelieu, includes accounts of the early French voyages to Florida. It reprints, with some changes, Champlain's earlier *Des Sauvages* and *Les Voyages* of 1613. Translated and edited by W. F. Ganong.

Vol. IV, 1608–1620, Toronto 1932
English translations by H. H. Langton

Continuation of *Les Voyages* (1632), Books III and IV.
Addition to Champlain's Marriage Contract, 14 January 1619.

Vol. V, 1620–1629, Toronto 1933
English translations by W. D. LeSueur

Vol. II of *Les Voyages* of 1632, called *Seconde Partie des Voyages du Sieur de Champlain,* covering events from Champlain's return to Quebec in 1620 through 1629.
Champlain's receipt for royal pension of 600 livres in 1618.

Vol. VI, 1629–1632, Toronto 1936
English translations by LeSueur, Langton, and Ganong

Vol. II of *Les Voyages* of 1632, continued through 1631.
Traitté de la Marine et du Devoir d'un Bon Marinier, par le Sieur de Champlain, n.d. A fresh translation will be found at the end of my text.
Appendix of documents: Champlain's agreement with "Sieur Querc" (Kirke), 1629; inventory of the fort at Quebec when surrendered; his lengthy *Appel au Roy* of 1633, enumerating the valuable commodities of Canada; his letters of 15 August 1633 and 18 August 1634 to Cardinal Richelieu.

[Unnumbered] Portfolio of Plates and Maps, Toronto, n.d.

This indispensable part of the set includes full-scale reproductions of Champlain's manuscript map of 1607, now in the Library of Congress; of the 1612 Map of New France from the 1613 *Les Voyages;* and all illustrations from the John Carter Brown manuscript of the *Brief Discours.*

In quoting from this great work I have followed the practice of French historians of modernizing the spelling and punctuation of French, and have ventured in many instances to make my own English translation. Those in the Champlain Society edition are generally good but occasionally fall down in matters maritime.

The John Carter Brown Library at Providence has the best collection in the United States of Champlain's original editions.

Most English-speaking readers will be satisfied with the volume in J. Franklin Jameson's Original Narratives series, *Voyages of Samuel de Champlain, 1604–1618*, edited by W. L. Grant (Charles Scribner 1907, Barnes and Noble 1952, latest imprint 1959). This comprises translations of *Les Voyages* of 1613 and *Les Voyages et Découvertes* of 1619, by Charles P. Otis, which first appeared in the now rare *Voyages of Samuel de Champlain* edited by Edmund F. Slafter and published by the Prince Society (Boston, 3 vols., 1878–81).

For fifty years Canadian historians have been combing the national, provincial and notarial archives of France for fresh material, and the Canadian Department of Archives has published most of these, through 1622, in *Nouveaux documents sur Champlain et son époque*, W. K. Lamb ed. (Vol. I, 1560–1622, Ottawa 1967). Volume II unfortunately was not ready while I was writing.

The Champlain Society has also published a bilingual edition of Marc Lescarbot's *Histoire de la Nouvelle France*, (3 vols., Toronto 1907, 1911, 1914). This, originally published in 1609, long enjoyed greater esteem than Champlain's works because Lescarbot's French is literary and his narrative is larded with allusions to classical antiquity, flattering the readers of that epoch. There were later editions in 1611, 1612 and 1618. At the instance of Richard Hakluyt, Pierre Erondelle translated the most important parts of Lescarbot as *Nova Francia* (London: George Bishop 1609). This was reprinted in the *Broadway Travellers* series (New York and London: Harper 1928), which has a good bibliographical introduction by H. P. Biggar.

It is sad to relate that Lescarbot and Champlain fell out. The Paris lawyer, with his classical education, probably considered himself superior to the self taught Saintongeois who knew no Latin; and Champlain resented Lescarbot's rushing into print instead of letting him, as official chronicler, be the first to tell about the Acadian venture. And, still more, of describing himself on the title page "ocular witness of a part of the things here related." Champlain snorted at this, alleging that Marc had only once stirred from Port-Royal, when he sailed in a pinnace to Sainte-Croix (where he picked up a fine assortment of fleas at an Indian conclave). This infuriated the lawyer, who in his next edition deleted all complimentary references to Champlain and accused him of believing in the "Gougou," the legendary Micmac forest monster. Although Lescarbot does not cover later events, he is an indispensable source for Champlain's Acadian phase. William F. Ganong rightly attributed Champlain's annoyance to "the antagonism between the man of action and the man of letters, when the latter makes literary material of the former's exploits."

2. SECONDARY WORKS

There is no contemporary or even early biography of Champlain. The two leading French Canadian historians, Gustave Lanctot (*Histoire du Canada*, 3 vols., Montreal 1959–1964; English translation *A History of Canada*, Harvard University Press 1964) and Marcel Trudel (*Histoire de la Nouvelle-France*, vols. I and II, Montreal 1963, 1966) supply accounts superior to any modern biography of our hero. Trudel's volume III, from 1627 on, was not out in time for me to use; but Lanctot covers the last decade of Champlain's life. Both have woven in the numerous bits and pieces of information published by French Canadian historians during the last fifty years. Professor Trudel has also written a too brief *Champlain* (Montreal 1956), and compiled an excellent bilingual *Atlas de la Nouvelle France* (Quebec: Université Laval, 1968), including Champlain's maps and those inspired by Cartier. Among those not reproduced in this book are Levasseur's of 1601, which shows the "Coste de Cadie"; Wytfliet's, from his 1597 *Ptolemy;* Lescarbot's of 1609; and Hessel Gerritsz's of 1612, showing Hudson Bay, upon which Champlain drew (this is also in *Works* II 257).

By far the best work in English is Francis Parkman's classic *Pioneers of France in the New World*, Part II, *Champlain and His Associates*. Although first published in 1865, this work, for its matchless narrative style and hearty appreciation of Champlain, should endure when all other works on him are forgotten. Extracts on Champlain's Acadian phase may be found in my *Parkman Reader* (Boston 1954), chs. iii and vi. The best biography in English is Morris Bishop *Champlain: The Life of Fortitude* (New York 1948; reprinted as a paperback Toronto 1963). L'Abbé H. R. Casgrain, Parkman's friend, wrote a short biography, *Champlain, sa vie et son caractère* (Quebec 1898), which is very understanding.

In my opinion, the two best French biographies are (1) N. E. Dionne *Samuel Champlain, Fondateur de Québec et Père de la Nouvelle France* (2 vols., Quebec 1891). He has a useful appendix on the early sailings to Canada at I 388–95. (2) Gabriel Gravier *Vie de Samuel de Champlain, Fondateur de la Nouvelle France* (Paris 1900).

Many writers on early Canada, including myself, feel that de Monts has never had a fair break. William Inglis Morse *Pierre du Gua, Sieur de Monts* (London 1939) is a collection of documents, not a biography. Morse also edited *Acadensia Nova* (2 vols., London 1935), which is full of interesting items on L'Acadie. His fund in the Harvard College Library has made that collection very rich in early Canadian history.

There was a great interest in Champlain both in New England and in Canada during the second half of the nineteenth century. The key to this literature may be found in Justin Winsor *Narrative and Critical History of*

America, vol. IV (Boston 1884), chs. iii and iv by Edmund F. Slafter and Charles C. Smith, with valuable critical notes by Winsor himself.

A good critical bibliography of this period in Canadian history is published in *Centenaire de l'Histoire du Canada de F.-X. Garneau,* published by the Société Historique de Montreal in 1945 (pp. 166–254). And *Sixteenth-Century Maps Relating to Canada: A Check-List and Bibliography* (Ottawa, Public Archives, 1956) is indispensable for geography.

Notes to the Chapters

I CANADA BEFORE CHAMPLAIN
(pp. 3–15)

See my *European Discovery of America: The Northern Voyages A.D. 500–1600* (Oxford 1971); Lanctot *History of Canada*, chs. i–vii; and Trudel *Histoire de la Nouvelle France*, I, *Les Vaines Tentatives, 1524–1603* (Ottawa 1964).

The Huron Indians. I seem to have made a mistake in following the classic historians and calling Donnaconna's subjects, as well as the natives of Hochelaga and Achelacy, *Huron.* The tendency of living ethnologists and anthropologists is, largely on the evidence of excavated artifacts, to give them names such as Laurentian Iroquois or Canadian Iroquois, terms confusing to the reader. Admittedly the natives of the St. Lawrence River encountered by Cartier were of the Iroquoian language group, and the same goes for the Huron of Old Huronia encountered by Champlain; but were they the same people? The confusing state of recent knowledge of the subject is well reflected in Bernard G. Hoffman, *Cabot to Cartier* (Toronto 1961), pp. 210–12. Dr. Frederick Johnson of the R. S. Peabody Foundation for Archaeology, Andover, Mass., wrote to me (17 May and 3 June 1971): (1) that Cartier's friends "may have been Iroquois but culturally . . . they were probably not much different from most eastern Indians of the period"; (2) that the Huron whom Champlain later encountered in Old Huronia had been there a long, long time; and (3) that there is no certain answer yet to the question of what happened to Cartier's friends on the Great River between his departure and Champlain's arrival. Thanks also to Mr. P. Schuyler Miller of the Society for Pennsylvania Archaeology, Harrisburg, for raising the question, warning me against accepting nineteenth-century hypotheses, and for a long, informing letter of 22 July 1971. He points out that Christopher Carlile, in his *Briefe and Summarie Discourse* (1583), states that Cartier's "outrage and injurious dealing" broke off relations between French or other Europeans and the river Indians, who only began "to admit a trafique" two or three years ago, since when French ships had made fabulous profits. (Hakluyt Society facsimile of the 1589 Hakluyt's *Voyages*, 1965, II 723.)

II EARLY LIFE AND WEST INDIES VOYAGES
(*pp. 16–22*)

The dates usually given for Champlain's birth are c.1567 and c.1570. Both are guesswork, calculated from the statement that c.1593 he was *maréchal-des-logis* in the French army and so must then have been in his middle twenties. But could not a smart, tough lad have made that grade at eighteen or so? Of Pont-Gravé, Champlain wrote in his 1632 *Voyages* (*Works* IV 363), "I was his friend, and his age would make me respect him as my father." The *Dictionary of Canadian Biography* states that Pont-Gravé was born c.1554, but the *Nouveaux documents* of 1967 prints his baptismal certificate, dated 27 November 1560. Adding eighteen years, a reasonable father-son gap, you have Champlain born not before 1578. Shuffle these *circa* dates as you will, nothing comes out but more variables; so I follow Trudel by assuming Champlain to have been born c.1570. Yet I suspect that he was really several years younger.

For Brouage, see David R. Jack "Brouage, Birthplace of Champlain," *Acadiensis* IV (1904) 226–33, and W. G. Tyrrell *Champlain and the French in New York* (Albany 1959), both with illustrations. "Today," wrote Jack, "the town is silent and deserted; its streets poorly paved, its buildings ill kept."

Because of his Old Testament name, and his birth in a region where Protestantism flourished, some have concluded that Samuel Champlain was born and baptized a Huguenot, a member of the Reformed Religion. There is no real evidence for this. In all his writings and dealings, Champlain showed himself to be a Catholic in faith and practice, and he supported the exclusion of Protestants from Canada by the Duc de Vantadour in 1628. Use of the name Samuel means nothing; for as Gustave Lanctot pointed out to me in a letter of 20 October 1955, it was fairly common in the sixteenth century for French Catholic parents to give children Old Testament names; e.g., Isaac de Razilly, Isaac du Pas (Marquis de Tenquières), Emmanuel Philibert (Duc de Savoie), and Abraham Martin, an early settler of Quebec from whom the Plains of Abraham were named.

For items on Champlain's army career, and for "*le capitaine Provençal*," see *Nouveaux documents* pp. 2–14 and 17–21.

Besides the Providence manuscript of the *Brief Discours* there is one in the University Library of Bologna, which lacks eleven of the illustrations. Jean Druchési in *Champlain, a t'il menti?* (Montreal 1950) raised a literary storm by arguing that his account of the West Indian voyages was a phony. Jacques Rousseau answered him in a pamphlet, *Champlain botaniste mexicain et antillais* (Montreal 1951). L. A. Vigneras discussed this in *Revue d'Histoire de l'Amérique Française* XI (1957). Vigneras finds so many inaccuracies in the *Brief Discours* as to suggest that Champlain never left Spain and composed it ashore by picking the brains of sailors! That hypothesis, to my mind, is refuted by the quality of the colored sketches, which (excepting some of the bird's-eye views of towns) could not possibly have been copied from existing books, and are obviously from the same hand as those of Champlain's books on Canada. I conclude that, as a Frenchman in a ticklish situation (the Inquisition was already well established in Mexico and his very presence there was illegal), he dared not take notes or make sketches, but wrote the text and painted the illustrations from memory after his return to France. That would explain his sometimes mixing up characteristics of two different plants in one painting. The style of Champlain's work is evidently based on that of Théodore de Bry, some of whose illustrated works on the New World came out early enough to be seen, or even owned, by him.

The only authentic portraits of Champlain known to exist are the three sketchy self-portraits in his pictures of battles with the Iroquois, the best of which we have enlarged and reproduced as frontispiece. The one usually reproduced in French lives of the explorer, with or without a Quebec background, is that of a certain *controleur des finances* (Trudel *Champlain* p. 17). This has inspired all the recent statues of Champlain. Victor H. Paltsits "A Critical Examination of Champlain's Portraits" in *Acadiensis* IV (1904) 305–11 exposes a number of phonies.

III FIRST VOYAGE TO CANADA
(*pp. 23–33*)

Des Sauvages (1603) and *Les Voyages* (1613), book I, are principal sources, best found in the Champlain Society edition of his *Works*, vol. I. There is an early translation of the 1603 book in *Purchas his Pilgrimes*, 1625 edition vol. IV pp. 1605–19 (MacLehose 1906 edition XVIII 188–228).

For Honfleur, see A. Labutte *Essai historique sur Honfleur* (Honfleur 1840) pp. 91–94. The chapel, swept away by a storm in 1558, was rebuilt in 1606 by the town; and when the local Capucins tried to annex it to their monastery the whole town rose to prevent it. Labutte reprints a poem "A Notre-Dame-de-Grâce" by a local poet, of which the first stanza reads:

> *La mer bouillone et gronde autour de ta chapelle.*
> *Vierge de grâce et de bonté,*
> *Le marin en péril te supplie et t'appelle,*
> *Pour fléchir un ciel irrité.*
> *Ces hommes durs et fiers, mûris dans les tempêtes,*
> *Ces pilotes noirs et velus,*

Otent le lourd bonnet qui pèse sur leurs têtes,
Et viennent t'adorer pieds nus.

IV L'ACADIE AND NORUMBEGA
(*pp. 34–70*)

The main sources are Champlain *Works* I and II, and Lescarbot. I have drawn freely on my own experiences and observations along these coasts, and am grateful to Edward Rowe Snow for reminding me of the Wood Island dog "sailor."

For the shifting east and north of Verrazzano's *Archadia* from the Carolinas to Nova Scotia, see Ernest H. Wilkins "Arcadia in America," American Philosophical Society *Proceedings* CI (1957) 4–30, especially p. 16 for Champlain's use of the name, which really fixed it in Nova Scotia–New Brunswick–Maine.

The best account of forming de Monts's company is in Trudel *Histoire de la Nouvelle France* II 9–15. I agree with him, "*Sans de Monts il n'y aurait pas un Champlain.*" The only biography of him, William Inglis Morse *Pierre du Gua, Sieur de Monts* (London 1939) is largely a collection of documents. The only memorial to him known to me is the Sieur de Monts spring near Bar Harbor, Mount Desert Island.

Champlain's pinnace. What the English then called a pinnace, Champlain called a *patache* or *barque*. I cannot give him good marks as a ship-picture artist, but on several of his harbor charts, especially in that of Port St. Louis (Plymouth), which is at page 65, he makes some attempt to show those used in his New England cruises. These pinnaces were two-masted, rigged with one square sail on the mainmast, one lateen sail on the mizzen, and occasionally a square mizzen topsail. They were not completely decked over, and with a crew of eighteen or more men must have been very uncomfortable.

Sainte-Croix. W. F. Ganong has an exhaustive article, "Dochet (St. Croix) Island," in Royal Society of Canada *Proceedings and Transactions* 2nd ser. VIII (1902) 126–231.

The shallop was primarily a rowing boat, small enough to be carried on the deck of a transatlantic ship, or to be towed across. She had one or two masts, square-rigged or lateen. The one illustrated (p. 279) is Poutrincourt's at Port Fortuné (Stage Harbor). Other examples are in Champlain's picture of Sainte-Croix. The shallop was the work boat for fishermen or fur traders.

Many large ships are shown on Champlain's big maps, but it is not possible to identify them, and they are not good examples of marine art. The ensigns and flags with a Latin cross are stylized; they appear on many maps of the time, and signify nothing.

Etienne Bellinger, who is probably responsible for erecting the cross that Champlain found in the Bay of Fundy, was a French friend of Richard Hakluyt's who was fitted out by the Archbishop of Rouen to make a fur-trading voyage along the shores of L'Acadie in 1583. See references in Morison *European Discovery of America: The Northern Voyages A.D. 500–1600* (1971) pp. 468, 489.

Fannie H. Eckstrom "Champlain's Visit to the Penobscot," *Sprague's Journal of Maine History* I (1913) 56–65, pinpoints Champlain's sojourn at the site of Bangor. The "little river" near which he dropped anchor was the Kenduskeag; the *"quantité de rochers"* which stopped his pinnace there were mostly removed in the nineteenth century so that lumber schooners could lay alongside the banks. The Indian village was on the

Poutrincourt's shallop at Port Fortuné (Stage Harbor, Cape Cod). From Champlain's engraving in Les Voyages *(1613). Courtesy Harvard College Library.*

easterly bank of the Kenduskeag, their favorite winter hunting ground for moose.

Norumbega is an Algonkin word meaning a stretch of quiet water between two rapids. For the Norumbega story see my *European Discovery of America: The Northern Voyages* (1971) chap. XIV. It was the common name used by both French and English from about 1550 for the region between Nova Scotia and Cape Cod. Champlain in his 1616 map places the name Acadia above the forks of the Penobscot, replacing the Norumbega on his 1607 and 1612 maps.

Mallebarre is the only name given by Champlain to any place south of Maine which has survived. As Malebar it was transferred to the long peninsula which makes the elbow of Cape Cod, and is found on English and French maps down to the present century. It also became the class name of a fleet of yachts designed by the late John Alden. See S. E. Morison ed. William Bradford *Of Plymouth Plantation* (New York 1952) p. 61*n*. In *Mitchell's New General Atlas* (Philadelphia 1864) plate 16, Cape Malebar is the cape just east of Chatham, behind Monomoy Island. It is at the same place, spelled Mallabarre, in T. G. Bradford *Illustrated Atlas of the United States* (Boston 1841).

Interesting contracts with masons and a tile-maker of Honfleur to go to Canada for at least one year, their wages being 81 livres each and found, dated 9 March 1605; and for carpenters and locksmiths, including the Jean Duval who was hanged, for 45 to 120 livres per annum, are in *Nouveaux documents* I nos. 59, 61. Louis Hébert the apothecary got 100 livres per annum, and he was the only one to start a farm.

Curiosities from L'Acadie. Nicolas-Claude de Fabri, Seigneur de Peiresce, an amateur scientist interested in curiosities, knew de Monts and described (*Nouveaux documents* no. 61) in November 1605 and March 1606, the six-months-old moose calf, the hummingbird and other birds, the horseshoe crab, lobster, merganser and other creatures brought home by de Monts, as well as a bark canoe, a bow and arrows, and other objects. Peiresce informs us that the caribou sent to the king by de Monts had been turned loose at Saint-Germain, and died for lack of water "or other commodities."

V PORT-ROYAL AND CRUISE TO CAPE COD
(*pp. 71–88*)

The main sources are Champlain and Lescarbot. The former's *Les Voyages* (1613) is divided between volumes I and II of his *Works*, and contains valuable notes by W. F. Ganong identifying localities.

When Parkman visited the site of the Port-Royal habitation in 1871, the outlines of it could be traced on the ground (Mason Wade ed. *Journals of Francis Parkman,* New York and London 1947, II 549). Early in the twentieth century Mrs. Harriette Taber Richardson of Cambridge began a movement to have the habitation restored, and restored it was by the Canadian government with the help of private contributions. See photo in Morison *European Discovery of America: The Northern Voyages* (1971) p. 449. A visit to this restored habitation, situated at Lower Granville a short distance from Annapolis Royal, N.S., will give one a better idea of how Champlain and his associates lived in Canada than any amount of description.

The usually impeccable Ganong in his notes on Champlain's illustration of the Port-Royal habitation, in *Works* I 373, went wrong in saying it looked too smooth and must have been built of unfinished logs. As H. R. Shurtleff shows in his *Log Cabin Myth* (1939) pp. 66–67, the early French and English were sawyers, not loggers. Moreover, comparison with Champlain's pictures of the habitations at Quebec and Sainte-Croix proves that the exteriors of all were finished smooth. There is no indication that they were painted.

VI THE ORDER OF GOOD CHEER
(pp. 89–101)

Le Théâtre de Neptune, which first appeared in Lescarbot's *Les Muses de la Nouvelle France* (Paris 1618), is reprinted in his *History of New France* (Champlain Society edition, Toronto 1921) III 473–79; and also, with translation, in Harriette T. Richardson *The Theatre of Neptune in New France* (Boston 1928). This charming little book includes the music to which Marius Barbeau thinks the ode to Neptune was sung.

The story of the black interpreter d'Acosta is told in William Inglis Morse *Pierre du Gua, Sieur de Monts* (1939) p. 51. A document of 1609 about "Mathieu de Costa, naigre" is in *Nouveaux documents* no. 106.

For L'Acadie after Champlain's departure in 1607, see Trudel II 80–149, Gustave Lanctot *A History of Canada* (1964) chaps. xxi–xxiii, and Parkman *Pioneers*, part 2, chap. vi. H. Leander d'Entremont *The Forts of Cape Sable of the Seventeenth Century* (Halifax 1938) is most useful.

For Poutrincourt's later life, see Trudel II 240.

For the Sieur de Monts's action against one Captain Couillard, a prominent poacher, winning his furs and 1500 livres costs, and other similar litigation, see *Nouveaux documents* nos. 78–84, 92, 94–97, 102, 112. The arrêt of the Conseil d'Etat restoring his monopoly for a year, 29 March 1608, is no. 93. In no. 99 we find 200 beaver skins sold for 1200 livres at Saint-Malo in 1609. In no. 104 is an arrêt of the Conseil d'Etat allowing Malouins and Basques free trade in Canada, provided they pay de Monts 6000 livres.

VII QUEBEC FOUNDED AND IROQUOIS ATTACKED
(*pp. 102–122*)

This is covered by *Les Voyages* (1613), second livre, in *Works* II 3–110.

Champlain and de Bry. Anyone who peruses the many works illustrated by Théodore de Bry and his sons (as I had the privilege of doing at the Bibliothèque Royal, Brussels) can see that he was Champlain's artistic inspiration. For instance, in his *Americae Tertia Pars* (1592), plate I has naked Indians, like Champlain's, attacking a French fort in Brazil; page 120 shows boats exactly like the "canoes" at Ticonderoga.

The Five Nations' rôle and French Indian policy initiated by Champlain are highly controversial. George T. Hunt *The Wars of the Iroquois* (Madison 1940) presents the Iroquois as the innocent, defensive, put-upon side, which certainly would have made our ancestors — whether French, Dutch, English or Irish — roar with laughter. Allan Forbes Jr. has made a convincing attack on Hunt's thesis in an article "Two and a Half Centuries of Conflict," *Pennsylvania Archaeologist* XL (nos. 3, 4, 1970) pp. 1–29.

The arquebus or harquebus, decisive weapon in Champlain's first two fights with the Iroquois, was a handgun developed by Spain in the previous century. Muzzle-loading, it was fired by a match or fuse the diameter of a thin pencil, impregnated by a substance for slow burning. This would be lighted before battle by flint and steel. A short length of the fuse would be attached to the hammer (generally in the form of a snake and called "the serpentine"), and when the arquebusier wished to shoot he blew this red-hot, pulled the trigger, and thus ignited the gunpowder in the pan, which set off the charge at the base of the barrel. Gunpowder was carried in a waterproof brassbound flask whose spout (with a steel cutoff) held just enough for a charge; and round lead bullets were carried in small pouches. Champlain does not depict these, but de Bry did, and the Arms Museum in the Castel S. Angelo, Rome, has an example of the pouch and of an arquebus just like those depicted by Champlain. I found this gun to be surprisingly light and handy, just the thing to carry into the wilderness. The arquebus was the handgun of the conquistadores, of the French civil wars, and of the Dutch rebels against Spain. Already, in Champlain's time, European armies were using the longer and more lethal musket, so heavy that it had to be supported by a rest.

The quotations from Lescarbot are from the Champlain Society edition of his *Nouvelle France* III 472, 480.

S. H. P. Pell prints a fresh translation of Champlain's account of the 1609 campaign in his *Fort Ticonderoga* (Ticonderoga 1970); and Edward P. Hamilton has a chapter devoted to the fight in his *Fort Ticonderoga: Key to the Continent* (Boston 1964).

Arquebus of c. 1600. From the Museo Nazionale, Castel
S. Angelo, Rome. Courtesy of the Director, Signor Marcello Terenzi.

Powder flask such as Champlain carried. From the Museo Nazionale, Castel S. Angelo, Rome. Courtesy of the Director, Signor Marcello Terenzi.

VIII CHAMPLAIN MARRIES AND RETURNS TO CANADA
(*pp. 123–129*)

Documents on Champlain's marriage to Hélène Boullé, edited by Emmanuel de Cathelineau, will be found in the periodical *Nova Francia* V (1930) 142–55. Samuel is therein described as "noble homme," which the editor, quoting Loyseau *Les Cinq Livres du droit des offices*, says meant no more than the particle "de" which he then adopted. *Sieur* was supposed to mean that the person so designated owned landed property; Champlain describes himself as *sieur* in some of his captions, but is not known to have been a landowner unless in Canada. See also Robert Le Blant "La Famille Boullé," *Revue d'Histoire de l'Amérique Française* XVII (1963) 55–69. Among the witnesses to this marriage contract there were three *sieurs*: Pierre du Gua, sieur de Monts, described as "*gentilhomme ordinaire de la Chambre du Roy et son lieutenant général dans la France Nouvelle*"; Jehan Ravenal, sieur de La Merois, and Pierre Noël, sieur de Cohingne. Another important person to sign was Antoine de Murat, "*conseiller et aumonier du Roy*." Simon Alix, Hélène's uncle, turned up, but not one relation of Samuel although his father is described as living. Two merchants, one of Rouen and Martial Chanut, a shipowner of Paris, signed, as did François le Saege, "*appoticaire de l'escurye du Roy* — the royal horse-leech. Also, a barber-surgeon and a midwife. In other words, a rather mixed crowd socially. In the document on the dowry, the child bride's signature is that of a little girl whose fingers have not yet mastered the pen.

IX FIRST WESTERN EXPLORATIONS
(*pp. 130–146*)

Most of this chapter is based on Champlain's *Les Voyages* of 1613 and *Quatrième Voyage* of 1613, as printed in his *Works* II 236–316. Trudel (II 184–5) tells about the La Rochelle régime. The merchants' diatribe against Champlain is in *Nouveaux documents* no. 125. Those on Hélène are in the same, nos. 149–50; no. 126 gives their address as Rue Troussevache paroisse Saint-Jacques de la Boucherie. Several documents on Champlain's negotiations at this period with the merchants are in *Nouveaux documents* nos. 128–131, 137, and the "Acte de constitution de la Compagnie du Canada" is no. 145; and in no. 146 of 21 November 1613, Champlain pays 1800 livres to the Sieur de Monts for his share in the company.

The Prince de Condé was heir to the throne prior to the birth of Louis XIII, husband of Charlotte de Montmorency (granddaughter of the Constable), and father of the "Great Condé." His secretary Charles Deslandes was brother-in-law to Hélène (Boullé) Champlain.

The "Imposter" Vignau. Professor Trudel has come to the rescue of

Vignau's reputation. He believes that Vignau really did visit Lakes Huron and Nipissing, but confessed himself a liar under duress, as Tessoüat did not wish the French to trade directly with either lake. In my opinion, Vignau "knew what he was talking about," even if he never left the village.

The canoe trip. An astrolabe, discovered near Green Lake in 1867 at the place where Champlain had surmounted a windrow of fallen trunks, has since found a permanent home in the New York Historical Society. Trudel (II 196*n.*) argues that there is no evidence of this astrolabe's having belonged to Champlain. I am inclined to believe that it did, but was not lost by him; Champlain left an astrolabe by will to Père Lalemant, who did a great deal of portaging between Quebec and Huronia, and why could he not have lost it?

The 1616 map, original of which is in the John Carter Brown Library, has been reproduced full-size by that library. Lawrence C. Wroth wrote a pamphlet, *The Champlain Map of 1616*, for the Champlain Society (1956), and an article on the second edition, "An Unknown Champlain Map of 1618," for *Imago Mundi* XI (1954) 85–94.

X REORGANIZATION AND MORE
WESTERN EXPLORATIONS
(*pp. 147–168*)

The canoe journey and campaign against the Onondaga fort are covered by *Voyages et Descouvertures* (1619) in *Works* III and, with slightly fewer details, in *Les Voyages* (1632) in *Works* IV. Note that the 1619 *Voyages* has two title pages. I have quoted the printed one; the engraved one is called simply *Les Voyages du Sr. de Champlain . . . 1615–1618* (Paris: chez C. Collet, 1619).

For details on the Récollets and their recruitment, see Trudel II, especially pp. 459–60.

At this point we begin to profit from the works of Père Gabriel Sagard, to whose name "Théodat" is sometimes added. *Le Grand Voyage au Pays des Hurons* (Paris 1632) is printed with English translation (*The Long Journey to the Country of the Hurons*) by H. H. Langton with notes by Victor H. Paltsits and George M. Wrong, by the Champlain Society (Toronto 1939). His *Histoire du Canada et Voyages que les frères mineurs récollets y ont faicts pour la conversion des infidèles depuis l'an 1615* (Paris 1636) was reprinted in four volumes by M. E. Tross (Paris 1866).

Father Le Jeune's Guide to Good Manners is in R. G. Thwaites ed: *Jesuit Relations* (Cleveland 1896–1901) XIII 116–23. In another place we have the story of a priest, fresh from France, who was expected his first day to be guest at an Indian feast. The other Frenchmen present told him to express gratitude in their language by "Ho! Ho! Ho!" The poor cleric, confronted by a particularly smelly samagité that he dared not touch, turned pale. His hosts then produced their greatest dainty, a slab of broiled bear fat. The poor man tasted it; then, unable to contain himself any longer, rushed from the assembly, not forgetting to utter a feeble and unconvincing "Ho! Ho! Ho!" between vomitings.

Topography of Champlain's western journeys. Here the most important monograph, based on local as well as library research, is Arthur Edward Jones S.J. *"8ENDRAKE ENEN" or Old Huronia* in Bureau of Archives for Ontario Fifth Report (1909). Father Jones identifies the Huron villages visited by Champlain and tells the story of the Récollet and Jesuit missions in great detail. Others are Orsamus H. Marshall "Champlain's Expedition of 1615," *Magazine of American History* II no. 8 (1878) 470–83, and William G. Tyrrell *Champlain and the French in New York* (Albany 1959). Morris Bishop (*Champlain* pp. 355–59), who examined evidence on the location of the fight, favored Onondaga Lake where the city of Syracuse is located, as does Mansfield J. French in *Champlain's Incursion Against the Onondaga* (1949). I favor Atkins Pond, but only archaeology can decide. Parkman's map of the entire expedition, in his *Pioneers,* has never been surpassed.

For the Trent Canal see *Encyclopedia Canadiana* II 219, with map.

XI MADAME CHAMPLAIN COMES TO QUEBEC
(pp. 169–184)

Champlain's map of 1616 was reproduced in facsimile collotype by the John Carter Brown Library in 1956, together with a three-page description by Lawrence C. Wroth, which the Champlain Society published that year. The successive versions appeared in 1653, 1664 and 1671. I take issue with Wroth's statement that in the 1616 version *Acadie* is "improperly" located on the New England area. *Acadie* is placed just north of the forks of the Penobscot; and as the French then considered that this regional name embraced both Nova Scotia and Maine, it is well placed.

The quotation about psalm-singing is from Parkman *Pioneers* (1898) 436. Champlain's statement about Pont-Gravé is in his *Works* IV 363.

For proof that Champlain made a round voyage to Canada in 1617, see Trudel II 241. *Ibid.* 250–58 for his excellent analysis of Champlain's proposals of 1618. For the Caëns and their religious affiliations see Trudel II 271–286. The rare pamphlet of 1622, *Plainte de la Nouvelle France dicte Canada, à la France sa Germaine* (Complaint of New France called Canada, to France her Cousin), written by the Récollets, may be found in the Houghton Library, Harvard.

Trudel II 369*n.* throws doubt upon the Mohawks' descent on Quebec in 1621 or 1622, as it is mentioned neither by Champlain nor Sagard, only by LeClerq, who picked up the story at Quebec no earlier than 1675.

The item on Champlain's sending home the two farmers who did nothing is quoted from Odoric-Marie Jouve *Les Franciscains et le Canada* I (Paris 1934) 186.

For the beginning of the seigneurial system, see Trudel II 309–13, with map. William B. Munro *The Seigniorial System in Canada* (New York 1907) is still the best general account. This system of land grants and settlements, corresponding to the head-right system in Virginia and the townships in New England, was admirably suited to the French people; they became devoted to their seigneurs, and even, in some instances, went on paying feudal dues after the system was abolished in mid-nineteenth century.

XII THE ENGLISH CONQUEST
(pp. 185–199)

The period of the English capture and occupancy of Quebec is covered in Champlain's *Voyages* of 1632. The English sources on this brief conquest, as printed in Henry Kirke *The First English Conquest of Canada* (London 1871), agree with Champlain. The chapter in Parkman's *Pioneers* is still the best secondary account of the English at Quebec; but Lanctot's *History of Canada* (1963) chaps. 11–13 contains new material. Sagard (Paris 1866, IV 886–912) also covers events at Quebec.

Père Lalemant's vivid letter about his shipwreck is included in the 1632 *Voyages* (*Works* VI 161–67).

XIII THE HUNDRED ASSOCIATES
(pp. 200–210)

XIV LAST PHASE
(pp. 211–227)

Trudel's *Histoire*, so far published, ends in 1627, and Champlain's last work (*Les Voyages*, 1632) does not take him beyond 1631; but *Le Mercure françois* XIV (1632) 232–67 contains a detailed account of the Cens Associés with its charter and earliest regulations. It also contains (XVIII 56–74) an account of the rendition of Quebec, probably by Père Le Jeune.

The English ballad is quoted from C. H. Firth *An American Garland* (1915), p. 24. Samuel L. Morison procured the data about French warships named *Champlain*.

Les Voyages of 1632 was apparently too much for Collet to handle alone, because some of the surviving copies are published "Chez Pierre Le-Mur dans la Grand' Salle du Palais," and others "Chez Louis Sevestre Imprimeur-Libraire, rue du Meurier près la Porte S. Victor & en sa Boutique dans la Cour du Palais." In those days, if a second or third bookseller wished to sell copies, he printed his own title page.

Champlain's petition to Louis XIII was printed as a quarto pamphlet of twenty-five pages, no title page or date; the *incipit* is "Au Roy, SIRE, Le Sieur de Champlain démontre tres humblement." Copy in the John Carter Brown Library. Champlain's receipt for an earlier payment of the pension is in *Works* V 330.

Le Mercure françois XIX (1636) 771–867 reprints Père Le Jeune's *Jesuit Relation* of 1634, and concludes with an original account of Champlain's last voyage to Quebec and events there by an "honest person" unnamed, who accompanied him. This narrator returned to France with du Plessis in August of 1635 (p. 867).

The *Jesuit Relations* are one of the best sources for this period. In the R. G. Thwaites edition the most important volumes are V and VI, Père Le Jeune's Relations of 1633–34; VII and VIII, his Relations for 1635 and 1636, and Brébeuf's for 1635; IX, Le Jeune's Relation for 1636 continued, including Champlain's death; XI, Le Jeune's Relation for 1637, and two letters of Brébeuf.

There are documents on the purchase of a house in Brouage from Champlain by Jacques and Marie (Cameret) Hersan in *Nouveaux documents* (1967) nos. 165, 166, 170, 171.

Lanctot's *A History of Canada* is the best general history for this period, and contains the results of fresh research on the English conquest and the rendition.

The Paris book world. Lucien Febure and Henri-Jean Martin *L'Apparition du Livre* (Paris 1958) pp. 420–25. There is still more on the subject in Geoffroy Atkinson *Les Nouveaux Horizons de la renaissance française* (Paris 1935), including an analysis of a curious exotic novel *Coppie d'une lettre envoyée de la Nouvelle France, en Canada, par le Sieur de Combes* (Lyon 1609), which is based on Champlain's *Des Sauvages*. This very rare book is reproduced, with translation by Samuel E. Dawson, in Royal Society of Canada *Proceedings and Transactions* 2nd ser. XI (1906) sec. 2, pp. 3–30.

The first edition of Jacques-Auguste de Thou, called *A. Tuani Historiarum sui temporis pars prima* (Paris 1604), was too early to include Champlain, but the author and his successors updated it in later editions. In the London (1733) edition a few pages on de Monts and Champlain appear, but they take the story only to 1609.

Two books on Bosse in which the Galerie du Palais engraving is reproduced are André Blum *Abraham Bosse* (Paris 1924) and Nicole Vila *Le XVIIᵉ siècle vu par A. Bosse* (Paris 1967). Corneille's comedy *La Galerie du Palais* (1634) was reprinted in his *Oeuvres* (Marty-Laveaux ed. II, Paris 1862).

Champlain's proposed anti-Iroquois task force is printed in *Le Mercure françois* XIX 841–44. He wants one hundred élite troops, with necessary logistics so as to be independent of the savages for food and drink. Eighty are to carry a *carabine* three to four feet long, with a musket's caliber; ten to be armed to fight with sword and pistol; four to employ *artifices* such as hand grenades to blow breaches in wood palisades; ten good halberdiers, four carpenters, four *serruriers* (locksmiths); each of these eighteen carrying a battle-axe and pistol; ten pikemen, each also armed with a cutlass; two surgeons. For extra arms and munitions, plenty of good steel swords, steel helmets, powder and lead. A coat of chamois or well-cured leather is preferable to armor. Also, 600 little and 400 big axes, 4000 steel arrowheads, and 100 steel sword blades, for our savage allies. And a supply of hardtack, dried peas and prunes for the inevitable feast before a campaign.

Champlain's will, discovered in the Archives Nationales in 1959, is printed with discussion in *Revue d'Histoire de l'Amérique Française* XVII (1963) 269–86. On the location of his remains, see Paul Bouchart d'Orval *Le Mystère du Tombeau de Champlain* (Quebec 1951).

Père Le Jeune's tribute in his Relation for 1636 is as follows:

"Truly he had led a life of great righteousness and equity,* with perfect loyalty towards his King, and the Company, but at his death he crowned his virtues with such great sentiments of piety that he astonished us all. How his eyes filled with tears! How his love burned for the service of God; what love he had for the families here, saying that they must be powerfully assisted for the good of the country and supported in every way possible in their new beginnings, and that he would do it himself if God gave him health! And he was not caught unawares in the account he had to render to God; he had prepared long ago a general confession of his entire life, which he made with great contrition to Père Lalemant, whom he honored with his friendship."

Last days of Hélène de Champlain. D. Toussaint du Plessie *Histoire de l'Eglise de Meaux* (1731) I 453 says that in excavating the old college before building a new Ursuline convent, workmen came upon a medieval Jewish cemetery — "*Mais aujourd'hui que des vierges chrétiennes ont sanctifié cette terre maudite.*" The Ursulines gave up, or were expelled from this convent at the time of the French Revolution, and the college moved back. "Nothing is left of it," states Jacques Herissy *Les Massacres de Meaux* (1935) p. 8, "but a fair porch and a mutilated coat-of-arms."

The fate of the Huron. Even before Champlain's death in 1635, the Iroquois began a yearly harassment of the Huron, attacking them on their canoe route to and from the annual peltry fairs on the St. Lawrence. Huronia itself, which Champlain found so mellow and peaceful, became a dark and bloody ground from 1642, when the Iroquois began attacking the fortified villages. The following year, on one of these raids, the Jesuit missionaries Jean Brébeuf and Gabriel Lalemant were captured and tortured

---

* Le Jeune's words are *justice et equité;* the former obviously in the sense that the *Dictionnaire de l'Académie* defines as "*la rectitude que Dieu met dans l'âme, par sa grâce*"; and the latter, "*la justice exercée avec une modération et un adoucissement raisonnable.*"

to death. Huronia was completely broken up. Many thousand took refuge with the friendly Tionontati and the so-called Neutral Nation; but the Five Nations implacably pursued them thither, and both were involved in a common ruin with the Huron. A few hundred escaped to Quebec or to the Andastes, or to tribes further west where they merged with the Wyandot. Even the few hundred who sought French protection and were given the Ile d'Orléans as a new home were attacked there by Mohawks in 1656 and lost 76 of their number, including girls carried back to Iroquoia to become brood-mares for the warriors. For details of this sad history see Frederick W. Hodge *Handbook of the American Indian North of Mexico* (Washington 1907) I 587–90.

Index

(Illustration page numbers are in italic.)

Marsolet, Nicolas, 108, 195–6
Martin, Abraham, 179, 224, 276
Martin, Marguerite, 224
Mary Otis, 87
Massé, Ennemond, 185, 204, 214
Mayflower, 64, 79
Medici, Marie de, 4, 17, 121
Membertou, sagamore, 72–3, 77–8, 89, 95
Mercure françois, 200–1, 205, 219, 287–8
Messamouet, sachem, 78
Michel, Capt. Jacques, 192, 196–7
Micmac, *see* Souriquois
Miller, P. S., 275
Missionaries, 12, 145, 148–9, 220, 286, 289. *See also* Jesuits; Récollets
Mohawk, 22, 290; 1690 fight, 109–16, 189; attack Quebec, 179–80, 286
Mohican, 111, 189
Monopolies, 15, 25; Caën company's, 180, 183, 189, 200; de Monts's, 34, 97, 102–3, 137, 173; Hundred Associates', 201
Monsters and marvels, 6, 32–3, 271
Montagnais, 3, 13, 14, 30–1, 138, 149, 190, 214; customs, 173; described, 29; fight Iroquois, 107–17; peace treaty, 180; rescued by Champlain, 107; trade with, 128
Montmagny, Charles de, 225
Montmorency, Duc de, 169, 176, 180, 185
Montreal, 6, 8, 14, 30, 126, 134, 149, 218
Monts, Pierre du Gua, Sieur de, 15, 130, 272, 278, 284; in Acadie, 35–9, 52–5; lawsuit, 95; monopoly, 34, 97, 281; moves to Port-Royal, 71–2, 77; New England cruises, 55–70, 87; Quebec venture, 102–3, 106, 116, 124, 133–7, 147; death, 148
Morieu, Capt. Michel, 214
Morison, S. L., 287
Morse, W. I., 272, 278, 281
Motin, poet, 131
Mount Desert Island, 46–7, *48–49*, *50*, 56, 78, 98–9, 148, 171, 260
Mouton, Port, 37–8, 99

Murat, Antoine de, 284
Muses de la Nouvelle France, 89–93, 100, 281
Mutiny, 106

Nauset (Indians), 64, 68–9, 82–3, 87. *See also* Mallebarre
Nauset Harbor, *68*
Navigation, 247–56, 261–2, 267
Nebicerini, 142
Nesle, Capt. Pierre de, 214
New Brunswick, 35, 38
New England, 13, 60, 99, 202; explored, 55–70, 73–80; named, 132*n*
Newfoundland, 3–7, 12–3, 23, 27
Nibachis, chief, 140
Nields, J. F., xii
Nipissing, Lake, 117, 142–3, 150, *151*, 224, 285
Noël, Pierre, 284
Noirot, Père, 199
Northwest Passage, 5, 13, 31, 173
Norumbega, 13, *96*, 132; explored, 45–47, 52–3; name, 280
Notre-Dame-de-Grâce, 27, 277
Notre-Dame de la Recouvrance, 216, 221–4
Nova Scotia, 35–7, 47, 63, 99, 286

Onondaga, fight with, 122, 157–61, *159*, *160*, 167, 174, 285–6
Oqui, 165–6
Onemessin, chief, 78
Order of Good Cheer, 94, 122
Ottawa (Indians), 150–1
Ottawa River, 7, 31, 125, 138; explored, 139–43, *141*, *144*, 147–50

Panounias, 55–6, 78
Parc, Sieur du, 121, 173
Parkman, Francis, 145, 162*n*, 280; *Pioneers of France*, 272, 281, 286–7; quoted, 39, 54, 175
Patache, see Pinnace
Patents, 14, 34, 97